SCHOOL FOR GENIUS

SCHOOL
FOR
GENIUS

The Story of the ETH—
The Swiss Federal Institute of Technology,
from 1855 to the Present

By
THOMAS MOORE

FRONT STREET PRESS
Rockville Centre, NY

Published by
FRONT STREET PRESS

© 2005 by Thomas Moore

ISBN 0-9725572-2-9

Cataloging-in-Publication Data is available from the
Library of Congress.

First edition, first printing.

PRINTED AND BOUND IN THE UNITED STATES OF AMERICA.

CONTENTS

Foreword

When Americans tell me they're making their first trip to Zürich, I urge them not to miss hitching a ride on the charming old red funicular—the Polybahn—which carries students, professors and the curious from the bank of the Limmat River up the hill to the ETH Terrace. They'll enjoy a spectacular view out over the city and usually find a worthwhile exhibition in the 19th-century Zentrum, the center of the school's original facilities. The colorful flow of bright, animated young ETH students at work and play is fascinating. Albert Einstein was once one of them—and his like could be there today. The ETH is something that should not be missed.

I hope this small book will help inform Americans about how much this unique institution—the MIT or Caltech of Switzerland—has contributed to the world, and what a beehive of activity it is today. Our own graduate students, advanced researchers and corporate scientists are already beating a regular path there. The projects and research initiatives that involve cooperation or collaboration between the ETH and U.S. schools grows every year.

These robust science and technology relationships—often linked to private sector R&D exchanges—support the extraordinary trade and investment relationships which are highly beneficial to both "Sister Republics." In 2004, bilateral trade between the U.S. and Switzerland increased 8.1%, reaching roughly $21 billion. The Swiss are big investors in the U.S., with capital holdings here of approximately $113 billion. Swiss companies operating in the U.S.

provide jobs to about half a million Americans, a demonstration of outsourcing not always recognized. And besides products, Switzerland puts money into U.S. services—the eighth largest buyer of U.S. services worldwide. That is an astonishing number, given Switzerland's size.

These deep economic relationships benefit the Swiss as well. The U.S., for its part, invests heavily in Switzerland, being by far the biggest foreign investor in that country. And the Swiss export more to the U.S. than to any other nation except their immediate neighbor Germany. The ETH is a large link in a chain which brings economic well-being to both our countries. The exchange of people makes Zürich a hub for academic and commercial interchange. You can see it in the streets.

There's little language problem for Americans. Knowing a little Swiss-German can prove helpful—and is decidedly useful in the lovely garden restaurants and wine verandas along the Limmat—but today English is almost universally accepted as the basic language of the sciences, and most Swiss are comfortable with multiple languages, including English. Conversations flow smoothly into English at the ETH and indeed all over Zürich. Prospective students, graduate students or emerging researchers exploring the school will find a cosmopolitan reception. Many advanced courses are taught entirely in English—another sign of the globalization of science. Americans join students and professors from leading knowledge centers worldwide, and they are warmly welcomed.

After all, Switzerland—despite its long-established political neutrality—is a country which is like the U.S. in many ways. It shares a traditional commitment to the bedrock values of morally ordered liberty and human rights, and it has a long-standing harmonious social order. Historians know that our founders like Adams, Jefferson, Hamilton and Franklin closely studied the unique Swiss democracy founded in 1291. And the Swiss have borrowed from us in their Constitution of 1848 and are generally well informed about the United States, too.

There are important differences, as *School for Genius* tries to point out. Government funding of science is a subject of debate in both countries. The U.S. massively outspends Switzerland in the amounts poured into pure and applied science and puts resources into a space program and military R&D at a rate the Swiss could never match—not unexpected given the sheer size of the U.S. economy. U.S. science dollars are spread out over multiple departments, agencies and organizations in what often appears to be an inefficient and overlapping disarray. Swiss expenditures are less in amount but much more tightly focused on creating and maintaining Switzerland's first-class scientific centers.

Both countries, however, have been effective in producing new science and also new applications of science. We Americans take Swiss-created life-saving pharmaceuticals, build aircraft with Swiss-designed machine parts, and drive across bridges like the Verrazano designed by ETH-educated engineers and architects. Swiss biotechnology, on the other hand, draws lessons from American breakthroughs. American developments in computer science, medicine, nanotechnology and sub-atomic physics fuel Swiss research. The mutually beneficial relationship between the science and technology platforms of both countries is a model of productive international cooperation.

Americans—academics, students, educators at all levels and informed citizens—should know more about this relationship and about the "big league" institution situated in a relatively small but highly advanced country. At the ETH, researchers and world-class architects in training are keenly aware of what is happening in their fields in the United States. We Americans would do well to repay the favor.

I hope you will find *School for Genius* good reading, informative and useful.

FAITH WHITTLESEY
Former U.S. Ambassador to Switzerland
(1981–1983 and 1985–1988)

Acknowledgments

The author is indebted to Dr. Olaf Kübler, President of the ETH; Dr. Konrad Osterwalder, Rector; Dr. Meinrad Eberle, in charge of the ETH 150th Jubilee; Dr. David Gugerli, ETH History Department; Dr. Christine Bärtsch, ETH Library and Director of the Picture Archive; Petra Hieber, ETH Public Relations (Corporate Communications); Gabrielle Rollé, ETH Director of Admissions; Dr. Reza S. Abhari, Head of the Department of Mechanical and Process Engineering; Thomas Eichenberger of the President's staff; Colonel Marco Cantieni of the MILAK-ETH; ETH student Georg Wilckens; and especially to Nicole Schwyzer for her cheerful and able research and administrative assistance in Zürich.

Also, the author is grateful to Daniel M. Hofmann of Zurich Financial Services; Dr. Anton E. Schrafl, ETH graduate and retired Vice Chairman of Holcim; Georg Gyssler, ETH graduate and retired engineer; Dr. Hans Halbheer; Dr. Jürg Stüssi-Lauterburg; and Dr. Jean-François Bergier.

The author owes special thanks to Thomas M. Ryan for his invaluable research, editorial support, and contributions to the text, and to former two-term Ambassador of the United States to Switzerland Faith Whittlesey.

I would like to thank the Ernst Göhner Foundation in Zug, Switzerland, and the Jacobs Foundation in Zürich for major funding of this book. Additional funding was kindly provided by F. Hoffmann-La Roche AG in Basel, Dr. Fritz Schnorf-Lüthi in Meilen, Ernst Basler & Partner in Zollikon, and Basler and

Hofmann AG, Julius Baer Foundation, Credit Suisse Group, Swiss Re and UBS AG, all in Zürich. I am also most grateful for the innumerable smaller donations made by unnamed parties.

Introduction

The Swiss Federal Institute of Technology, or ETH as it is abbreviated in German (short for *Eidgenössische Technische Hochschule*), is ranked as one of the top scientific schools in the world. A recent evaluation named Zürich's "Poly" the best scientific university on the European continent, ahead of similar institutions in Germany and France, and behind only Oxford and Cambridge for the whole of Europe.

Since its founding in 1855, this Swiss "School for Genius" has been a phenomenal success story. But sitting quietly on the hill above Zürich's picturesque Limmat River, the ETH remains little known outside scientific circles. Mention the ETH—the school that produced Einstein, Röntgen (who discovered the x-ray) and close to two dozen other Nobel laureates in advanced science—and you're likely to get a blank stare, at least in the Anglo-American world. Yet, applications of ETH breakthroughs have been part of our working environment in the U.S. for decades. And the school's leading-edge research teams continue to open new paths into the world's common future—in fields like biotechnology, nanotechnology, pharmacology and advanced imaging.

The purpose of this book is to open up this enigma called the ETH (pronounced either "AY-TAY-HAH" or "EE-TEE-AITCH"). The story of its founding and development offers fascinating insights into how a coherent national science strategy can contribute to a modern nation and create broad-based prosperity.

Today, the ETH's lift-off into the new interdisciplinary and globalized sciences is of interest to anyone curious about the structure and evolution of research in the next century, and especially to policymakers and planners. Our hope is to establish a broad and fruitful link to the ETH for both emerging American scientists and the American public in general. There is much to be learned.

The ETH is a Swiss *federal* institution, funded since its inception by the Swiss national government. In the U.S., apart from our military academies, there are no federal institutions of higher learning. In contrast, within Switzerland the impact of the ETH is impressive and widely recognized. Indeed, designs coming from the Poly have literally shaped the landscape of Switzerland. The railroads, bridges, tunnels and hydroelectric networks that link this modern nation of seven million people were by and large the achievements of ETH engineers.

That was the intention at the founding. But we learn that it was not long before ETH engineers, having honed their skills building infrastructure links within the challenging Alps, moved out into the rest of the world in the first great age of reinforced concrete and structural steel—to Europe, America, Russia and Asia. This was a Swiss tradition, because the Swiss are of necessity an outward-looking people. The country has few natural resources, and ever since the first waves of industrialization swept Europe, the Swiss have been forced to go abroad—for raw materials, for markets larger than their own, for larger workforces, for food and fuel, for clients and partners.

The Swiss are a clever, practical and hard-working people. Over the past two centuries, they have developed a cosmopolitan business culture and learned the skills that make for success in places far from home. They learn languages; they know international law, banking and finance; they have learned to keep a close eye on factors affecting international trade and politics. They know currency exchange and move money efficiently. Their financial and engineering expertise allows them to size up opportunities and scientifically assess risk virtually anywhere in the world. The importance of a reliable and timely knowledge network is hardly new to the Swiss.

At an early stage of the Industrial Revolution, Swiss visionaries recognized a direct connection between a superior university system —one focused on innovative technologies—and the long-term prosperity of the nation. A university was not to be an intellectual playpen where the next generation would be polished before its work life begins. Rather, it was to be a machine for output and results driven by innovation. The Swiss wanted to give free rein to genius and pure research. But today, more than ever, advanced Swiss schools are also seen as the driving engine of Swiss material culture, as well as the training ground and laboratory for Swiss multinational corporations. In this regard, Swiss culture has a high level of self-awareness, and the Swiss share a broad agreement on policies deemed necessary to maintain the country's success in global economic competition.

Swiss economic policy has been forward-looking, largely less concerned with how existing wealth is distributed than with the creation of new wealth. The electorate for the most part understands and agrees with this position. Switzerland has been governed since the advent of socialism in the 19th century under a so-called magic formula, a stable balance between socialists, social democrats and the center-right. The Swiss contribute their wealth generously to humanitarian projects around the world. But the practical impulse predominates over the utopian in Switzerland.

What's more, although individual Swiss—and cantons—prize their autonomy and independence, they form a united front in advancing Swiss national interests. That united front includes the government, the universities, the corporations, labor, the media and the general public. Of course there is debate, disagreement, at times rancor, but a unique Swiss consensus system makes possible collaboration between government, science and capitalist enterprise that would be almost unthinkable in the more diverse and chaotic United States. An American industrial policy, whatever it may be, is not easy to discern or articulate succinctly, and certainly would ignite heated controversy if initiated by the central government.

Through the first industrialization of the late 19th and early 20th centuries, Swiss international business expertise, coupled with a focus on value-added technology products like watches, machine tools, optics and instruments, put Switzerland on the road to becoming a prosperous nation, though it could never become a self-sufficient one. New revenues, besides providing funds for the huge investment in Swiss infrastructure, made possible additional and, by the standards of the day, generous funding of the ETH—and indeed of an outstanding educational system up and down the line. This exceptional level of funding, the reliance on experienced business-men and technologically sophisticated leaders, and an uncanny abil-ity to attract the right geniuses—created the first great age of the ETH, the time of Einstein and Röntgen and so many others, both in engineering and in fundamental science.

This book tells that fascinating story in some but not exhaustive detail. As we move into the present, it is clear that the foundations upon which Swiss prosperity rests have been shifting. The Swiss are keenly aware that their fragile niche in the production of value-added machine goods is shrinking. The watches, tools, optics and instruments—where they once dominated—are now increasingly being produced more cheaply in Asia. It's also clear that manufac-turing and its associated logistics are everywhere undergoing radi-cal change. Looking forward as they do, the Swiss realize they have to transform their economic model if they are to maintain them-selves in a globalized world. That transformation—the much-heralded strategic shift to the production of knowledge itself—is under way. Of course, the restructuring of today's ETH complex plays a big part in what the Swiss call their "re-industrialization." This also is a story worth reading.

It is perhaps one of the ironies of history that the United States, so much more diverse, rowdy and undisciplined than the "man-aged" states of Europe, was successful in producing so many of the breakthroughs at the first level of industrialization—in steam, elec-tricity, powered flight, electronics and nuclear energy. Now, during what may be called the second great technology revolution, America's very tumult and absence of tradition and precedent seem somehow a good fit for the open frontiers of so much of contem-porary science.

The media, and people generally, often focus on the social problems in the United States. Meanwhile, almost unnoticed, the robust muscularity of research in the U.S.—coupled with the harvest provided by a huge influx of scientific refugees—has made the U.S. a uniquely productive hothouse for new ideas. Everything is in play. There are vigorous venture capital markets and little stigma of failure in visionary business ventures.

Switzerland is changing rapidly, too. Yet, the Swiss are not comfortable with disorder. At every level they pay attention to precision and detail, to the Swiss way of "doing things right." Perhaps Switzerland may share the tendency of other European societies to defer to tradition—be it only to the new "tradition" of the comfortable life. Certainly the penchant for deliberate, managed reform can be a disadvantage when the pace of change accelerates, and when educational funding, based on the health of national economies, becomes less certain.

Swiss planners are clearly aware of these hurdles as they import corporate management theory at the same time that they work to build a more freewheeling entrepreneurial culture within and around the ETH. They have been given a mandate for fundamental reform and considerable freedom to make it happen. The federal government may attempt to help the Swiss people understand the importance of the revolution at the ETH, but it does not micromanage ETH planners. Indeed the entire ETH budget is but a single line in the Swiss budget, signaling an extremely "light hand." However, there is clearly a demand for measurable results.

Swiss cantons remain extraordinarily autonomous, and the Swiss central government is more limited in its powers than those in other European states. But small as it is, the Swiss federal government offers the ETH certain advantages. The school has a reasonably secure ongoing source of funding so that it doesn't, for example, need to rely primarily on tuitions. There is a limited control bureaucracy and considerable operational freedom. The various institutes of today's ETH are encouraged when they take up new projects or initiate cooperative ventures with other schools, organizations and even corporations on an increasingly global basis.

Technology transfer—the ability to guide knowledge breakthroughs into private sector production—is a central concern of Swiss planners. We now enter a world of intellectual property rights, licenses, patents, spin-offs and startups where the U.S. has been blazing the path. Suffice it to say that the Swiss are working hard—and not just within the ETH—to find the best balance between creating useful knowledge and making that knowledge pay off for the Swiss people. *School for Genius* provides a valuable perspective on some, though not all, of these issues.

For its 150th year celebration, the ETH conducted an essay contest to predict the shape of the ETH in the year 2030. Professors, students and outsiders participated, and the final selection was provocative. The school is streaking into a future that is bright and challenging, but in so many ways unknown. For the English reader, *School for Genius* provides a foundation for understanding the ETH today and following its path as it "Welcomes Tomorrow."

PART I
TOWARD AN IDEAL OF EXCELLENCE

CHAPTER ONE

The Transforming Power
of the Mind

An event unnoticed by the rest of the world unfolded on a hill above the picturesque Swiss city of Zürich in October 1855. With a 55-gun salute to mark the occasion, the Swiss Federal Institute of Technology, then known as the Polytechnic School, or informally as "the Poly," opened for business.

The hopeful cannonade notwithstanding, the new school's beginnings were decidedly modest. It was the first federally supported institution of higher education in a country where education was strictly a local matter, and many Swiss were ambivalent, if not outright opposed. Switzerland was not then a wealthy country, and many begrudged the expenditure of public money on an uncertain venture. The Poly did not even have its own quarters but had to share housing with the University of Zürich, founded 22 years earlier. Two hundred and thirty-one students reported, but most of them were auditors. Only 71 were enrolled in the full diploma track. Yet from this modest beginning grew one of the finest institutions of science and technology in the world and one of the best overall universities—a school which has been instrumental in transforming Switzerland into the prosperous country it is today while at the same time providing incalculable benefits to the rest of the world.

The subject of this book, the Swiss Federal Institute of Technology (ETH), is the jewel in the crown of Swiss education. It also represents an object lesson in how a school founded and supported by a practical-minded government of a relatively small country can rise to the highest pinnacle of scientific achievement. Yet most Americans have never heard of the ETH or know it exists. Accustomed to U.S. preeminence in science and technology, Americans might be surprised to learn that Switzerland hosts an institution specializing in science and technology with a record of achievement often equaling—and in some respects exceeding—any comparable institution in the United States, the United Kingdom or Switzerland's neighbors in Western Europe.

The Swiss Federal Institute of Technology was the first Swiss "national" school, in contrast to existing educational institutions in the cantons and private or religious schools. Guided and funded by the Swiss federal government, the ETH had to struggle through a controversial beginning as an advanced institute of higher learning. Today it has evolved into a complex enterprise consisting of undergraduate and graduate programs and a wide range of advanced research groups. Worldwide it is known by the German acronym ETH for *Eidgenössische Technische Hochschule*, the official Swiss name.

The ETH's wide-ranging successes demonstrate how strategic public investment in advanced studies can produce well-educated and well-trained people capable of overcoming seemingly insurmountable obstacles—in Switzerland's case, size, terrain, limited population and lack of natural resources. The ETH has succeeded beyond its founders' wildest dreams in transforming Switzerland both directly, through the physical and intellectual contributions of graduates, and indirectly, by creating an affluent and forward-looking civic culture across the whole nation. From its inception, the experience of the ETH has proved that the best investment a country can make is in the intellectual capital of its people, because the transformational power of the human mind is virtually unlimited.

Graduates of MIT or Caltech, of Oxford or Cambridge, are justly proud of their institutions and might argue that their school's contributions to scientific knowledge equal or surpass those of the ETH. It is not the object of this book to rank the world's science and technology schools, and in any case, with typical Swiss modesty (not necessarily shared by this author), the ETH makes no excessive claims for itself. Suffice it to say that the ETH has had the capacity, through some strange alchemy of factors, to find, ignite and sustain the spark of human genius.

The story of the ETH is a kind of adventure story, for the greatest adventure is not necessarily a voyage across remote seas but the inner voyage that expands the frontiers of knowledge.

THE GENESIS OF AN IDEA

In the fall of 1855, Europe and the wider world were paying scant attention to the academic procession and the saluting guns on the heights of Zürich. The Western world was focused on cannon fire of a far more dramatic nature, and events in small, at the time relatively remote, Switzerland hardly registered on the popular mind. The Crimean War between Russia and Turkey, Britain and France was approaching its climax. The strategic Russian city of Sebastopol had just fallen after a long siege that dominated the headlines for a year. Czar Nicholas I, the "Iron Czar," who led his country into this disastrous war, had just died and been succeeded by his son Alexander II. The world waited in suspense to see if Alexander would continue as Autocrat of All the Russias or open his country to the liberalizing forces sweeping Europe.

The mid-19th century was a time of rich intellectual ferment. England and France bestrode the literary world, and names like Browning, Tennyson, and Dickens, Hugo and Dumas were celebrated throughout Europe. The upstart United States was also making its mark in the world of letters. A potboiler called *Uncle Tom's Cabin* had been published only a few years earlier. By 1855 it had become an international best-seller and its author, Harriet Beecher Stowe, a celebrity; and the slow fuse it had helped ignite would soon erupt into America's bloodiest war.

The intellectual ferment of the times had produced huge strides in science and technology, fields in which Great Britain, France and Germany led the world. Scotland's University of Edinburgh, home of a race of legendary engineers, had just instituted its first chair of technology. Ferdinand de Lesseps received a concession from the French government to dig a canal though the Suez Peninsula, linking the Eastern Mediterranean and the Indian Ocean and saving weeks of sailing time around Africa's southern cape. The first all-iron steamer, of the British Cunard Line, crossed the Atlantic, making the trip in an unprecedented nine and a half days.

Technology expositions and trade fairs were wildly popular events, reinforcing hopes that the mid-century would usher in a new era of human potential. In 1855, the Exposition Universelle de l'Industrie in Paris followed similar technology fairs in Munich, New York, and especially the 1851 exposition in London's Crystal Palace, capturing the public imagination. Citizens of Europe and North America began to see the combination of science and technology as a pathway to undreamed-of improvements in the condition of mankind.

Leading Swiss academics and politicians began to ask: What about Switzerland? Why shouldn't the Swiss partake in the benefits of science and technology? Neighboring countries had founded polytechnic schools expressly to train chemists and engineers, people with the skills and knowledge to translate new scientific discoveries into new industries and other practical benefits. Why not the Swiss?

Compared to its far larger and better-endowed neighbors France, Germany, Austria, and Italy, Switzerland appeared to have little going for it. It was—and is—a small country, with comparatively few natural resources. It is landlocked, with no outlet to the sea for direct foreign trade. With the exception of the fertile plains along its northern and western periphery, the country is dominated by a forbidding mountain landscape that limits agriculture and other productive activity. Not even a "nation" in the classic sense, it is a confederation of states built over the centuries—almost entirely voluntarily, it should be noted—by a polity embracing four different languages and cultures—German, French, Italian, and Romansch (a neo-Latin dialect descended from ancient Roman occupiers).

In 1855 Switzerland was relatively poor as compared to neigh-

boring France, Germany and Austria, with agriculture, light manufacturing and cottage industries predominating. At the time it also
had an infant mortality rate of approximately 28 percent. However,
the Swiss did have a strong tradition of cross-border commerce,
largely because their country lay astride key trade routes between
Italy and northern Europe, and it controlled the vital Alpine passes
along those routes. Switzerland also held great promise in the
innate energies and abilities of its people and in its accommodative
culture and politics—stable despite the potential for internal conflict among different religions and cultures because the Swiss had
perfected the art of compromise and local self-government.

Economists Nathan Rosenberg and L.E. Birdzell, Jr., have written a history of world commerce, *How the West Grew Rich: The
Economic Transformation of the Industrial World,* in which they
analyze the capitalist free enterprise system that has conferred so
much on the Western industrialized democracies. The essential elements were, first, an ideology of individual freedom assuring that
the state would not simply confiscate private property. Then came
the development of moral and religious beliefs "compatible with the
needs and values of capitalism," the development of commercial
law and commercial courts, the advent of insurance to reduce the
risks of international commerce, deposit banking, capital markets,
and double-entry bookkeeping that made economic calculation
possible, among other things. Looming over all and woven through
all was the forward march of technology.

All these elements—except for the wide availability of modern
technology—were abundant in Switzerland in the 1850s or were
rapidly developing in the country's favorable commercial climate.
The people of the Swiss Confederation enjoyed a remarkable degree
of freedom, along with political and social stability flowing from
the country's decentralized organization. The individual cantons,
rather than a central government, held the greatest power (and still
do), including collection of most of the taxes, and retained a high
degree of local autonomy. French-speaking Protestant Swiss in
Neuchâtel or Geneva did not intrude on the daily lives of German-
speaking Catholic Swiss in St. Gallen or Lucerne, and vice versa.

But there was one major deficiency. In the mid-1850s, the Swiss made a conscious decision to provide that essential prerequisite to the country's development they lacked—namely, scientific know-how and technological prowess. The result was the ETH.

A GAMBLE ON THE FUTURE

In 1855 Switzerland's population consisted of only two and a half million people. To found a great scientific enterprise on such a slim human foundation was a bold undertaking. Yet Switzerland's greatest resource, and export, had always been its people—intelligent, industrious strivers who had frequently overcome great odds. From medieval times the Swiss were known as fierce and skilled warriors and were in great demand as contract soldiers throughout Europe. The Vatican's Swiss Guard is a lingering remnant of that tradition. However, the Swiss eventually grew tired of providing fodder for Europe's endless wars, so often dead-end struggles involving greed or dynastic ambition. The Swiss aspired to a better life than selling themselves as soldiers-for-hire to foreign princes, or alternatively remaining farmers and small tradesmen. But the country possessed few natural resources, farms were often isolated, and farm work itself in a land largely dominated by the Alps could literally be a daunting uphill task. Opportunities in traditional skilled trades were scarce. Then the intellectual ferment of the Enlightenment and finally the French Revolution at the end of the 18th century swept across Europe. The Swiss took in many refugees, and the excitement and challenge of revolution reverberated across Switzerland.

For all their excesses, these two revolutions—one intellectual and one political—imbued Europeans with a new sense of possibility. People began to see the potential of invention and industrial knowledge as a path to solve age-old problems of transport, communications, sustenance, and self-defense. Knowledge could produce wealth, and wealth brought power and freedom. Visionary Swiss soon came to believe that an "advanced" nation could only come from skilled and well-educated craftsmen and inventors. Early on they took up the new technical education movement that had started in France and urged investment in Switzerland's people, focusing on research, applied science and technology. A nationally sponsored school would help unify the country and bring practical benefits for their resource-poor country.

Today, with the wisdom of hindsight, this may seem to have been an obvious conclusion. But the advantages of unified advanced education were not so obvious in the 1850s. Science was as ever entangled in religious and political traditions. The benefits of research and technology—especially coming from an institution controlled by a central government—were nowhere as clear as they are today. To conservative Swiss, "modern" education—tied in the public imagination as it was to the Enlightenment, the darker aspects of the French Revolution, and the uprisings and chaos in Europe of 1848—was considered dangerous and subversive of the prevailing social order. Switzerland was already divided by language and religious denomination, as well as by divergence of interests between its trading and manufacturing cities and its agricultural cantons. Advanced learning was also clearly "foreign," having its origins in nations which the Swiss saw as troubled—primarily France and Germany. Some Swiss were sure that a unified federal school would change Switzerland, but *for the worse*, opening the nation to overwhelming German or French influences, robbing autonomy from the cantons, or serving the interests of the cities but not the countryside.

Ultimately, the Swiss were willing to take a chance on the new school. It was a flash of genius for the Swiss to commit themselves to invest in the *intellectual capital* of their people—an investment in what was then largely an unknown. But they were in step with their times. The 19th century became the age of industrialization and offered unique opportunities to Switzerland and to the ETH. Today we have to remember that at the time all other institutions of higher learning were cantonal and dedicated to "humane letters," theology and law. It took determination to establish the institute, especially for a culture with a strong political consensus against increasing federal power. The Swiss, by voluntarily establishing an institution like the ETH—funded, thus ultimately controlled by their national government—were going against their own traditions and beliefs, a difficult undertaking for any people at any time.

Since its founding the ETH has been the only higher education institution supported by the Swiss federal government, as distinguished from the 12 cantonal or state universities. By 1864 the Poly had its own imposing neo-classical edifice on the ridge above the Limmat River, with a panoramic view of downtown Zürich and the hills beyond. In 1855 it began as the *Eidgenössische Polytechnische Schule*, or "Poly"; and visitors can still see vestiges of the old name. The cog tram that carries students up the steep hill from central Zürich to the ETH, for example, is called the Polybahn. In 1911 the school's name was changed to the *Eidgenössische Technische Hochschule*.

The original ETH grew enormously in size and scope from its relatively humble origins. That growth continues today with the new sciences of lasers, computer design, informatics, microbiology, genetics, nanotechnology and a host of new areas of exploration. A federal law in 1991 created the *ETH Bereich* ("domain"), or "Greater ETH." It now includes the ETH in Zürich, the *Ecole Polytechnique Fédérale de Lausanne* (EPFL) in Lausanne, and four subordinate research centers in various regions of Switzerland: the Paul Scherrer Institute; the Federal Institute for Forestry, Snow, and Landscape Research; the Federal Institute for Materials Testing and Research; and the Federal Institute for Environmental Science and Technology.

The term *Eidgenössische* is one of those compound German words that sound like someone clearing his throat and is a unique Swiss construction that roughly means "federal." It is the Swiss equivalent of the better-known German word *Bund*, as in *die Bundesrepublik Deutschland,* the Federal Republic of Germany. The root words are *Eid*, which means "oath," and *Genossen*, the fellows united in the swearing of that oath (as an adjective, the root noun *Genosse,* or "fellow"—plural *Genossen*—picks up an umlaut to become *genössisch*). It is distinctly Swiss because it harkens back to the founding of the Confederation in 1291, when representatives of the central "Forest Cantons," Uri, Schwyz and

Unterwalden, met at the Rütli Meadow above Lake Lucerne to form a defensive alliance—*die Eidgenossenschaft*—against Habsburg domination. All participants swore an oath to come to the aid of the others if attacked. *Technisch* should be easily recognizable to English speakers. And *Hochschule*, while literally translatable as "high school," does not carry the U.S. definition but refers to a school of higher education. (What we call high school is *Gymnasium* in German-speaking Switzerland, although the curriculum of a European *Gymnasium* does not correspond to that of an American high school.)

In its early days, the ETH curriculum was closely confined to "accepted" disciplines. The school was set up as a polytechnic with little pretension to university status. Before the 20th century arrived, the ETH placed heavy emphasis on practical pursuits in six departments—architecture, civil engineering, mechanical engineering, chemistry, forestry, and mathematics. Limited generalized course work in the natural and social sciences rounded out the school's program. Just after the turn of the century, the Poly was restructured into a genuine university, though retaining its emphasis on science and technology. It not only took on the new name but created new departments and began granting doctoral degrees. The institution's explosion in creative output during the early 20th century paralleled the breakthroughs in the hard sciences across Europe. The benefits of advanced science and technology followed breathtaking discoveries in physics, chemistry, electronics and structural engineering. New fields and subfields emerged one after the other, and the ETH both produced and attracted some of the world's best scientists—a story which will be told in some detail in the following chapters.

Today the ETH curriculum has grown to offer degrees in architecture, civil engineering, electrical engineering, environmental engineering, mechanical and process engineering, computer sciences, materials sciences, industrial management and manufacturing, mathematics, physics, chemistry and chemical engineering, pharmaceutical sciences, biology, earth and environmental sciences, agricultural sciences, forest sciences, human movement and sports sciences. Moreover, in keeping with Switzerland's reliance upon a citizens' army built around a small professional cadre, students can also earn a federal diploma in the professional officer program. The ETH also offers a wide range of practical postgraduate studies for university graduates who have already embarked upon a career.

In the 2005–2006 academic year the ETH was transitioning to the European Bachelor's/Master's degree structure under the so-called Bologna Reforms, named for the agreements reached among European education ministries in Bologna, Italy. This will make European degrees, including the Ph.D., uniform with the system in place in the U.S. and the U.K., and much of the rest of the world.

From the beginning the ETH's focus was on teaching as well as research, and even today it remains a teaching university that strikes a deliberate balance between classroom activity and research. At many U.S. universities top professors have relatively little contact with undergraduates, and basic courses are turned over to the junior faculty or even graduate student teaching assistants. The ETH ethos demands that all teachers teach, including the introductory courses for new students.

The ETH benefited from the beginning—and was able to succeed—because of three vital requisites. First, as a federal instead of cantonal institute, its funding base was solid, anchored and allocated by the Swiss Parliament. That funding, along with an intelligently executed commitment to excellence, drew an outstanding faculty—the second requirement for a first-tier school. Ample financial support, a fine faculty, and the support of national policy brought the third element of success—good students. Swiss culture imbued in its young people an ethos of hard work and civic virtue. They were disciplined, eager to learn, and intelligent; or, if not, they didn't remain.

In the 19th century, when people took religion more seriously than they appear to do today, some Swiss cantons were heavily Protestant and others strongly Catholic. But the ETH was successful in cutting across sectarian divides. The best faculty were hired on the basis of academic qualifications alone. That was an exceptional move for the Swiss, since Swiss devotion to local autonomy in education and other matters meant that cantonal universities tended to hire either Protestants or Catholics.

There are two additional factors of Swiss culture and policy that helped the ETH become successful in cultivating genius. In its early days the institute did not require graduation from a secondary school, or *Gymnasium*. Students with promise were allowed to enroll on the basis of an entrance exam. That provided an opportunity for a number of towering intellects who nonetheless had not been successful in their secondary schools, or who came from a different country. In a more restrictive system, they might never have been able to matriculate. The Swiss maintained a rigorous egalitarian meritocracy at the ETH, but the door was always left open a crack for late-blooming or eccentric geniuses, and the strategy paid off handsomely. Second, it must be recognized that throughout their history the Swiss have had a long tradition, as in the U.S., of welcoming refugees. The best and the brightest from France and Germany, in particular, found a haven in Switzerland from persecution and chaos in their own countries. That tradition continues and, while it is not an easy process to become a Swiss citizen, the ETH was and remains an immensely cosmopolitan and welcoming institution. Indeed, during the early days of the school, the ETH went out of its way to attract foreign talent, both as faculty and students.

Two of the ETH's most illustrious graduates were beneficiaries of these enlightened policies—men who might not otherwise have found a place to nourish their genius, including the winner of the first Nobel Prize, Wilhelm Conrad Röntgen (in 1901, for Physics), and perhaps the most famous man of science of all time, Albert Einstein, who won the Nobel in 1921.

Americans are generally fascinated by theoretical physics or quantum theory, especially in 2005, the centennial of Einstein's "miracle year" when he published five papers—including one on relativity theory—that began the transformation of modern physics and changed the way we comprehend the universe. Few Americans know that the ETH continued to play a pivotal role in the development of theoretical physics through such other graduates as Wolfgang Pauli, regarded by some as Einstein's spiritual heir, and through its work in creating the world-famous CERN (*Conseil Européen pour la Recherche Nucléaire*—the European Organization for Nuclear Research) near Geneva.

From 1901, when the first Nobel was awarded to Röntgen, to the present, ETH faculty or graduates have won 21 Nobel Prizes in physics, chemistry, and medicine, more than any comparable institution worldwide. Not all of the ETH's most illustrious graduates could aspire to the honor of a Nobel Prize—not least because so many of them followed a practical orientation toward architecture and civil and mechanical engineering, and there is no Nobel Prize for engineering. If there were, no doubt it would have been awarded to Swiss-American immigrant Othmar Ammann. "It is a crime to build an ugly bridge," declared Ammann, who graduated from the ETH in 1902 and came to the United States in 1904. True to his word, he designed bridges that are not only marvels of engineering but also majestic works of art in steel and concrete, including New York's George Washington Bridge. Completed in 1931, it was called the most beautiful bridge in the world, and was the longest suspension span of its type.

The impact of the ETH's groundbreaking science in physics and chemistry and also the achievements in architecture and mechanical and civil engineering have proven a boon to Switzerland and the industrialized world, all out of proportion to the country's small size and population. Almost from its beginnings, the ETH managed to create an environment in which people can dream, risk and invent—an atmosphere the present ETH administration calls "creative chaos."

While our modern technological societies are beneficiaries of hundreds of years of accumulated knowledge, scientific knowledge and technological prowess do not necessarily progress in steady increments, like a river of cumulative discovery, one tiny move forward piled upon another and another. As Thomas Kuhn has demonstrated in his seminal book *The Structure of Scientific Revolutions*, knowledge is cumulative; but it also advances in fits and starts and sometimes—appropriately in the context of the ETH story—in quantum leaps. Kuhn's term, which has now fully entered the modern lexicon, is "paradigm shift," a discovery or new approach that redefines reality. What follows, then, is the story of an unusual people, a unique country, and their world-renowned Federal Institute of Technology. It is the story of how an unassuming people did their part to shift the paradigm in science education, primarily for their own benefit, to develop their country and make it prosper. In so doing they also benefited the rest of the world. Let us learn what we may from it. Whether or not we wish to learn or the Swiss wish to serve as a model to emulate, the story of the ETH is still a story that cries out to be told.

CHAPTER TWO

The ETH and the Swiss Paradox

In the 1850s, when the idea of an ETH was being debated in Parliament, Switzerland had a population of only two and a half million. Much of its territory was mountainous to the point of being impassable, and difficult or impossible to farm. Switzerland was poor, landlocked, surrounded on all sides by potential enemies, and possessed few natural resources, with the notable but largely untapped exception of water power. There was no coal or other mineral wealth. Switzerland had its traditional crafts, maintained lively trading, banking and customs operations as a kind of gateway between France, Germany, Austria and Italy, but possessed hardly any industry. With the exception of age-old trade routes, there was scarcely any infrastructure knitting together the country's diverse cantons across rugged and inhospitable terrain. Communications were slow. Travel was difficult.

Thus, at the time, the ETH seemed an unlikely project for a nation made up mostly of farmers, herders, small craftsmen and traders. Yet the Swiss were successful within a relatively short period in producing a world-class institution where the very frontiers of human knowledge were explored and advanced. The story of how they conceived the ETH, conducted a national debate, enacted the law necessary to give it birth and guided its growth features a success of vision over seemingly insurmountable obstacles.

What prompted the Swiss to grasp the importance of higher education in science and technology at such an early date, and come up with a plan to make the ETH a reality? What led them to harness their inherent skills and brainpower to overcome first the limitations of their own environment and then reach out to the world, emerging today as one of the world's most successful countries? What role did the ETH play in this development, to which it was both primary contributor and, as time passed, a beneficiary?

Switzerland is a multi-cultural country with an intense commitment to independence and local autonomy. Despite its linguistic and religious diversity, it works without the heavy hand of a powerful central authority. Individual cantons (similar to U.S. states) vigorously define and defend their particular interests. Switzerland is a direct democracy, and on the national level much of its policy (such as whether to join the UN or European Union) is still decided by direct referendum by the people themselves. Thus the ETH had to make its way through a thicket of potential conflicts—four linguistic-cultural communities, French, German, Italian and Romansch; Catholics versus Protestants, urbanites versus rural dwellers, financiers against farmers. In the end, the Swiss created an institution that served the entire polity and not the narrow interests of one dominant community. To what extent did the spirit of voluntary cooperation and compromise derived from Switzerland's long historical experience as a direct democracy bring about the ETH's success? What was the impact of Switzerland's decentralized political system on the institute, and how have both flourished despite the natural tendency of governments and government creations to aggrandize their own power?

GEOGRAPHY IS DESTINY

In Switzerland's evolution, one can see the positive effects of many of the forces that have shaped what remains best in the modern world. The Swiss have achieved democratic self-government without demagoguery, religious freedom with minimal sectarian conflict, industrial development without a permanent underclass, and modernity without the pervasive shabbiness and mediocrity that so often accompany the material plenty of mass production. They have created wealth without grave maldistribution, and prosperity without significant discontent, envy and social strife. Much of the country's success can certainly be attributed to sharp insights and prudent policy. But, as always, Swiss history has also been shaped by the country's location and topography.

Occupying the heart of Europe, Switzerland exists astride the Alpine watershed that sends the great rivers of Europe flowing down from its mountains in all directions—the Rhone and Ticino rivers to the Mediterranean, the Rhine to the North Sea, and the Inn to the Danube and the Black Sea. One could say the Swiss stood at the "top" of Europe. They were literally at the source of the great flows of the continent, and from time immemorial they have fiercely defended their high ground. The Romans feared them as among the most formidable warriors the legions faced. Invaders nearly always had second thoughts about venturing into their mountain fastnesses. The impenetrable and dangerous mountains helped the Swiss remain apart from Europe's frequent conflicts, and shaped and supported their sense of independence.

Switzerland, of course, is not all mountainous. Most of the country's population and productive economic activity are located in the narrow fertile plain—the "Plateau"—bounded by the Jura and the Alps, running roughly on a line from Lake Geneva in the southwest to Lake Constance in the northeast. The mountainous center of the Alps presides over all, offering an impregnable sanctuary into which the Swiss have always been able to withdraw when threatened and to fight an invader to a standstill. Even the Nazis, who coveted Switzerland and had conquered virtually all of continental Europe by 1940, were concerned about attacking the Swiss.

This fortuitous balance between this remote high plain and the still higher mountains is the essential factor that permitted the development of a viable, stable political entity in the European heartland between France, Germany, Italy and Austria. The fertile, productive Plateau fed Switzerland and provided the initial basis for local trade, serving as a connecting link between the great cities along the northern periphery. When danger threatened, there was the Alpine mountain redoubt. Geography added yet another blessing. The expanding Swiss Confederation found itself in a transit zone between both the east and west of Europe and the ever-growing trade routes between the north and south. Strategic passes like the St. Gotthard controlled traffic and commerce into northern Italy. Parts of Switzerland gradually became cosmopolitan through this trade. The country that emerged was robust, used to travelers within its high valleys and diverse in character, while containing within itself the requisite conditions for a free and autonomous existence.

WHO ARE THE SWISS?

In his *Annals*, the great Roman historian Tacitus wrote with admiration of a rugged Celtic people in central Europe. They inhabited a territory bounded in the west by the Jura range, on the south by the Rhone River and Lake Geneva, and on the north and east by the Rhine River, down to Lake Constance. Its inhabitants called themselves the *Helvetii*. Though most modern Swiss are descended from other peoples, this ancient term survives in Switzerland's historical and official name. To avoid favoring any one linguistic community, and in keeping with their spirit of compromise, the Swiss cleverly adopted the Latin version of "Swiss Confederation," *Confoederatio Helvetica*, symbolized by the letters CH. This is why one sees "CH" national stickers on the backs of Swiss automobiles and "ch" as the tag on Swiss e-mail addresses and Internet websites.

By 50 A.D. Rome had conquered the area. Julius Caesar regarded the Helvetii as the toughest opponents he encountered in his numerous campaigns. Later, when these Celts of the central Alps had been Romanized, they proved to be the most effective of Rome's military auxiliaries and proved trustworthy to the end of the Empire. An enduring consequence of the Roman occupation was the early adoption of Christianity, and the faith remained deeply entrenched even when the Romans departed.

With the decline of Rome, the Latinized Celts of Helvetia were increasingly pressured by migrating tribes primarily from the north and east; and east of the Jura the Celts became heavily Germanized.

While the Alemanni (who gave their name to *l'Allemagne* and *les allemands*, the French name for Germany and the Germans) came in from the east, another Latinized tribe, the Burgundians, entered the region from the north and west. Where these two cultural-linguistic groups collided marks the rough boundary between French- and German-speaking Switzerland that remains to the present day. It also explains certain deep national feelings, not necessarily always positive, about the Germans and French, both of which descend from tribes other than the original Helvetii.

As a consequence of the migration of this unsettled post-Roman period, the majority of Swiss—about 72 percent—speak a German dialect and are stamped by Germanic culture. However, as the Swiss are quick to point out, they are not the same as Germans and Austrians, thanks to geography, the caprices of history and, above all, their own choices. Unlike Switzerland, most of Germany remained outside the Roman Empire and its indelible civilizing influences, and German tribes came only slowly to embrace Christianity. This historic difference marks a gulf between the two deeper than the dividing line between German-speaking and French-speaking Switzerland. In a similar manner, Alemannic Switzerland remained outside the influence of the Prussians and Slavs of eastern Europe and did not imbibe the aggressive spirit that took root in Germany. Anchored solidly in central Europe, the Alemannic Swiss share much in common with Germany and Austria, yet differ in major respects from their cousins across the Rhine and to the east.

French-speaking Swiss have much in common with France, yet differ in major respects from their cousins across the Juras to the west. These Swiss *Romands*, as they are called, make up about 21 percent of the population, and trace their roots back to the migration of Burgundians and Rhodanians, Gallic tribes of the Rhone region. It is noteworthy that, like German-speaking Swiss, French-speaking Swiss are not a monolithic religious community. Just as there are Protestants and Catholics among German Swiss, there are Protestant and Catholic areas in *Suisse-Romande*. French Protestantism is the legacy of John Calvin and the thousands of French

Huguenots who fled to Geneva and Lausanne to escape religious persecution in Catholic France.

Like their German-speaking countrymen, the Swiss *Romands* are culturally oriented toward a powerful neighbor but politically oriented toward the Confederation. In fact, they are well aware of the benefits of being a "necessary" cultural minority. In *Suisse-Romande,* status as a minority does not denote inferiority or less favored treatment. In the direct referenda traditional to Swiss democracy, they retain the clout to block policies that threaten their interests. What's more, the German Swiss seem to hold the French Swiss in high regard for their Latinate creativity, vivacity of temperament and style. Once again, autonomous self-determination protects minorities in Switzerland, and these necessary processes of negotiation and compromise played a large role in the creation of the ETH.

Finally, we come to the two smaller communities: the Italian- and Romansch-speaking Swiss, who together make up about three percent and one percent, respectively, of the population. The Italian Swiss are concentrated almost exclusively in Canton Ticino, which abuts Italy's northwest border, with a smattering in the nearby Grisons (the Canton of Graubünden, in German). They are Catholic and descendants of the Lombards, who have dominated northern Italy since post-Roman times. They look toward Italy as the basis of their civilization, as the Alemannic Swiss look toward Germany and the Romands toward France.

Although the Romansch speakers are a tiny minority, even they have been accorded a place in the Swiss mosaic. Romansch is a surviving form of the Celtic-Latin spoken by the Rhaetians under Roman occupation. Its spoken effect has been described as someone speaking Spanish with a heavy German accent, and it lingers in enclaves in the Grisons and as far north as Chur. While most Romansch-speakers are fluent in one or more of the country's other languages, their ancient tongue was accorded status as an official language in 1938, attesting to the Swiss desire to recognize the interests of minorities, however miniscule. The Swiss believe that official recognition of four linguistic communities supports the demographic equilibrium of the Confederation better than a simple French-German bifurcation.

To summarize, the Swiss created a stable, life-sustaining society of four different communities held together by peaceful, cooperative forms of behavior. Persuasion, conciliation, and a respect for the inviolability of other individuals, their language and their culture became the hallmark of Swiss society. This was in marked contrast to the social and political patterns in neighboring countries, where so often coercion ruled over cooperation, and conscription over contract. Despite cultural similarities to their neighbors— drinking from the same wellsprings of literature, folkways, and the arts—the Swiss forged their own path through an active effort to find consensus. They avoided the French pattern, which spawned bloody revolution and war in the late 18th and 19th centuries, and the Austro-German pattern, which culminated in a sociopathic cataclysm in the 20th century. The centralization and top-down rule of the powerful states on their borders never held any appreciable temptation to the Swiss. Individual liberty and local autonomy were enshrined within the Swiss society. Moreover, as prickly and individualistic as Swiss society could be, it was still capable of fielding a large, fierce army of citizen-soldiers to defend its independence. No foreign power has invaded the nation since Napoleon's army in 1798.

THE WORLD'S OLDEST INDEPENDENT REPUBLIC

The Romans and most of their Alemanni successors preferred living on the Plateau, avoiding the rugged terrain and harsh winter weather of the *Innerschweiz*, the central Alpine region. This area around Lucerne and its lake was steep, heavily wooded and largely unpopulated, a kind of "Alemannian Siberia." The Rhaetians, a tribe of the earliest Celtic Helvetians, gradually moved into the region of eastern Switzerland to escape the increasingly onerous demands of feudal civilization. Schwyz and Uri are two of the earliest place names in Switzerland, dating to about 750 A.D. These two communities, along with Unterwalden, made up a territory known as the

Waldstätte, or "forest districts," centered on Lake Lucerne—in German the *Vierwaldstättersee*, the Lake of the Four Forest Districts. The early Swiss of the *Waldstätte* were tough and self-reliant. They had to be to survive the high mountains and brutal winters. But they bonded together to resist any and all incursions by outsiders. Determined to be free from foreign overlords, the Forest Cantons formed the Swiss Confederation in 1291, arguably the oldest continuous republic in the world. Some historians might dispute this assertion, since the form and scope of the Confederation have undergone significant changes over its 700-plus years of history. Nevertheless, though the Swiss have changed their constitution several times—one might say, updated it—these changes have not fundamentally altered the republican essence and decentralized structure of the Confederation.

THE EARLY CONFEDERATION

Until the late Middle Ages, the lands occupied by the Swiss were simply unrecognized. They were neither a political nor even a cultural entity. However, the eastern portion lay within the sphere of influence claimed by the Austrian Habsburgs, who sent their tax collectors into the area of the Forest Cantons. It was this period of Austrian aggression that produced the world-famous legend of William Tell. Modern scholars doubt the existence of Tell, and there is little evidence to prove he actually lived. But he is alive in folklore and in the Swiss national consciousness as an abiding symbol of Swiss independence and resistance to tyranny.

In August 1291, the burghers and freeholders of the *Waldstätte*—Uri, Schwyz and Unterwalden—determined to resist Austrian domination, met in the Rütli Meadow, a shelf of level land on a hill that slopes steeply down to Lake Lucerne. Significantly, there were no great noble houses or princes of the church present, just ordinary men. They were undaunted by the arrogant Habsburgs and their armies. Most astonishing, in an era of rigid social castes and feudal obligations, the fellows assembled asked permission of no one; they simply acted as free men in their own interests. Simple, unassuming, but with clarity of purpose and dedication to liberty, these "Comrades of the Oath" (*Eidgenossen*) swore the bond of mutual support that was the beginning of the Swiss Confederation. Their proclamation, though virtually unknown outside of Switzerland, rings down through the ages as a declaration of liberty. It is a worthy companion of other great affirmations of self-government and political freedom such as the Magna Carta of England (1215), Scotland's Declaration of Arbroath (1320), and even America's Declaration of Independence 485 years later.

The Swiss Confederates swore in the name of God and on behalf of the public welfare, which is served "when leagues are concluded for the proper establishment of quiet and peace," that "the people of the valley of Uri, the democracy of the valley of Schwyz, and the community of the lower valley of Unterwalden, seeing the malice of the age, in order that they may better defend themselves and their own and better preserve them in a proper state, have promised in good faith to assist each other with aid . . . with might and main, against one and all, who may inflict upon any one of them violence, molestation, or injury, or may plot against their persons or goods. . . . To this end they have sworn a solemn oath." In our own Declaration, we hear a not so distant echo of this oath, and indeed our founding fathers knew it and the nation of Switzerland that grew from it.

The Rütli site is still there, easily visited by regular tour boat from Lucerne. Unlike places of similar historic importance in other countries, the Meadow boasts no soaring marble arches, no martial statues, no towering obelisk. (In fact, there are comparatively few such monuments in Switzerland as a whole.) There is a tall flagpole flying the white cross on its red field, the one concession to nationalism. There are a couple of unremarkable log buildings housing a small museum and a teashop, and a few crude benches. The visitor is bemused by the presence of a herd of goats, which announce their presence by a characteristically pungent aroma before one arrives uphill from the landing. This is the subtle message of the Meadow—it does not exalt the state. It does exalt something dis-

tinctly Swiss in its quiet modesty; and it speaks far more eloquent-
ly for the principle of liberty and independence, which is a simple
proposition, however difficult it may be to sustain.

The founding communities of Uri, Schwyz, and Unterwalden
were rural, pastoral and agricultural. As such, they managed a feat
unique in medieval Europe; they succeeded in attracting prosperous
city-states to their infant *Eidgenossenschaft*. First came Lucerne,
then Zürich. In 1353 the Confederation reached an important milestone when the city of Bern, a true military and economic power at
that time, entered the Confederation, which then consisted of eight
cantons. With the city cantons came the power of the guilds and the
businessmen of Zürich, Bern, Basel, and Lucerne. The expansion of
crafts and commerce inside the Confederation brought money interests into conflict with farmers and herdsmen. Yet the Confederation
managed to hold together, despite the occasional outbreak of tensions. The saving grace was the steady growth of the cantonal coun-
cils, the *Landsgemeinden*. These were a distinctly Swiss form of par-
ticipatory democracy that sustained the tradition of independence
and self-government against the trend of centralization. They
allowed maximum autonomy over local matters. Farmers and
herdsmen could maintain their way of life while the traders and
capitalists pursued theirs.

THE PROTESTANT REFORMATION

After the thirteenth canton, Appenzell, joined in 1513, the expansion of the Confederation came to a temporary halt because of a
development that shook Europe to its foundations—the Protestant
Reformation. The ensuing religious strife in Switzerland hardly
compared to that in the rest of Europe, which was ravaged by the
Thirty Years' War. It was proportionately the most destructive conflict in Europe's history, taking the lives, directly or indirectly, of a
third of the population where the armies struggled. The Swiss
remained neutral, and the horrors of this war, for the most part,
passed them by.

The Reformation in Switzerland, while not without its outbreaks of sectarian violence, did not overturn the Swiss political system. Internal religious conflicts were resolved with a minimum of force. The minimalist state of the Swiss proved resilient, adaptable, and capable of coping with a fundamental revolution that had plunged most other countries in Europe into cycles of strife, recrimination and retaliation.

The immediate political consequence of the Reformation was the splitting of the Confederation into two camps: a largely rural Catholic league of cantons and Protestant city cantons. The Protestants in turn were divided between the followers of Ulrich (or Huldrych) Zwingli in Zürich and German-speaking Switzerland, and followers of John Calvin in Geneva and some—but not all—French-speaking cantons. Lutheranism made only minimal inroads. The differences between the Protestant doctrines were sufficiently minor that in 1566 the followers of Zwingli and Calvin were able to subsume them in a common creed, the *Confessio Helvetica posterior*, giving the Protestant camp increased political solidarity. The success of Swiss Protestant solidarity caused the Reformation to acquire a particular Swiss coloration in the minds of Switzerland's neighbors. In an interesting historical footnote, the French pronunciation of *Eidgenosse*, corrupted into "u-ge-noh," or Huguenot, came to serve as a general word for Protestant.

The Protestant Reformers had the support of two-thirds of the population and of the main economic centers. The Catholic cantons managed to protect their religious and political identity, but still felt threatened by the greater numbers of Protestants and the superior economic and political power of the cities. This spurred them to greater efforts to safeguard their ancient privileges. In an accommodation typically Swiss, they demanded—and received—narrow Catholic corridors throughout the country enabling them to communicate with their co-religionists in Switzerland and abroad. These "joint dependencies" were co-administered by bailiffs of both confessions, which laid the basis for toleration of opposing faiths. Though grudging at first, this accommodation helped to heal a breach that had shattered domestic peace in neighboring France, Italy and the German principalities, and it kept the country from falling apart in sectarian strife. It proved to the Swiss that, despite differences in matters even as important as religion, the Confederates could still work together where their interests converged.

The Reformation also had profound economic consequences that ultimately affected the creation of higher education in Switzerland and the founding of the ETH. Protestant cantons welcomed refugees from Catholic persecution in the rest of Europe, many of whom were entrepreneurs, merchants and manufacturers, especially in the dye, textile and watch-making industries. Zürich, Geneva and Basel especially benefited from the influx of these industrious and disciplined immigrants. Their skills, experience and commercial connections gave a boost to early industrial growth, first in those regions where they settled, and then in the rest of the country as the effects of their enterprise rippled outward. Cottage industries sprang up as suppliers were needed to feed burgeoning industries. Peasants who until now had mostly engaged in subsistence agriculture found new income from the land in supplying raw materials—for example, wool and flax for textile producers. Even though most of the country remained pastoral, it was not lost on the Swiss that the path to prosperity lay in manufacturing and trade.

THE EXPANDING CONFEDERATION

Among all the paradoxes in Switzerland's evolution to its present state, one of the most striking is the Swiss military record. Today people with only a passing knowledge find it hard to accept that the seemingly pacific Swiss, who avoided the modern conflicts that wracked Europe, were also for centuries regarded as Europe's finest soldiers.

Like most things Swiss, the country's early military practice and traditions were a marked departure from the pattern in neighboring France, Austria and the German states. In those highly stratified feudal countries, military leadership was reserved for the monarch and the nobility. The emperor, king, duke or local lord maintained a cadre of full-time professional soldiers, often heavily armored and mounted men-at-arms. They were officered by nobles and supplemented in time of war by the feudal levy or hired mercenaries.

In contrast, Switzerland had a far less stratified society and few noble houses. The Swiss preferred the aristocracy of merit and followed leaders who showed the most competence in the field, whether aristocrat or burgher. The army was primarily a foot army of volunteer citizen-soldiers raised from each canton. It was composed of tough, hardy men who were highly skilled in the use of arms, especially the long pikes that played havoc in countless battles with cavalry and infantry alike. Of more significance, they were usually well motivated, self-disciplined, and confident in the manner of free men, with a high degree of mutual trust among themselves and between leader and follower. These superior qualities of morale, mutual trust and *esprit de corps* gave the Swiss a decisive edge over armies composed of the unwilling, led by lords indifferent to the lives of their men, and forced into battle by either greed or fear.

Space does not permit a full catalogue of Swiss military campaigns over the centuries. For our purpose it is enough to note that the Swiss acquired a fearsome reputation for raw courage, doggedness and skill on the battlefield. Their reputation for victory was instrumental in the late-medieval defense and expansion of the Confederation. Their shattering defeat of the Duke of Burgundy in 1476, for example, persuaded Fribourg and Solothurn to join the Confederation; an outbreak of war with the Habsburgs after a long truce led to the conquest of the Canton of Aargau.

In time, Switzerland's neighbors learned to leave her alone. There were two noteworthy results. First, Switzerland's policy of political neutrality was no mere inclination. It had teeth, a deterrent made all the more credible by centuries of Swiss military superiority. Second, as Switzerland's external wars subsided, the Swiss found themselves with an abundance of martial energy and ability in contrast to a lack of economic opportunity at home. Thousands of young men hired themselves out as contract soldiers, or, to use a more honest but less appealing word, mercenaries. For three centuries, until the practice formally ended in the 19th century,

Switzerland's principal export was regiments of tough, well-trained soldiers, usually contracted by agents who recruited them for service with foreign princes and grew enormously rich in the process. Though this practice ended long ago, it has left an historic echo in the Swiss Papal Guard. Often seen standing sentinel in colorful medieval uniforms at the Vatican (and when traveling abroad with the Pope, in dark suits), they are not comic-opera soldiers but tough and well trained in modern weapons and tactics. These hundred-plus guardsmen are recruited from Swiss men of good family and reputation exclusively in the Catholic cantons, and represent a lingering legacy of the once fearsome renown of Swiss regiments.

We have noted that Switzerland has comparatively few monuments to its soldiers. However, there is one that simply cannot be ignored in any discussion of Switzerland's military heritage—the *Löwendenkmal,* or Lion Monument, in Lucerne, which American writer Mark Twain termed the most moving piece of stone sculpture in the world. It depicts a reclining, dying lion, pierced with arrows, carved in deep relief out of the vertical face of a granite cliff. The inscription reads *Helvetiorum Fidei ac Virtuti*—"To the courage and loyalty of the Swiss"—and commemorates a tragic incident in August 1792, at the height of the French Revolution. An enraged mob burst into the Tuileries Palace where King Louis XVI, his queen Marie Antoinette and their children were under house arrest after attempting to flee France to Austria. Abandoned by their countrymen, the family's only protection was their regiment of Swiss Guards. Faithful to their trust and against overwhelming odds, the Swiss fought to the last man. Eight hundred guardsmen were massacred in an attempt to keep the royal family from being dragged off to the Conciergerie Prison, from which the King and Queen were later taken to be guillotined.

The poignant dignity of the Lion Monument suggests that the Swiss regarded mercenary service as an honorable profession. For a time it was indeed one of the country's major sources of outside revenue, even as Swiss parents longed for some other livelihood for their sons than fighting the battles of remote foreign lords. The mercenary system began to unravel when Swiss soldiers increasingly found themselves fighting against each other in the pay of rival rulers. Moreover, the advent of long-range firearms reduced the unique value of Swiss infantry tactics. By the 18th century the peasant pikemen, who had once found the answer to the mounted knight of Europe, had encountered a new, more impersonal, foe: artillery.

Since Switzerland itself managed to stay out of the many wars that periodically rocked Europe, thanks to her military reputation and policy of neutrality, it was the only country on the European continent able to maintain for over 200 years a tradition of liberal education uninterrupted by invasion, civil war, revolution or dictatorship. Thus, Switzerland's military system and foreign policy contributed to the story of the ETH by creating peace and stability, an environment in which education at all levels could flourish.

THE CONSTITUTION OF 1848 AND THE NEW SWISS CONFEDERATION

The Swiss have been conquered only once in modern history, and it took one of history's great captains to do it—Napoleon Bonaparte. In 1797, fresh from his conquest of northern Italy, Napoleon began to put military pressure on the Swiss. The Alpine passes were his strategic goal, for they would provide a direct route between Milan and Paris. As before, the Swiss had remained neutral during the war of the First Allied Coalition against revolutionary France, but Bonaparte was no respecter of such forms, and the French cry of *"liberté, égalité, fraternité"* appealed greatly to Swiss, particularly in the French-speaking cantons, who resented the rule of powerful guilds and leading families.

The Swiss oligarchs waited too late in their efforts to bring about democratic reforms. When the French pressed into the Jura and into Valais from Italy, a combination of battlefield success and Swiss unwillingness to fight them to the death led to French domination in 1798. The cities in the Jura and western Plateau, Basel, Bern and others submitted. The eastern and Alpine cantons were never conquered, though they were the scene of much fighting between the French and a counterinvading army of Russians. Nevertheless, the capitulation of the leading city-states sealed the end of the old Confederation, and the *République Helvètique,* allied with France, was formed in 1798. In 1803 Napoleon returned to Switzerland and attempted to quell public unrest with a policy compromise called "The Mediation"; however, most Swiss continued to chafe under French rule.

Swiss regiments marched off with Napoleon and, true to form, it was "the courage and loyalty of the Swiss," even in the service of an unworthy master, that shored up the vital rear guard in the ghastly retreat from Moscow in 1812. After the fall of "the Ogre," Swiss neutrality was accepted and ratified by the rest of Europe at the Congress of Vienna in 1815. For our purposes, it is interesting to note that the impact of the Bonaparte era was not just military and diplomatic. For all its horrors and excesses, the French Revolution spawned some new ways of thinking and a thirst to be free from oligarchical rule, ideas that were spread wherever Napoleon's armies marched. The Revolution opened the consciousness of men to new possibilities, including a belief in the power of the human mind to harness the natural world for the improvement of man's material condition. The faith in knowledge, science and technology that had begun in the Enlightenment period took deeper root as the 19th century opened. It was in this period of renewed intellectual ferment, of belief that all things were possible, that the idea of a polytechnic university for Switzerland was born.

If the remarkable peace, stability, and comity of the Swiss Confederation seemed at times too good to be true, the Swiss of the late 1840s would have agreed. Peace and stability had been established between cantons, between Catholics and Protestants, and between French- and German-speakers. Yet, within cantons, widespread dissatisfaction with the rule of the guilds, elite families, and ecclesiastical powers with their privileges and monopolies began to bubble to the surface. Against the backdrop of a massive crop failure in 1845 and severe economic depression, these latent differences began to break out across Switzerland in riots and armed demonstrations. Liberals took advantage of the turmoil to press for sweeping reforms. However, the more conservative Catholic cantons of the *Innerschweiz* defended the old order and formed a military defense pact known as the *Sonderbund*. The clash came in 1847 when Swiss General Henri Dufour, representing the Parliament in Bern, led federal troops against the recalcitrant Sonderbund. He defeated it at Gislikon near Lucerne, and the last holdouts in Valais.

The 1847 Civil War of the Sonderbund (in which about 100 were killed) did not destroy the deeply engrained Swiss spirit of conciliation and compromise. To be sure, the victors used their triumph to bring about liberal reforms in a new Swiss Confederation, including removing the remaining cantonal obstacles to economic growth and industrial development. The draft Constitution (*Bundesverfassung*) of 1848 proposed standardization of coinage, weights and measurements among the cantons, and eliminating intra-cantonal customs and duties, placing those functions in the hands of the federal government. (Napoleon had tried to institute some of these same reforms.) Crucially, local and cantonal rights were still to be respected. Education and taxation were left in the hands of the cantons, along with the right to protect local preferences in religion and language. Among the articles of the new Constitution was one calling for the establishment of two federal institutions: one a university for arts and letters and the other a polytechnic institute to promote science and technology.

UNITY IN DIVERSITY

Many people claim their country has achieved unity in diversity— perhaps none more so than Americans, especially in these contemporary times. "Diversity" is now the catchword of political correctness. In fact, few countries and people have actually achieved it. The motto of the United States is *E pluribus unum*—"Out of many, one"—signifying that the 13 original sovereign states came together in 1789 to form a voluntary union. At the time it was chosen as a credo, *pluribus* certainly did not mean a diversity of peoples, cultures and languages, for the original America was remarkably homogeneous. It consisted mainly of English-speaking peoples from the British Isles, with a leavening of others, almost all from Western Europe: French Huguenots in South Carolina, German and Swiss immigrants in Pennsylvania, and the original Dutch settlers in New York. The cultural differences were minor and not unbridgeable, and non-British peoples rapidly assimilated to the predominant Anglo-Celtic culture, the English language and Christianity. (Native Americans and black slaves were not considered part of the body politic.)

Switzerland could also claim to be *E pluribus unum*. It cannot be overemphasized that Switzerland grew not by forced unification but by peaceful aggregation. With only a few exceptions, the 26 cantons that now constitute the Swiss Confederation joined voluntarily. Some even petitioned to join and had to wait in the queue, as it were.

One of the most formative facts of Switzerland today is that it alone among its European neighbors managed to live through two catastrophic world wars without being swept into the maelstrom. Moreover, the Swiss have not only been spared invasion, they have also been spared revolution. The French Revolution did have an impact on Switzerland, but nothing remotely compared to the vast civil bloodletting in France and the interminable wars that followed. Indeed, one cannot even imagine anything like the Great Terror of the Jacobins happening in Switzerland. The Swiss also felt the reverberations of Europe's revolts in 1848. Still, the fundamental nature of their society and political structure was never overturned; the roots reaching back to the founding spirit of the Middle Ages were never severed. The normal flow of civilized life was sustained throughout all Europe's turmoil via a continuity that nourishes a still living tradition.

The effects of this peaceful continuity are incalculable. Peoples who have been invaded and despoiled can only envy a civilization in which there lives a serenity and amiability—if also a kind of innocence and good will—that comes from an absence of *Sturm und Drang*, and from never knowing the bitterness, privation, violence, misery and despair which are the fruits of war and revolution. Remaining at peace with their neighbors and with themselves enabled the Swiss to practice the high arts of civilization and to create a fertile environment for exemplary education—including, in due course, the ETH.

ZÜRICH: A REFUGE AND ECONOMIC CENTER

A discussion of the historical, political and cultural setting for the ETH would not be complete without a look at Zürich, which was the "stage" for its founding and which continued to influence the institution over the years. Though small in comparison to New York, London, Paris or Tokyo, Zürich—Züri, as the locals call it— is one of the world's great cities, though it today holds only 360,000 inhabitants.

Turicum, from which the modern name derives, was founded in 15 B.C. by the Romans, who established it as a customs station overlooking the junction of Lake Zürich and the Limmat River to control the region's lucrative trade. By the Middle Ages the city had become a thriving commercial center dominated by rich and powerful craftsmen's guilds. Wealth brought an emphasis on the arts and learning, along with openness to new ideas, including the revolutionary religious doctrines beginning to disturb the peace of Europe.

As noted earlier, Zürich proved a receptive host to one of the Protestant Reformation's most active men, Ulrich Zwingli, a former priest from the countryside. He proved a dynamic politician and warrior as well as theologian. Zwingli pastored the city's famous Grossmünster cathedral and helped implant the Reformed Protestant faith in the canton until his death in battle against the Catholics in 1531. The twin towers of this ancient church, said to have been originally founded by Charlemagne, remain an imposing landmark in old Zürich, just as Zwingli's brand of Protestantism has left its permanent mark on the culture—an influence that can be seen almost five centuries later. Zwingli's statue still stands in a place of honor on the banks of the Limmat in downtown Zürich.

The Reformation in Alemannic Switzerland was neither Lutheran nor Calvinist, but Zwinglian. One could say it bore less of

the personal imprint of its leader than did Lutheranism and
Calvinism, paradoxically because of the personality of the man
himself. Zwingli was no less forceful and charismatic than his co-
religionists in Germany and in Geneva; but his emphasis on "pure"
doctrine and ecclesiology prevented his church from becoming a
cult of personality. The result was a form of Protestantism, still
more or less extant in this secular age, marked by less of the spon-
taneous mysticism of Luther and less of the juridical spirit of
Calvin, but truly Swiss at its core, with a more solid rationalism and
tending to the practical. It harmonized citizenship with religion,
providing unshakeable support to the development of Swiss republicanism. It also opened doors to expanded industrial development,
manufacturing and trade.

In 1877, some years after the founding of the ETH, Zürich
entered its heyday as a commercial and financial center with the
establishment of a stock exchange, now among the most important
in the world. Zürich's centrality as an intellectual center grew parallel to its importance as a hub of trade, industry and finance as the
city attracted emigrés and expatriates, ranging from "artistic
refugees" like James Joyce to political dissidents like Vladimir
Lenin. It was from Zürich that Lenin set off in a sealed railway car
provided by the Germans in 1917 to St. Petersburg, a journey that
still casts a baleful shadow over modern history.

As Switzerland's unofficial capital (Bern would become the official one in 1848), Zürich emerged as a leader in experimentation,
artistic ferment and inquiry, hosting such names, by the early 20th
century, as the iconoclastic Swiss architect Le Corbusier and the
counterculture of its day, the Dadaist movement. The cantonal
University of Zürich was established in 1833 as the *Universitas
Turicensis*, the first university in Europe to be founded by a democratic state rather than by a monarch or the church. When it opened
its doors, its founders hoped it would one day develop into a university for the whole of Switzerland. Its spiritual father, Johann
Caspar von Orelli, wrote to a colleague, "We had to found a Zürich
university to get things off the ground. But it and it alone should
become the Swiss university."

Alas for Dr. von Orelli, it was not to be. The University of Zürich emphasized theology, philosophy, law and medicine. At the same time it was being created, the Swiss began to understand their need to invest in science and technology to develop their country and make it prosper. This turn to the sciences did not incline the Swiss toward the University of Zürich, despite its illustrious beginning and its high academic qualities, but toward something entirely new and different; and that, of course, is the story related in subsequent chapters. Zürich was the natural choice for the new federal institute that would focus on the sciences. Despite early resistance from the cantonal university for fear of being superseded, the ETH and University of Zürich were able to overcome professional jealousies—demonstrating the Swiss spirit of consensus—and arrived at a cordial working relationship that thrives today.

Upon its founding in 1855, the ETH shared space with its sister school until moving into the magnificent edifice Gottfried Semper built next door. In 1908 an agreement between the Canton of Zürich and the Swiss federal government formalized the partnership. New agreements followed, leading to a close collaboration between the two schools, including 21 shared academic chairs and five joint institutes. The ETH long ago outgrew its original building in the Zentrum, spilling over to many buildings nearby, to the modern Hönggerberg campus north of the city, and to the subsidiary institutes. But the heart of the ETH remains on the ridge overlooking the Limmat River and downtown Zürich, where the round dome at the epicenter of the ETH Zentrum proudly shares the skyline with the square cupola of the University of Zürich.

A CONGENIAL ENVIRONMENT

From the early Confederation of 1291 to the new Swiss Confederation formed by the Constitution of 1848, the Swiss developed a civic culture and brand of politics that led to the birth of the ETH and its nourishment. Given their historical experience, the Swiss could hardly have produced anything but a politics focused on practical solutions. To them, the end work of politics and government was to create beneficial results, not to give voice to sweeping ideological abstractions. Government's role was to enable the people to better meet their basic practical needs and to secure their welfare. Resisting the temptation to authoritarian centralism that so beguiled their neighbors, the Swiss limited the administrative machinery of their centralized state to act for the people and the cantons as their fiduciary agent. The government was to be their servant, not their master.

Differences between communities—both major and minor—were able to flourish without generating hostility. Each community respected the right of the other not merely to exist but to maintain its linguistic-cultural identity without encroachment. This attitude was especially noteworthy of the German Swiss, since their restraint and respect of others was crucial. Representing almost three-quarters of the population and the country's principal manufacturing and economic centers, had the German Swiss ever gotten it into their heads to run roughshod over the other linguistic communities, they would have provoked a vigorous backlash and irreparably ruptured Swiss unity and stability.

The Swiss were wise enough to embrace industry and trade while keeping the two in balance with agriculture and small crafts. Their mechanization and industrialization proceeded along other than mass-production lines and never at the expense of quality. The Swiss benefited from a dual tradition, both artisan and scientific. One was born in the ingenuity of the peasant and yeoman, the other in the rich civilization that grew up in Swiss towns beginning in the Middle Ages. The whole was protected by a fortuitous geography, a military tradition that kept aggressors at bay—wrapping the country in the protective mantle of peace for centuries—and sustained by a stable, consensus-driven political and social system.

The ground had been prepared, all the conditions were ripe, the tools were in hand, the tillers and husbandmen ready. All that was needed to bring forth the ETH was to plant the seed.

CHAPTER THREE

The Seed Is Planted

Switzerland's most notable achievements are not the country's advances in science and technology, development and material success, as impressive as these are. They are only the results of even greater achievements—a society that respects cultural differences and a political system of republican self-rule that strikes a balance between cantonal autonomy and central government authority. The Swiss evolved a way to settle internal conflicts, for the most part peaceably, and were able to produce outcomes acceptable to the country's diverse peoples and interests.

There is nothing in Swiss history like the atrocities of the Peasant's Revolt in Germany in the 1500s, the Great Terror of the French Revolution, or the rise of fascism in neighboring Germany and Italy in the 20th century. Indeed, it is almost impossible to imagine such excesses in Switzerland. The Swiss Sonderbund conflict of 1847—with its 100 dead—was their civil war. When it ended, the Swiss created a new constitution drawing on influences from the U.S. Constitution.

The existence of internal and external peace was of vital importance to Swiss education and the development of the ETH in particular. It instilled a belief in the Swiss that their investment in education and in the development of their country would not be lost in war or revolution.

Objectivity, however, requires us to acknowledge that the Swiss are also subject to the failings to which all flesh is heir. They have known their share of pursuing personal or regional interests over the common good. Though more republican than the rest of Europe, Switzerland was never a classless meritocracy. Oligarchs, guilds, moneyed interests and other special pleaders have schemed to expand or preserve their power, just as in the rest of Europe or the United States. Pride, prestige, and religious or economic concerns have often pitted canton against canton. All these tensions played out in the birth of the ETH.

The inherent conservatism of the Swiss people and the obstacles posed by their divergent interests allowed 50 years to pass between the conception of the ETH, roughly in 1798, to the article of the Constitution authorizing the *Polytechnikum* in 1848. Then it took another seven years to actually open for business. At many junctures, the founding could have taken a very different direction, or perhaps not occurred at all.

THE FOUNDATIONS OF TECHNICAL EDUCATION

Prior to the end of the 18th century, universities had not changed materially from a structure established in the Middle Ages. Curricula were still heavily influenced by the medieval *trivium*—grammar, logic and rhetoric—and subsequent *quadrivium*—geometry, astronomy, arithmetic and music. The typical European university emphasized theology, law, Latin, Greek and classical literature, a program typically described as "humane letters," or what we today call humanities or liberal arts. At this time it was rare in the European experience to earn a university degree in the hard-lab sciences and engineering, something we take for granted today. Education at all levels was primarily the responsibility of the church, and students were graduated from the university principally for a career in the clergy, the law or teaching. For the sake of perspective, Americans should remember this was also true of the earliest colleges in North America—Harvard and Princeton Universities are prime examples—where students majored in theology and the classics, Latin, Greek and Hebrew, to prepare for careers in the church.

Since the fateful year of 1798—the year of the French invasion—many of the best minds of Switzerland were preoccupied with
the goal of creating an all-Swiss university, or a *Hochschule* (not
quite synonymous with "university" but still denoting an institute
of higher learning). This was a lasting result of the broader revolution in social and political thought spawned by the French
Revolution. The Revolution was responsible for vast atrocities in
the Vendée, the Great Terror, and the despotism of Napoleon; yet,
it also created a great hunger for liberty throughout Europe. Most
notably for Switzerland, the influence of the secular Enlightenment,
the French Encyclopedists, and the Revolution introduced the concept of an all-powerful central state, an idea largely alien to the
Swiss until then. The leaders of the Helvetic Republic under the
sway of France also imported into Switzerland strong doses of
materialism and faith in the burgeoning powers of science. They
helped institutionalize the belief that mastery of one's physical environment, not just of the human mind and soul, could bring about
happiness and mitigate, if not solve, the age-old challenges to
mankind—war, poverty, hunger and pestilence.

It is human nature to follow familiar patterns, and there were
few patterns to serve as a guide for the new "technical education."
The Swiss began to realize they needed a school to train young men
(and women, too, as it turned out later) in the sciences, but how
exactly? In the Switzerland of 1798, there was virtually no formal
education of this kind. Existing technical schools were basic "art
schools" which hardly went beyond the level of today's secondary
education. Apprenticeships with the guilds, private instruction, or
simply learning by doing were the basis of technical education.

These questions were not only faced by the Swiss. In fact, the
story of the ETH is merely one chapter in the larger story of the
emergence of modern technical education, a challenge faced by the
entire Western world on the threshold of the Industrial Revolution.
As the Swiss struggled to reconcile their political ethos of decentralized government with the idea of a federal institution, a parallel
development in technical education was unfolding in America. The
United States, at the time also a highly decentralized federal repub-

lic, founded the Military Academy at West Point as a polytechnic college to train military officers. Concurrent with their military training, West Point cadets received training as civil engineers. President Thomas Jefferson signed the law establishing the Military Academy in 1802. From 1784 to 1789 he had been U.S. minister in Paris, where he observed French plans for the *Ecole Centrale des Travaux Publics* (Central School for Public Works), later to become the Ecole Polytechnique. Influenced by the French concept, Jefferson wanted a federal college to train U.S. officer-engineers who in peacetime could superintend the development of the national infrastructure—canals and roads as well as military fortifications. Over time the federal academy concept expanded to include the other service academies, the only four-year colleges supported by the U.S. government, and where until recent years all cadets were graduated with degrees in engineering.

The renowned Ecole Polytechnique, founded in Paris in 1794, was the "mother institute" of all higher technical education and the world's first college specializing in the technical disciplines. Like many things in France at the time, it was revolutionary. It severed higher education from the church and made it the responsibility of the central state; and it specialized in training scientists and engineers for service to the state.

A number of specialist schools had been created in Europe as early as the 18th century to meet the state's increasing need for qualified workers in individual technical disciplines. Civil engineers were needed in centralized France to improve the roads. The *Ecole des Ponts et Chaussées* was founded in 1747 in Paris to alleviate this shortage. The Freiberg School of Mines (1765) in Saxony and the Schemnitz (now Banská Stiávnica) School of Mining and Forestry (1770) in the southwestern part of Slovakia's Ore Mountains had an influence on mining and smelting that extended far beyond their own countries' borders.

However, it was not until the French Revolution and the Ecole Polytechnique that the pathway was laid for other polytechnics in Europe, opening a new dimension in the understanding of the technical sciences. Lazare Carnot, a military engineer and member of the French National Convention, was the principal founder of the French *Polytechnique*. His premise was that all technical disciplines share a common scientific basis, and he helped establish the *Polytechnique* to provide this basic training. Here the elite of French engineers followed a two-year course in mathematics, physics and chemistry, which they had to complete before entering a specialist school such as the School of Mining or the Military Academy. Engineers were trained there exclusively for the civil service and were subject to military discipline. The students wore uniforms, lived in barracks and had to drill and exercise in the courtyard on Sunday mornings.

THE IDEA OF A CENTRAL SWISS POLYTECHNIC

Philipp Albert Stapfer of Brugg, Minister of Arts and Sciences of the newly created Helvetic Republic, was among the first to recognize the epoch-making significance of the new French institution. He envisioned the establishment of an all-Swiss university or "central school," combining the advantages of German universities with those of the new French polytechnic college. In a November 1798 memorandum, Stapfer laid out a comprehensive plan for public instruction for all of Switzerland. The principal feature of the plan was a single "comprehensive institute, where all the sciences and arts useful to the new republic" would be taught. It would be supported by the best resources of the nation and would produce "insightful and careful physicians, enlightened teachers, clear thinking legislators, capable regents, adept judges, meaningful scholars." This proposal followed the traditional pattern emphasizing studies and careers based on the liberal arts or humane letters. But significantly, he departed from the norm with an emphasis on producing "invention-rich artists, skillful building masters, and engineers."

In other words, Stapfer's vision for a "central school" incorporated the best features from existing universities in Europe while adding something unprecedented. This led him to search for a name that would set it apart and convey its uniqueness. He wrote: "If one looked over the wide range of institutes of learning, one would immediately recognize this Swiss university. It would stand out like the Ecole Polytechnique in Paris," but would have an even more comprehensive scope. It would be "polytechnical" in creating skills and resources for the common good—specifically, for the physical development of the country. It would also be "liturgical" in the old sense, meaning that, in contrast to the basic instruction in lower schools, it would develop the mind and character of the individual. The new institute would also encompass the "political" in that it would provide for the education of an enlightened class of public administrators. In modeling his idea on both German universities and the new Polytechnique in Paris, and in combining both the theoretical and the practical, Stapfer proposed something distinctly new and distinctly Swiss.

Stapfer's bold vision of a national institute sketched out in 1798 was only conceivable in the Helvetic Republic, which was heavily influenced by Revolutionary France. Its constitution had radically set aside the old Swiss Confederation, disregarding its deep roots in the country's history. Switzerland's polytechnic was to be all-Swiss, or federal—that is, supported by and accountable to the central government and not to any one canton. It was to be at the level of advanced learning, combining traditional liberal arts with a polytechnic course of study. But neither Stapfer nor anyone else could quite figure out the latter issue: how to reconcile the idea of a Swiss institute for higher learning or advanced technical studies with subjects that heretofore had been the province of apprenticeships, on-the-job training and vocational schools. Thus, the seed was planted, without becoming quite apparent at this early stage, for two federal institutes. One would resemble the traditional university with an emphasis on liberal arts, and the other would be a polytechnic. As the years unfolded, this wish solidified into policy and became the subject of contentious debate surrounding the eventual launch of the ETH.

Stapfer believed his project would create a rebirth of the Swiss as a people. He wrote:

This institute will be the focal point of the intellectual

strengths of our nation, in which the diverse peoples which comprise it will be reforged into a unity. It will be a fount of culture of a "three-peopled" nation joined in Switzerland. It is perhaps our destiny to unite the thoughtfulness of the German, the skills of the French, and the taste of the Italian into a new creation.

Perhaps naively, Stapfer believed it was possible to create an all-Swiss institute with little financial support from the federal government. To start, he only wanted to bring together resources then scattered over Switzerland, turning existing academies, lyceums and the rest into mere preparatory schools for his institute, and freeing up resources otherwise unused. To this end, in February 1799 the education ministry requested the Swiss legislative council to grant authority to bring a polytechnic into being. However the Swiss Parliament did not accept this idealistic, wide-ranging proposal. The strain on Swiss finances and the very real possibility of war with Revolutionary France made this an inauspicious time for such an initiative. The request of the ministry was turned over to a study commission. In effect, the project was put on hold.

The misery and chaos which swept over the new republic during the war of the Second Coalition against France in the final years of the 18th century left Switzerland exhausted and ended any possibility the project would be resurrected again soon. Yet the dream of a central institute remained alive throughout the turmoil of the period. Stapfer himself came back again and again to the idea. In September 1800, while serving as an emissary to Paris, he once more pressed the Swiss government to establish a national advanced technical school, although of more modest proportions. In his view, it was the only way to build a national identity among the Swiss peoples and to raise Switzerland's prestige in the eyes of the rest of Europe.

Virtually all the different constitutions proposed for the Helvetic Republic of 1798–1803 had listed the establishment of a polytechnic as one of the tasks of the cantons. In discussions held in Paris in the winter of 1802–1803, all Swiss parties present continued to support the idea. It was only with the sudden ascension of Napoleon as Emperor and the subsequent return of Switzerland to the old confederate system that the idealistic goal was abandoned. The short-lived Helvetic Republic under the sway of France ended in 1803. In the state acts of 1803 restoring the old Swiss Confederation, control over education was returned to the individual cantons. The cantons in turn redirected and expanded their learning institutions, albeit with scant resources, toward the "old way"—that is, higher education principally for the preparation of churchmen. The concept of a federal Swiss university, in which engineers and architects would be educated alongside doctors and lawyers, was laid aside for the time being. Philipp Stapfer, the farsighted Minister of Education, was not to see his dream materialize in his lifetime, and Switzerland was not to have the honor of establishing the first new institute of higher technical learning after the French. Nevertheless, the seed had been planted and the idea was not forgotten.

STEFANO FRANSCINI AND THE REVIVAL OF SWISS FEDERAL EDUCATION

Toward the end of the 1820s, many Swiss sought to reinvigorate the Confederation, and concurrent with that effort the idea of a federal institute surfaced once more. The first to publicly advance the subject was a young schoolmaster, Stefano Franscini from Canton Ticino, later a Federal Councilor. In his seminal *Statistics of Switzerland* (*Statistica della Svizzera*), published in 1827, Franscini lamented that Switzerland had nothing to compare to the famous universities of Europe and expressed the wish that all the cantons would unite in setting up a common university. Such a university would have enormous intellectual and moral advantages both for the cantons and the republic, making possible a stronger new union of the Confederates of the Oath.

The career and influence of Stephano Franscini is worth a deeper look, and not just because of his role in the development of the Swiss educational system. He was one of the most influential figures of 19th-century Switzerland, a founder of the modern science of statistics, and a leading voice in the creation of a new, liberal Switzerland—itself a result of the intellectual revolution that swept Europe in the 1830s. Franscini's career attests to the fact that members of the smaller linguistic communities could enter fully into the affairs of the country. An Italian speaker from Ticino, he was not merely tolerated but rather celebrated in German- and French-speaking Switzerland as well as in his own canton.

Major historical developments often begin with a period of ferment of new ideas, followed by a period of sudden and rapid movement when those ideas achieve critical mass and break down the old order. A more or less chaotic period of rapid change finally ends in a period of consolidation and reconciliation as the new ways of thinking become institutionalized. So it was in Switzerland in Franscini's lifetime. The old system eroded and was supplanted by the new worldview with its roots in the Enlightenment and in the French Revolution.

Stefano Franscini lived his formative years in Milan, Italy. Born poor in nearby Bodio, he went to the local school and then to a seminary. At the age of 19 he moved to Milan to complete his studies at the archiepiscopal seminary. Three years later, in 1818, he decided not to become a priest, left the seminary, and continued his studies largely on his own while earning his living as a teacher. In his autobiography, of which only fragments survive, he wrote: "My readings of those days had a decisive influence on my later life. They covered essentially two branches: education and political science. As concerns the latter, there were the books on political economy and statistics by Melchiorre Gioja, who was still alive then. They caught my attention constantly."

Gioja had been a student of Diderot in France and is one of the many links between Franscini and the Enlightenment and the French Encyclopedists. Besides Gioja, another friend, Carlo Cattaneo, influenced Franscini's thinking for the rest of his life. Like Franscini, Cattaneo began as a student of theology, only to become an ardent foe of religion, and in particular of the Catholic religiosity of his time and place. He emerged as an eloquent and powerful advocate of a new public educational system, free of church control and based on the ideas of the Enlightenment. To Catteneo, and subsequently to Franscini, state schools were a prerequisite for a free, independent and liberal state whose basis was an educated and civilized citizenry.

Cattaneo knew German and introduced the language and the works of both Germans and Swiss to his friend and colleague. Franscini learned German and continued his studies while he and Cattaneo taught together at an elementary school in Milan. There they tried out innovative courses in chemistry and mechanics, which induced them in turn to master mathematics, opening the door to a common interest in the emerging science of statistics. In this learned climate Franscini enlarged the narrow circle of ideas in which he had grown up and struggled to overcome the limitations of the poor education he had received before coming to Milan.

During this period Italy was not a unified country but still a patchwork of independent principalities. Northern Italy was ruled by an oppressive Austrian government, and Cattaneo decided to immigrate to Switzerland's Canton Ticino, as did many liberal refugees from Milan and northern Italy. There he became one of the best-known advocates for the liberal cause, authoring two major articles on setting up a new educational system. Cattaneo proposed that education should be a means of teaching young students to become autonomous in their thinking, freeing them from the ballast of old ideas so they could better serve the community of which they were members. This was in contrast to the idealists' doctrine that focused on the individual for his own sake, a position advocated in Germany and articulated, among others, by Wilhelm von Humboldt, who wrote, "The first law of true morality is to educate yourself, and only its second is to act on others by the way you are."

As a disciple of the Enlightenment, Cattaneo was convinced that public education was a task specifically reserved for the state, or at least that there had to be a guarantee of state control. By implication, education had to be taken out of the control of parents and traditional institutions like the church which would always continue to inculcate old ways of thinking and feeling. His book *On the Reformation of High School Teaching in the Ticino* is a detailed program for a modern public educational system, beginning with an estimate of total costs and continuing with all the details, such as curricula, textbooks, number of students and so forth. The book had an impact, something of which Franscini took note. The Minister of Education of Canton Ticino said at the same time that Cattaneo's work "corresponds optimally to our needs and its publication will have the best possible effect on public opinion. It will convince the public of the enormous advantages of this new organization and thus of the necessity to secularize the present institutions that are not, in any way, at the level of today's civilization."

In 1824 Franscini moved to the Ticino, convinced by Cattaneo's example that it was there that he had to try to realize his ideas. He worked for the next six years as a teacher and writer, launching his own fight against "reaction," still in evidence in the Ticino at that time, and for a liberal state built on the idea of a sovereign will of the nation and on the full participation of all citizens in public life. In 1827 Franscini published the first edition of the *Statistica della Svizzera*, an enormous compilation of facts and descriptions of the state of affairs in Swiss education, with an accompanying analysis of many of the problems of his day. In 1828 there followed *On Public Education in the Canton Ticino*, in which he criticized the government for misapplying the 1803 federal law on education and in which he proposed a completely renovated system of federally supported schools.

In 1830 he was instrumental in the defeat of the canton's conservative, anti-liberal government with his text *On the Reform of the Ticino Constitution*, which marked his entry into the world of politics. In 1837 he was elected a member and soon afterward head of the Ticino cantonal government and led the liberal reform of the canton. Franscini was one of the main influences that kept the Ticino from joining the mostly Catholic Sonderbund, a courageous decision with Catholic Austrian Lombardy to the south and Sonderbund forces to the north. As a consequence, when the Sonderbund War broke out, the northern part of the Ticino was invaded, and the cantonal militia proved too weak to offer serious resistance. Fortunately the conflict came to an end before serious damage was inflicted on the canton.

In the fall of 1848, Franscini went to the first Parliament of the new Swiss Confederation as a representative of the Canton of Ticino and was elected to membership in the Federal Council. Here he became Minister of the Interior, an office he held until his untimely death in 1857.

Originally, Franscini and his liberal allies had hoped that with the new Constitution of 1848 three federal schools of higher learning would be created: a teacher's college, a liberal arts university and a polytechnic institute. The first idea was dropped almost immediately. The other two survived—barely—by means of an article in the Constitution stating that "The Confederation is entitled to set up a university and a polytechnic school." As the first Minister of the Interior, Franscini went to work to bring the constitutional grant of authority to fruition as soon as he took office. He now had a seemingly perfect opportunity to implement the ideas about federally supported higher education he had developed through his friendship with Carlo Cattaneo.

In using his office to promote a Swiss technical institute, Franscini played the key role in the founding of the ETH. He would like to have created a comprehensive Swiss federal university, but finally settled on the polytechnic concept. He also saw himself as a prime candidate for a chair at the ETH while he was still Federal Minister of the Interior. He actually offered himself as candidate for three different chairs, and to his chagrin was turned down for all three positions by Johann Kern, the first President of the ETH, whom Franscini had himself installed in the post. Franscini's great personal disappointment aside, this episode raised fundamental questions that the Swiss struggled to resolve and that have relevance even in our own time: What does it take to be a scientific and academic teacher and researcher? What are the proper connections between the academic world and politics, commerce and industry?

The next chapter recounts the decision in 1854 to drop the idea of a federal university and establish a polytechnic institute in Zürich that later became the ETH. Franscini's letters to political friends in the Ticino document that laborious process along with his hopes to be appointed as a professor at the new *Politecnikum*. Yet he failed to grasp that by the 1850s prospects were poor for an amateur and autodidact, no matter how gifted, to become a professor at a modern institute such as the ETH.

Deeply disappointed and disenchanted with federal politics, Franscini decided not to seek reelection to the Swiss Parliament. He had decided to leave government service in 1857 to return to the Ticino, but he died in the same year. Despite his personal setback, the institute he helped create would enshrine his legacy.

THE CANTONS COMPETE

As the 19th century unfolded, the Swiss had begun to accept the need for some sort of federal polytechnic school. The public service of Stefano Franscini accelerated the process. However, difficult questions logically followed. What kind of school would it be? Should its course of study be purely practical, or encompass a base curriculum in the arts and letters? What rung would it occupy in the educational hierarchy? Should it be something on the order of a university, or less elevated? Should it perhaps represent something new—halfway between secondary school and university? Where would it be located, and how would it be paid for? Could the Confederation save money by building onto an existing school? Moreover, the Constitution authorized two federal institutions: a university, presumably with an emphasis on humanities, *and* a polytechnic institute. But the constitutional article did not define either or lay out criteria for their establishment. Each institution had its partisans, while many Swiss opposed the entire idea as a violation of cantonal prerogatives. At the same time the richer and more developed cantons vied for the privilege of hosting whatever new institution would emerge from this thicket of uncertainty and competing interests.

In 1829, the Lucerne philosopher Ignaz Troxler observed that Switzerland had a primary school system, or *Volksschule*, superior to almost any in Europe, but had sadly neglected higher education. Its "advanced schools" were in no way comparable to those of other nations on the continent. Troxler maintained that Switzerland did not possess a single university worthy of the name where a student could receive a complete and fundamental education in any area of learning. "Whoever seeks such an education has no alternative but to leave Switzerland and flee to Germany or some other neighboring land, so backward are we. For a studious youth, what stands in the way [in Switzerland] is not an absence of . . . knowledge, but the lack of organization and centralization." Troxler appealed to the spirit of the Confederation, insisting that, through one of the many accords (*Konkordat* in German) struck between the cantons, it should be possible to create a high-level national academy fitting to any people who aspire to independence. In effect, he proposed the same united Swiss polytechnic that Philipp Albert Stapfer had dreamed of.

Troxler's comments attracted great notice, and his proposal coincided with a renewed wave of liberal opinion that swept Europe in 1830 and which affected Switzerland as well. Echoing the views of his contemporary, Stefano Franscini, his voice helped develop the perfect environment for nurturing the idea of reforming public education and creating a common Swiss institution of higher learning.

One of the early leaders of liberal Switzerland, Dr. Kasimir Pfyffer of Lucerne, in his *Appeal to the Confederate City of Lucerne*, brought up the issue of the *Hochschule* in 1831. At a meeting of liberal cantonal representatives in Schinznach he maintained that the creation of a Swiss university was the necessary consequence of the ongoing political movement. "What the [new] Federal constitution is for our political life, the Federal university is for our spiritual life, even though years may pass before that university is fully realized," he said. Indeed, the first serious steps toward the realization of the ideal also revealed the almost hopeless difficulty of the undertaking.

As these currents roiled Switzerland's placid surface, individual towns and cantons took their own halting steps to upgrade their schools. In 1804 Zürich had added a "medical-surgical" institute to its ancient college, the *Carolinum*, and in 1807 had established a "political institute." Bern completely reorganized its city academy in 1805, and Vaud added new professorships to its academy in 1806. Geneva maintained its renowned Calvin School through the period of French domination, while Basel undertook wide-ranging reforms between 1813 and 1818 to revitalize the 450-year-old institution it called a "university," although that term was of dubious validity at the time. Despite these initiatives, however, the institutions, though designated "higher learning," occupied a position somewhere between a secondary school and a university and served for the most part as the capstone of a theological education. Many Swiss themselves had a low opinion of these schools. In Aargau, for instance, the school commissioner who provided funds for advanced study forbade recipients of Aargau scholarships from going to the university in Basel, requiring that they attend German universities instead.

In addition to these internal developments in Switzerland, a number of polytechnic institutes had come into being in neighboring countries, a trend that did not go unnoticed by the Swiss, and by Zürich in particular. The Austro-Hungarian Habsburg monarchy began working on plans to set up a polytechnic, as long as its pursuit of modern science was not tainted by the revolutionary spirit of the times, and thanks to the initiative of the Bohemian districts of the Habsburg Empire, the second polytechnic after Paris was opened in Prague in 1806.

Similar schools opened in Vienna (1815), Karlsruhe (1825), Munich (1827), Dresden (1828) and Stuttgart (1829). Most of these grew out of existing schools teaching crafts or trades and were intended to benefit both private industry and the state. However, these early institutions lacked the necessary substructure to elevate them to the level of a *Hochschule*. Forced to provide their own foundation courses, they were comparable to today's post-secondary two-year technical schools, not true colleges.

In Canton Zürich, the liberal revolution of 1830 ushered in a creative period affecting all aspects of the city, but it was especially

noticeable in public education. A Council for Education was elected and organized in two sections, one for the reform of the upper
or secondary schools and the other for the primary schools. At the
first meeting of the upper school committee in July 1831, the decision was made to undertake sweeping reforms. The committee proposed a reform of the canton's post-primary education according to
fundamental and internally consistent principles. First, they would
start from scratch to create a cantonal secondary school where new
scientific and technical instruction would take place alongside
instruction in the traditional humanities. Above this bifurcated secondary school would be an advanced institute with faculties of theology, law, medicine and philosophy that "could be called a
Hochschule," according to Johann Caspar von Orelli, who took on
the responsibility, with the help of other experts, of mapping out the
initial plan.

In April 1832, the Great Council of Canton Zürich removed the
choir section of the Grossmünster, Zwingli's historic church, which
in the past had been a venue for the church-school, to make room
for the new school. Orelli and his associates completed plans for the
new secondary canton school (*Kantonsschule*) that would comprise
a *Gymnasium*, with the humanities-based curriculum, and an
Industrieschule, or a School of Industry. They also asked for legislation establishing the advanced school for theology, law, medicine
and philosophy, the exact name for which was still under debate.
From the beginning, Orelli had insisted that "Zürich should have
the courage and power to name this highest school a *Hochschule*."

However, a majority on the education council disagreed. They
pulled back from the possible financial consequences of a
Hochschule for fear it would raise expectations and confront them
with the difficulties of having to come up with the resources to support it. They settled instead on the more modest term "Academy."
The council also raised the question of whether neighboring cantons should be solicited to participate financially. Thus, the wide-
ranging reforms in Zürich coincided with the establishment of an
advanced all-*Swiss* institute only to the extent of establishing higher education for *eastern* Switzerland. After lengthy debate, it was

decided that the best course was to rely solely on Zürich's resources to establish this school of advanced learning, and thereafter, perhaps, approach other cantons.

Just as things seemed to be moving forward in Zürich, however, another canton proposed that *it* set up a full-fledged university for all Switzerland. In June 1832, the Great Council of Canton Vaud, under the spirited urging of Professor Charles Monnard, made the decision to request the establishment of a *Swiss* university in the grand style via the route of a *Konkordat*, an agreement between cantons. In pre-meeting proposals circulated in July, prior to an upcoming Diet in Lucerne, the Vaudois government laid out its case and requested other electoral groups to provide their representatives instructions concerning the basic principle of a university and its administration, as well as financial means for its creation.

The Vaud proposal was taken up in August 1832, and Professor Monnard had the chair as the first representative of Vaud when the question came up for discussion. Zürich, Bern and Basel expressed the wish that the proposed all-Swiss university be established in their cities. Vaud contented itself with the altruistic observation that a university was its idea. At length, the conference delegated a commission, with Monnard as president, consisting of senior officials from Zürich, Bern, Basel and Geneva, to study the options in detail—another testament to Swiss conciliation at work on a high-stakes issue.

The news of the Vaud proposal in the meeting at Lucerne spurred Zürich into immediate action. That city decided to create a fait accompli and thereby ensure that a federal *Hochschule*, if it came into being, would be established in Zürich. The Zürichers realized that, even if such a school remained unlikely, one thing was certain: an advanced institute would only be created in a location where some kind of university already existed. Further, if Zürich did not go ahead with its model, there was little chance that a federal *Hochschule* would be established at all, and then Zürich would not be considered as a location in any case. However, if Zürich went ahead vigorously with its school, then both of these possibilities would remain on the table. The city's earlier reservations against a federal institute in the city somehow disappeared. Zürich's Council for Education hastily cleaned up its previously rejected legislative proposal for comprehensive education reform and set out in its report the logic of an expansion of the existing institute into a true polytechnic with a reference to the issue of a Swiss university.

> This school can become not only a school for Zürich itself but, in accordance with its facilities, the *Hochschule* for Switzerland. For such an undertaking words alone will not suffice. We must act. Thereby we will show our seriousness and our will to promote the spiritual well-being of our nation, and so gain the participation and support of all the confederates of Switzerland.

In September 1832 the canton's Great Council debated the issue in a four-day session, during which it became apparent to all that the ensuing Zürich school would become *the* Swiss national *Hochschule*. The measure passed in the Great Council with virtually no opposition. Moreover, hardly a voice was raised against the proposal from the countryside, from which opposition had been feared because of potential costs. With a vote of 148 for and only 9 against, the Great Council of Canton Zürich approved the founding of the Zürich *Hochschule*.

At almost the same time, the multi-canton *Hochschule* commission in Lucerne completed a report drafted by Vaud's Professor Monnard and signed by the other members of the commission. The commission also issued a draft of a *Konkordat* for presentation to the full Diet that almost surely came also from the pen of Monnard. His essential point was that the goal of a national university could be achieved only if it was created by the whole of Switzerland. Further, despite the advantages offered by existing Swiss institutions, the only way the cantons could be moved to create a university equal to the best foreign universities was for the cantons to sacrifice their own schools for the good of the nation and support the national initiative.

Monnard laid out what he considered the basic requirement for such an institution—unconditional academic freedom. Without that freedom there could be no honest search for truth, no intellectual life worthy of the name. He also maintained such a project would be expensive and would require a strong central administration. The yearly expense would run to at least 200,000 Swiss francs, a part of which would go to the building of a capital fund until such fund reached the level of four million francs. Of that outlay, the canton that enjoyed the advantages of being home to the institution would be responsible for half of the yearly contribution as well as for maintaining support resources and buildings without additional compensation.

The university proposed by the commission would have five faculties—Catholic theology, Protestant theology, law and political science, medicine and philosophy—with a total of 40 fully funded chairs. In general, lectures would be conducted in German, and additional chairs in French or Italian would be created according to the participation of the cantons speaking those languages. The administration would consist of a chancellor (*Kanzler*) and a university senate, of which only half of the members could come from the professorate. Further, Monnard's plan stipulated that, outside the right to vote for the chancellor and the university senate, the cantons supporting the *Konkordat* would have the right for their students to pay lower fees and matriculation charges than students from nonsupporting cantons. Monnard foresaw Zürich or Bern as the most likely location for the university.

Monnard's proposal was not taken up officially by the full Diet session, but his ideas were hotly contested in private discussions between the representatives. Members for Glarus, Solothurn, St. Gallen, Neuchâtel and Geneva lodged so many objections that a consensus of the Diet seemed impossible. Monnard's proposals appeared headed for oblivion. Nonetheless, compromise prevailed. At the last conference of representatives in October, they decided to try to take the proposals to a public referendum.

The reception Monnard's proposals received back in the cantons seemed to match the contentious attitude of the Diet. It was as if the sudden push by Canton Vaud had only served to demonstrate the impossibility of general agreement on the project. Not a single canton stepped forward to support the proposal. Of course, all were united on the *desirability* of a common Swiss *Hochschule*. But each canton which already possessed a school of higher education thought it would be akin to suicide for its institution to support the establishment of a common institute elsewhere.

Thus, the Swiss *Hochschule* ran aground on the tumultuous shoals of Switzerland's diverse intellectual and political life. Zürich, Bern, Basel, Geneva and Lausanne each had a rich tradition in science and literature and were determined not to give way to a rival and thereby fall to the level of a mere commercial city. The Monnard project ended like a meteor that, after a momentary brilliance, plunges into darkness. In the attempts to revise the organization of the Confederation in 1832 and 1833, the question of a Swiss *Hochschule* hardly came up. But the short existence of the Monnard project was not wasted. It provided the impetus for Zürich's *Hochschule*, was the reason Bern's academy was reorganized into a university, and pushed Basel into keeping its school through difficult times.

Even Zürich, which had every reason to be more accepting, had been decidedly cool to Monnard's proposal. In November 1832, the Zürich Council for Education discussed the matter and unanimously declared that if a *Hochschule* was to be created, it must be established in their city. Given the diversity of the languages, educational methods and needs of the Swiss cantons, they asserted a common university was neither necessary nor beneficial. "Under no circumstances," they declared, "should we give up our own university if it comes to pass that a common school is established in some other place."

In the same vein, the *Neue Zürcher Zeitung*, the leading Zürich newspaper, clearly "inspired" by individuals in the Zürich government, editorialized in November 1832: "We will not beat around the bush but declare straightaway, Zürich has possessed an institution of learning for hundreds of years and is long accustomed to the intellectual life it stimulates. It is not conceivable that this city should abandon it and pay to send its youth to Bern or wherever else to a *Hochschule* which robs us of our own university. Also, the canton and city of Zürich at this moment in time are not in a position to supply the funds necessary to support a school of the size envisioned in the proposal, even if Zürich were to be the site of such a school."

The Zürichers assessed the projected financial burdens on the canton that would host the proposed federal institute, and concluded that Zürich's own university could be maintained with a yearly contribution of only 27,600 francs. As a result, the Zürichers set out to organize their *Universitas Turicensis* with no regard for Monnard or his *Konkordat* draft. The cantonal university opened on April 29, 1833. Zürich had created "facts on the ground" with its new institution, and though it was not foreseen clearly at the time, Zürich's university would play a pivotal role in the founding of the ETH.

Despite all the opposition, the ideal of an all-Swiss *Hochschule*, especially a polytechnic institute, refused to die, even as its realization seemed to recede. In fact, in some ways the contentious national debate had been beneficial, encouraging the individual cantons to improve their upper schools and to stay in the running against the day when a federal polytechnic institute might again be considered. The ground had been prepared and the seed planted. In the fullness of time it would bear fruit, and the ETH would emerge.

CHAPTER FOUR

Birth Pangs

The heady calls for freedom, equality and brotherhood that emerged from the French Revolution did not die completely with the final defeat of the French in 1815. Together with the example set by the more successful American Revolution, they set in motion waves of ferment that led to radical new ideas and spawned uprisings throughout the 19th century. All over Europe intellectuals became fascinated with the concept of "liberation" and explored the causes of "oppression." Social and cultural revolution—whether gradual or abrupt—was the goal, and intellectuals addressed the problem of how a truly liberated citizenry might be created. The key to a fundamental transformation of human society, they thought, lay in devising a new kind of education for children and impressionable young adults.

Liberation remained a nationalistic affair through most of the 19th century, but educational thinkers in many nations were soon devising reforms that would produce this "new man" able to create a new society. Tempering these idealistic concerns in Switzerland was a dose of hard-headed practicality—how to produce well-trained engineers and scientists.

Switzerland, occupied by the French from 1798 to 1803, was not immune from the prevailing *Zeitgeist* that called for dramatic change. Swiss intellectuals began to look hard at the existing system of education in their country to determine where they could have the most impact. The idea of an all-Swiss university and polytechnic institute seemed an obvious place to begin, though the chances of its establishment were in part dependent on the ebb and flow of liberal sentiment in Switzerland and across Europe.

The liberal impulse was renewed in France in 1830, when popular revolts broke out in Paris and Lyons. Frenchmen were reacting to the abuses of the Bourbon dynasty, restored to power after the final fall of Napoleon. The Bourbons, as it was said, "had learned nothing and forgotten nothing" from the French Revolution and its aftermath. The old King Charles X abdicated, and Louis-Philippe, "the Citizen King," assumed the throne. Similar outbreaks of violence asserting the popular will against class and privilege occurred in Brussels, in Prussia and the German states, and in Warsaw. The excitement, with its renewed sense of possibility, carried over into Switzerland. Mass demonstrations led to legislation to expand the franchise of citizenry, to broaden the principle of popular sovereignty and to diminish the power and privileges of elite families and ecclesiastical officials.

Proposals on educational reform were in the wind almost everywhere. As noted earlier, Canton Vaud called in 1832 for the creation of a university commission, and under Vaud's own Charles Monnard it proposed a national university to be established by *Konkordat*. However, this commission had an effect opposite to its unifying intent. Its recommendations pushed some cantons to accelerate plans for their own universities. They feared the federal institute would jeopardize their cantonal interests and sought to preempt the national project on behalf of their own schools, hoping theirs might become the seat of the national institution.

Zürich stole a march on all and opened its new university in April 1833. However, the events of the 1830s were ultimately to have far greater impact on higher education in Switzerland than the Monnard Commission and the founding or upgrading of various cantonal institutes. At first, the excitement led nowhere. The idea of a Swiss national institute remained just an idea. It took the Sonderbund War and the resulting Swiss federal state under the new Constitution of 1848 to make the proposals for a unified federal school a national policy.

In 1845 Switzerland suffered not one but two crushing blows. There was a severe depression, especially in textile production, and widespread crop failure. The resulting distress brought to the surface latent conflicts between the capitalist bourgeoisie and suddenly unemployed and destitute urban workers. Food became scarce and expensive, aggravating an already explosive situation. The old tensions between Catholics and Protestants as well as French-speaking and German-speaking cantons threatened to break into the open.

Entrepreneurs in cities like Zürich and Basel were mostly Protestant and mostly interested in commercial and industrial expansion. Led by moderate liberals like Züricher Alfred Escher, they wanted a stronger, rational central government to bring order to the chaotic arrangement of inter-cantonal trade, with its different weights, measures, currencies and tariffs. The old order of rural and agricultural interests was championed mostly by the Catholic cantons of central Switzerland. In Lucerne citizens organized the military defense pact known as the Sonderbund to preserve the existing structure. The Sonderbund drew Jesuit activists and other Catholics from neighboring countries to the colors in hopes of restoring the ancient faith to ascendancy in Switzerland. This provided a convenient pretext for the liberals and their radical allies, who had only half the votes in the Swiss Diet but represented about 80 percent of the population. They launched a furious attack on Catholic conservatism (while not necessarily addressing its underlying political and economic grievances).

Fighting broke out on a large scale in 1847. Henri Dufour, appointed the first general in Swiss history, led a "liberal" army of 100,000—an enormous force for Switzerland at the time—to victory over Catholic conservative forces in Canton Lucerne and the Valais, but only 100—some say fewer—Swiss died in the exchange. Incidentally, it was during his campaigns in Switzerland's unmapped mountainous terrain that Dufour recognized the need for trained surveyor-cartographers. The need for this essential science was a minor but contributing influence in the founding of the ETH.

To their credit, in the midst of triumph, Swiss liberals did not forsake the old spirit of moderation, conciliation and compromise. Still, they were now able to deal from an unchallenged position of strength, and they insisted on a *Bundesverfassung*, or federal constitution, that would create a new Swiss Confederation.

The new federal state of 1848 marked the end of two decades of civil strife that had culminated in the bloodshed of the Sonderbund War. From here on, liberal Protestant dominance was a settled matter, and the old conservative, Catholic and patrician forces were relegated to the margins of Swiss political power. Still, the new constitution codified a wide range of traditional liberties— the right to live where one wished, freedom of association and religion, and equality before the law. It recognized the legitimate claims of the defeated minority with guaranteed provisions of cantonal sovereignty in local matters.

At the same time it paved the way for capitalist development and expansion, eliminating the principal obstacles to economic growth. The individual cantons lost the right to levy customs duties and to coin money. Weights and measures were standardized throughout the country. Among these steps toward national improvement was an article in the Constitution that finally raised the idea of an all-Swiss university and also polytechnic to the level of national policy in a way that had not been possible before. Like so many Swiss decisions, it was a compromise. Article 22 of the *Bundesverfassung*, adopted on September 12, 1848, stated: "The Federal Government shall be authorized to set up a university and a polytechnic school." The Constitution authorized the federal government to create the new institutes, but the *obligation* to do so had been dropped.

FROM DREAM TO REALITY

Swiss progressives had advocated both a university and a polytechnic since the days of the short-lived, French-dominated Helvetic Republic, and each had its strong advocates. In the event, the national polytechnic was founded, while the university was not. Yet, at the outset, discussions about how to comply with Article 22 were dominated by talk of a federal Swiss university. The committee set up by the cantonal representatives to implement the federal constitution addressed the issue of the university in February 1848. On that occasion Colonel Frédéric Jacques Louis Rilliet of Geneva was the first to suggest that, given the needs of Swiss industry, consideration should also be given to founding a polytechnic. Rilliet had served as an officer under Napoleon and in the Swiss Guards under Louis XVIII, and had seen for himself the achievements of the technical education system in France. His proposal was initially rejected on the grounds that there was already enough uncertainty about the prospects for a national university.

In May 1851, the new Federal Council established by the Constitution—that is, the new federal executive—received two bills drafted by Canton Zürich's extremely influential President Alfred Escher and others for both the university and the polytechnic, pursuant to the idea that had refused to die. In the report accompanying the polytechnic bill, the drafters stressed the fact that Switzerland's future prosperity depended on building roads and railways, and that its rivers could be adapted as sources of power. These tasks demanded the utmost in technical know-how and a corps of trained engineers, which meant that a federal polytechnic was required. The proposed federal law was moderate in scope and focused on the practical benefits. "The purpose of the polytechnic school," stated Escher's report, "is to provide engineers with a theoretical and, as far as possible, a practical training (1) in building roads, railways, waterways and bridges, (2) in industrial machinery and (3) in industrial chemistry, always bearing in mind the particular needs of Switzerland. The polytechnic school may also be used for the partial training of teachers for technical educational establishments."

Some forms of industry had come early to Switzerland, compared to other countries in Europe, partially as a result of the country's involvement in trade and its historic openness to refugees. Swiss industry, such as it was, was created by inventors and entrepreneurs whose training was through guild apprenticeship or on-the-job, trial-and-error experience. Mechanization of the textile industry had started at the beginning of the 19th century, first as a cottage industry and then transitioning to factory work, which intensified the development of engineering, especially mechanical engineering, as a separate discipline.

By 1850 this development was coming to an end. Technical knowledge was increasing exponentially with the pace of the Industrial Revolution and could no longer be mastered without systematic scientific and practical training. The country faced its own specific manufacturing limitations: a lack of coal and other raw materials and, more significantly, a work force largely consisting of peasants who still owned a small holding or Alpine farm, even though they could barely earn a living from agriculture. However, they were independent-minded as well as highly motivated, in contrast to the poor, malleable proletariat crowded into wretched slum cities in England or France, for example. These conditions naturally forced Swiss industry less toward mass production and more toward high-quality, value-added goods, enhancing the arguments for founding a polytechnic before—or in lieu of—a liberal arts university. Moreover, the estimated annual cost for the polytechnic was only 80,000 Swiss francs. The projected cost to the central government for the larger university was nearly five times that amount; thus, the polytechnic also represented a significantly better return on the federal investment.

Since Bern had become the federal capital, Zürich expected to be given the federal university as compensation, while the polytechnic was to be located in Lausanne. But the political winds veered once more. Francophone western Switzerland had supported the creation of the new federal state, but now feared that a Swiss federal university would encourage "Germanization." The proposed theological faculties for the university generated a heated backlash from the Catholic camp, still smarting over the expulsion of the Jesuits and their defeat in the Sonderbund conflict in 1847.

In January 1854 the battle for minds and hearts began in the Swiss Federal Parliament. It was filled with passionate debates, primarily about the university bill, with coalitions forming and reforming along political, cantonal, linguistic and confessional lines, depending on the proposals being discussed at any given time. In

January the National Council (the lower house of the new bicameral Parliament, known as the Federal Assembly) voted 59 to 39 in favor of a compromise proposal to combine the university and polytechnic on one site and thus save money. In Canton Vaud the decision was met with a storm of protest. Some 15,000 opponents from hundreds of municipalities claimed that federalism, the fundamental strength of the new federal state, was already in danger and urged the Federal Assembly (the upper and lower houses) to reject the proposed university law.

On February 1 the Council of States (the upper house) voted 27 to 15 not to endorse January's compromise bill from the National Council, which *ipso facto* threatened the polytechnic, the fate of which was tied to the university. The polytechnic was rescued in the session by the political leadership of the highly respected Alfred Escher and Johann Konrad Kern, with the critical support of Stefano Franscini, whose voice as the first Minister of the Interior carried considerable influence. On that same day, February 1, the Council of States adopted a second decision, to wit:

1. The decision is taken in principle to set up a Swiss federal polytechnic school in connection with a school for the advanced study of the exact sciences, the political sciences and the humanities. 2. This institution shall be located in Zürich. 3. The committee is required to present Parliament with an appropriate legislative bill together with a calculation of the costs involved.

The third item spelled a delay of several days for the required calculation of costs, which gave opponents of the other half of the national project, the university, time to marshal their forces against it. The Council of States gave the humanities and political subjects short shrift, approving the polytechnic only on February 4. By then the supporters of the university, outmaneuvered and outvoted, folded their hand. On February 7, 1854, the National Council adopted the unchanged bill by a large majority, spelling the end of a national humanities university.

Although Canton Vaud had vigorously protested setting up the polytechnic in German-speaking Zürich, the opposition of Francophone western Switzerland to the institute was not directed at technical training per se. Indeed, its necessity had been recognized at an early stage by leading public figures in Vaud, Geneva and other French-speaking cantons. It was this foresight that prompted the foundation in 1853 of the *Ecole Spéciale de Lausanne*, which began as a private institute for engineers. Later it was integrated into Vaud Academy, which became a university in 1890. This was the forerunner of the *Ecole Polytechnique de l'Université de Lausanne* (EPUL), which was taken over by the federal government in 1969 and became a sister school of the ETH Zürich in 1991. It is now known as the *Ecole Polytechnique Fédérale de Lausanne* (EPFL). This was yet another form of characteristic intra-Swiss conciliation, ensuring that Lausanne, which had pioneered technical education in Switzerland, would not go unrewarded.

The critical role of Stefano Franscini in promoting the all-Swiss polytechnic has already been highlighted. At this point in the story, it is fitting to credit the equally vital contribution of Zürich's most prominent political leader, Alfred Escher, without whose persistence and masterful guiding hand the story of the ETH might have turned out differently.

Escher was not only Zürich's leading figure but also one of the most important and influential men in all of Switzerland. He is a towering figure known to almost every Swiss—and this in a country where political leaders do not enjoy the celebrity status so common in the rest of Europe and in the United States.

In 1848 Escher was elected head of Zürich's cantonal government and then, upon the creation of the new National Council, he was elected to that body and served four times as its President. In addition to championing the ETH and locating it in his hometown, he was a strong advocate of the development of Swiss railroads. Though he favored a private rather than nationalized rail system, he became the driving force behind the construction of the Gotthard Line through the epic tunnel completed in 1880–1882. He helped secure the necessary agreements with Germany and Italy, and presided over the St. Gotthard project during its crucial and difficult early years.

AN AUSPICIOUS BEGINNING

The law passed by the National Council in February 1854 authorized the foundation of a polytechnic but did not spell out the operational details. Although passed in its final form in great haste, the law proved to be far-sighted and did not need to be revised until 1969, when the EPFL joined the ETH as a sister school. Subsequent modifications in the law were made in 1992 and 2002. The actual organization of the institute was laid down in the "Statutes for the Swiss Federal Polytechnic School," drafted by prospective professors of the ETH, along with members of the National Council Alfred Escher, Johann Kern and Johann Kappeler, and approved by the Federal Council in July 1854.

These leaders proposed a School of Building, where future master builders would study "civil and monumental building." The School of Engineering would train traditional road, railway, bridge and hydraulic engineers, along with topographical engineers specializing in the new science of geodesy. The School of Mechanical Engineering was to teach both theoretical mechanics and practical mechanical engineering. Courses in these three departments lasted six semesters. Courses in the School of Technical Chemistry along with the School of Forestry, which had been added at the suggestion of the Solothurn's member of the Council of States, could be completed within two years. The idea of training pharmacists had not been foreseen in the law authorizing the polytechnic, but was added to the Technical Chemistry department when the importance of the pharmacological sciences became apparent. Although no separate department had yet been set up for prospective teachers, the sixth department was in essence designed to train teachers for Swiss primary and secondary schools. It covered the mathematical disciplines, the natural sciences, literary subjects and "subjects related to the national economy," including the literature of the three national languages (this predated the official status of Romansch, which became the fourth official Swiss language in 1938). This department also included instruction in world and Swiss history, the history of art, archaeology, national law, commercial law, economics and free-hand drawing.

An important milestone was reached in resolving the matter of the level at which the syllabus should begin. If, as was the case in comparable institutions abroad, foundation or college-preparatory courses had also been provided, it could have had an adverse effect on the regional institutions by duplicating and superseding their function. Instead, it was decided to foster the cantonal *Mittelschulen* (secondary schools) by asking them to raise their standards with a focus on the foundation courses. It was soon apparent that the Polytechnic was an institute of higher education since its Director and teaching staff made up the institute's Directorship and General Conference, corresponding to the posts of Rector and Senate in other universities. The Poly's department chairmen and the six department conferences corresponded to university deans and their faculties.

To perform its tasks of leadership and oversight, the Swiss *Schulrat*, the Higher Education Council appointed by the federal executive, and its President were given far-reaching powers. It decided how the funds granted by the Federal Assembly were allocated. Though it appointed the ETH Director and the department chairmen, in the case of professors and auxiliary teachers it was restricted to creating a pool of applicants. It deferred to the Federal Council in Bern, which retained final decision-making powers related to the ETH.

The Polytechnic was the first school of its kind to dispense with foundation courses from the outset and that sought to be a real university. It was able to capitalize on a more broadly based technical education system that had grown up in Switzerland after the founding of the federal state in 1848, when industrial and vocational schools began to do more than provide a general preparation for on-the-job training in the trades and business. One of the exceptions in that early phase was the upper school of the aforementioned Zürich *Industrieschule*, which counted among its teachers Ferdinand Redtenbacher, who, after being called to the polytechnic in Karlsruhe, Germany, in 1841, founded the science of mechanical engineering. The first Director of the Swiss Federal Polytechnic, Joseph Wolfgang von Deschwanden, born in Stans, had not only taught at the Zürich *Industrieschule* but had previously been a pupil of Redtenbacher. These personal links to Karlsruhe played a role in determining that the pioneering bill of 1851, which was influenced by Alfred Escher and his advisor Deschwanden, unlike the outline put forward by the French-speaking cantons, abandoned the French model in favor of the Karlsruhe model.

Depending on the department involved, the new institute was equipped with workshops and laboratories and a new library. The original budget was doubled when the federal government, relieved of the need to also provide for a national university, decided to make up to 150,000 francs available; the Canton and city of Zürich together had to contribute 16,000. A hundred students were expected. To ensure that enough students with the requisite qualifications applied, a one-time preparatory course had been started as early as May 1855. In the first academic year of 1855–1856, the total of 231 students far outstripped projections. Admittedly the majority of these were auditors, while only 71 students were working toward the final diploma. Still, the student turnout was an early indicator of the appeal of the new institute.

The ETH's reputation depended crucially on the quality of its teaching staff. In October 1854, 32 professorships and between 9 and 12 auxiliary teaching posts—we typically use the term "adjunct" today—had been advertised in the national and foreign press. Pay was comparatively poor. The Federal Council had put a 5,000 franc per annum ceiling on salaries, and there were no additional benefits. Nevertheless, 189 applications came in, of which over 100 were from the German states.

Switzerland was highly attractive to potential faculty in neighboring states because of political conditions at the time, still unsettled as a result of yet another period of turmoil that swept Europe in 1848. The universities of Zürich and Bern had already benefited greatly from the influx of German refugees in the 1830s. Many of the original professors of the University of Zürich in 1833 had been Germans because there were insufficient Swiss nationals to fill the posts. When the reactionaries triumphed over the German romantic revolutionary movements of 1848–1849, many of those persecuted fled to Switzerland, England, or even overseas to America. The Poly gained some of its most famous teachers from among those who had been persecuted because of their political views.

One of them was the noted architect Gottfried Semper, who helped to shape a whole building epoch. Because of his involvement in building barricades during the 1849 "May Uprising" in Dresden, he had had to flee Germany. Word of his appointment at the ETH, promoted by the composer Richard Wagner, reached him in London, where he was in exile. Pompejus Alexander Bolley, appointed as Professor of Technical Chemistry, had been a member of the *Burschenschaft* (a revolutionary movement campaigning for a free and united Germany) and had taken part in Germany's Hambach Festival demonstrations in 1832, earning him six months in prison. This spelled an end to his career in Germany, so he immigrated to Switzerland. He was first Rector of the Aargau vocational school, where he helped it to prosper, and later was Director of the Polytechnic from 1859 to 1865. Other refugee faculty included Hermann Behn-Eschenburg, Professor of English Literature, and Francesco de Sanctis, who had been targeted for his views by the Naples reactionaries and spent three years in prison. He taught Italian literature at the ETH and later returned to Italy, where he became Minister of Education in the United Kingdom of Italy. The well-known aesthete Friedrich Theodor Vischer, who in 1849 had been one of the stalwarts in the Frankfurt National Assembly, moved to Zürich to escape restrictions on the freedom to teach. Other notable émigrés of the turmoil of 1848 included Johannes Scherr, sentenced *in absentia* to 15 years in prison and appointed Professor of General History at the Poly in the autumn of 1860, and the former insurgent Gottfried Kinkel, who came late to Zürich (in 1866) as Professor of Archaeology and Art History.

The young school was filled with a spirit of technical and intellectual progress. This was also thanks to a number of qualified and mainly young teachers who were not political refugees: the architect Ernst Georg Gladbach, appointed at the beginning of 1857; Karl Culmann, Professor of Engineering Sciences and founder of graphostatics; and Gustav Anton Zeuner and Franz Reuleaux, who divided mechanical engineering into two separate disciplines—a theoretical one and a practical one—a concept then unheard of abroad. The chemists Georg Städeler and Rudolf J.E. Clausius, pioneers in the field of mechanical thermal theory, came from German states.

There were also well-regarded Swiss teachers who made up about half of the teaching staff. Joseph Wolfgang von Deschwanden took over as Professor of Descriptive Geometry. The physicist Rudolf Albrecht Mousson and the geologist Arnold Escher von der Linth, the son of the engineer of the Linth Canal (joining Lakes Zürich and Wallenstadt), had previously taught at the University of Zürich. To avoid duplication, a number of professors taught at both the ETH and the cantonal University of Zürich. Some of the teachers at the ETH were eager to hold parallel appointments as professors at the University, which helped to equalize the academic ranks in the two institutions. Jacob Burckhardt worked only for a short time at the Poly. At Easter 1858, he gave up his chair in the History of Art and Archaeology to take up a post at the University of Basel.

Despite assiduous efforts, it proved impossible to ensure that the other non-German-speaking parts of the country were appropriately represented on the teaching staff. Of the 83 lecture courses given during the second year, 70 were given in German, nine in French and four in Italian. A drive to attract more outstanding teachers from France took place under Johann Kern, but it met with only modest success. Still, no other European polytechnic had been able to start off with such a distinguished staff.

TOWARD THE INSTITUTE OF TECHNOLOGY

The Polytechnic had to wait in its temporary accommodations longer than expected. The construction of the main building was repeatedly delayed, mainly because of cost. It was up to Canton

Zürich to make the necessary land and facilities available. The definitive design for the new school's main building was undertaken by Gottfried Semper. His design took into account the diverse requirements of the departments and their various collections, and its handsome aesthetics met with enthusiastic approval, although construction ended up costing twice what the Zürich government had planned. The neighboring building for chemistry was ready by 1861, while in the northeastern part of the main building, where the School of Mechanical Engineering was located, the first lecture was given in April 1863. The wing to the southeast served as accommodations for the University of Zürich. In 1864 the Swiss Federal Observatory, constructed under Semper, began its astronomical observations.

Although the Polytechnic School, especially as far as the teaching staff were concerned, was an institute of higher education, it differed fundamentally from the University, which had its roots in quite another tradition. For the first 50 years the Poly still treated its students like lower school pupils. Classes were obligatory. Good grades determined whether students moved up to the next class. Students were subjected to checks on how hard they were working, and anyone who failed could expect to be disciplined. Soon friction grew between the ETH and University students, eliciting intervention from the *Schulrat* on the disputed issues. This friction was based mostly on the two institutions' different attitudes toward academic freedom, a fact exacerbated by the institutions inhabiting the same space.

As the Polytechnic's stay in temporary quarters drew to an end, order was maintained with difficulty. At the time there was a sharp increase in the number of new entrants. The entry requirements had perhaps been set too high initially. The expected growth in numbers failed to materialize, but the revised entry requirements and the introduction in 1859 of a one-year preparatory course in mathematics led to a significant improvement in matriculations. The preparatory course, which was abolished in 1881, was not intended as a back-door foundation course. Instead, its purpose was to help close the gap for those who came from other language regions or who could not go straight into the specialist departments because of deficiencies in the education they had received in their cantons. Official rules about the recognition of matriculation certificates later made it possible for them to be accepted directly.

These reforms bore fruit. In 1858–1859, only 109 students had been working toward a final diploma; five years later there were 500-plus diploma-track students. This put intolerable pressures on the high numbers in temporary accommodation, leading to a high rate of academic discipline. In 1862–1863, 22 percent of students were disciplined—reprimanded, threatened with expulsion or expelled. No sooner had the Poly moved into its new main building when a full-scale student mutiny broke out against Director Bolley.

In July 1864, because of malicious damage to Semper's new edifice by parties unknown but presumably students, Bolley instituted a disciplinary crackdown. His tough measures generated a backlash, a "declaration of war" by students against his strict regime, particularly when it turned out to be more stringently enforced in the new *Semperbau* (designed by Gottfried Semper) than it had been in the temporary accommodations. The conflict ended with the demand by some 300 Polytechnic students that Director Bolley himself be expelled. When the *Schulrat* failed to demand Bolley's resignation, many of them left. Although the conflict was exacerbated by Bolley's stiff authoritarian manner, the dispute was about more than personalities. The "struggle for a liberal principle," as University of Zürich students called it in a message of support, was also about improving the status of Polytechnic students, and was a dramatic prelude to their later efforts to acquire more student rights and greater academic freedom.

The 1863–1864 "year of revolution," as the Polytechnic Yearbook styles it, had only a very short-lived impact on the growth in student numbers. Many new entrants kept the enrollment boom going unabated. At the beginning of the 1860s, the ambitious Polytechnic had more teachers even than Karlsruhe, even though the latter had more students. Its counterparts in Stuttgart, Dresden, Berlin and Hanover were much smaller. Once the supplementary law of January 1859 was passed and opened the way for a pay raise for the teaching staff, the Poly enjoyed a generous budget in every respect. Annual expenditure was not the only way in which it surpassed the other polytechnics. There was also a significant effort to build up the Polytechnic's collections. Even in this early phase, a foreign expert described as "remarkable" the ETH's geology and mineralogy collection, which had integrated older stocks from the Canton and city of Zürich, the mechanical engineering collection and its geometric instruments collection.

Once the Polytechnic was installed in the *Semperbau* in all its glory, it became hugely attractive to Germans, Austrians, students from Hungary and many other countries. For a decade Swiss were actually a minority among matriculated students. For a short time, at the beginning of the 1870s, the Polytechnic was the largest—and some were already saying the best—institution of its kind in the German-speaking world.

Part II
A CENTURY OF ACHIEVEMENT

CHAPTER FIVE

The Age of Industrialization 1855–1905

The latter half of the 19th century was a time of accelerating change: intellectual, social, political and especially technological. These various streams of endeavor fed into one another, magnifying the effects of the 1848 revolutions, primarily in France and Germany, that were still rippling outward. Switzerland, after its own comparatively mild Sonderbund conflict, had wisely and generously made concessions to the defeated. Now, under a new federal government and constitution, the country had attained a level of peace and stability not enjoyed by much of the rest of Europe. This allowed the Swiss to concentrate on developing their potential. By 1855, when the ETH opened, Switzerland was well on its way to industrialization. It did not happen right away, but still relatively quickly in historical terms. Within a few decades of the ETH's opening, Switzerland had achieved a reputation as one of the advanced industrialized countries of the time.

We have earlier cited Thomas Kuhn's seminal work *The Structure of Scientific Revolutions*, but the point bears repeating: scientific progress is not necessarily a matter of small accumulated, incremental gains. It moves in leaps and bounds as people come to accept entirely new frameworks of thought—"paradigm shifts." The second half of the 1800s was a time of such leaps and bounds as knowledge expanded; more to the point, knowledge spread as the awareness of the possibilities flowing from a mastery of science and technology expanded.

In practical terms, the most observable leap forward in Switzerland was its internal development—Alpine roads and bridges, the electric railway, the ingenious new *Bergbahn* or *Zahnradbahn* (cogwheel mountain trams) and the *télépherique* (cable cars), hydroelectric power stations, the great Alpine tunnels, and flourishing engineering, chemical, dye and textile industries.

These achievements bore witness to the technical aptitude of the Swiss people, especially in light of their lack of raw materials. The great strides in the last half of the 19th century validated the insight of the Swiss that their greatest capital was not in raw materials, arable land or natural resources but in intellectual capital—knowledge, training and hard work. They had discerned that their future lay in science and technology, industrialization and engineering; and their new polytechnic institute was expected to lead the way.

SCHOOL, FACTORY AND LABORATORY

During its first 50 years, the ETH generated cooperation between education and industry, and the economic environment of Switzerland began to feel the impact of an increasing reservoir of trained scientists and engineers. First the country focused on the challenges of mastering its own rugged landscape with an amazing network—amazing even today—of bridges, tunnels, dams, cogways and roads. Later, Swiss industry and Swiss science reached out to undertake projects around the world. The knowledge gained from overcoming the daunting challenges of the Alps was made available to other countries. Knowledge, like today's digital algorithms, can be replicated on a scale far beyond the locus of the original insight or solution.

The development of modern Switzerland can be said to spring from two interlaced legacies in the national character. One is the ingenuity and fierce independence of the peasant and freeholder. The other is the culture of commerce and industry born in Switzerland's principal trade towns from the Middle Ages onward. These two legacies syncretise in the uniquely Swiss response to the modern world. It cannot be overemphasized that the technical sophistication of the Swiss has a cultural basis. Some of the world's greatest mathematicians—starting with the Bernoulli brothers and Leonard Euler of Basel in the 18th century—stand at the foundation of modern Swiss development. They helped give the country a head start in the branches of manufacturing and machine tools in which precision was the hallmark of success. The preeminence of mathematics is also discernible in the founding of the ETH. However, in keeping with the essential Swiss spirit of practicality, the ETH "model" was also directed toward application, not just theory. Swiss production, unlike that in the U.S. or Great Britain, thus tended toward specification and value-added quality, resulting in less heavy industry and more specialized manufacturing. Highest quality, not volume, was the watchword, and the phrase *klein aber fein* ("small but fine") still resonates today.

Competition from—and collaboration with—institutions in other countries had a decided effect on the ETH. Enrollments shifted with the perceived superiority of one school or another. In its first two decades, enrollment at the Polytechnic rose to a peak of 725 students, with 289 auditors in the School of Humanities. Then it began to decline rapidly, in what threatened to become a long-term crisis affected by geopolitical events. The unification of the north and south of Germany had brought far-reaching changes to the region, the consequences of which were felt by the Poly. A unified Germany began to flex its "imperial" muscle, giving top priority to higher technical education. Institutes of technology were created in Munich in 1868, Aachen in 1870 and Berlin in 1879, tempting experienced teachers, many of whom were Germans, to leave Switzerland for positions closer to home. For example, in 1871 the ETH's great architect Gottfried Semper moved to Vienna, where prestigious commissions awaited him, including the world-famous Hofburg and other monumental buildings.

One cannot pass over Gottfried Semper's tenure at the ETH without noting an incident involving Semper and another ETH notable, Johannes Scherr. It illustrates that, while the Swiss might have seemed restrained and accommodating in most areas of public life, they still had strong convictions—especially regarding their decentralized republic. It also illustrates a significant difference between German-speaking Swiss and Germans.

The background to this vignette was one of the most fateful events of the 19th century. In 1870, in a whirlwind war orchestrated by the "Iron Chancellor," Otto von Bismarck, the Prussians and their north German allies won a crushing victory over the French, in the process seizing the "mixed" provinces of Alsace and Lorraine for the new Germany. In 1871 Wilhelm I was crowned Kaiser of a new German Empire in the Palace of Versailles. The republican Swiss watched this development warily, though many German expatriates in Switzerland exulted. In May 1871 Gottfried Semper, as a member of the German community in Zürich, joined a committee inviting Germans in Switzerland to a victory party in the *Tonhalle* concert hall to celebrate the founding of the German Empire. During the event, an angry crowd of Swiss assembled outside. Semper's ETH colleague Johannes Scherr had agreed to take part and read a congratulatory speech. Though a Swiss by choice, Scherr was a German emigrant and a highly regarded man of letters who had fled to Zürich in 1850 to avoid imprisonment for his agitation for parliamentary reform in his native Württemberg. In celebrating the new German Reich, this flagbearer of republicanism was seen as betraying the cause he had previously championed. It goaded the Swiss demonstrators into an occurrence rare in Zürich, a full-scale riot, known famously as the *Tonhallekrawall* (concert hall riot). Scherr had to suspend his remarks, the victory party broke up, and for a time relations were strained between the ETH's German professors and their Swiss hosts.

Despite his temporary fall from grace, Johannes Scherr is still revered today in German-speaking Switzerland. Born in 1817 in the Kingdom of Württemberg that borders Switzerland on the north, Scherr studied philosophy and history at the University of Tübingen. He then joined his brother, who had moved to Winterthur in Switzerland. After teaching for several years at his brother's academy in Winterthur, Scherr returned to Germany and became active in the democratic movement that culminated in the upheavals of 1848. He fled to the safe haven of the Switzerland he knew and found work as a private tutor. Scherr later joined the arts and letters faculty at the ETH.

He was a versatile writer and researcher, specializing in the roots of Germanic (including Swiss) language, civilization, literature, manners and customs. His works are still studied in German-speaking Switzerland and especially in his home city of Zürich. Scherr's books have a heavy political emphasis, no doubt stemming from his encounter with reactionary zealots in 1848–1850. Yet, they also have a freshness and vigor still celebrated by Zürichers. They are included in the ETH's liberal arts syllabus, especially his works on Friedrich von Schiller, one of Germany's greatest writers and, along with Goethe, a leading voice of German Romanticism. Scherr's *Schiller and His Times* (1859) and the historical novel *Schiller* (1856) established him as a master in the field. Lest anyone miss the Swiss connection between Schiller and Switzerland, it was Schiller's drama *Wilhelm Tell*, first performed to intense public acclaim in Weimar in 1804, that helped inscribe the great patriotic tale deeply in the consciousness of all Swiss.

Scherr's special place in the ETH pantheon suggests that the pride and honor of the school do not rest entirely on its accomplishments in science and technology. Even in its earliest days, the liberal—and nationalist—achievements in the arts and letters were part of the curriculum. Scherr, one of the most sophisticated men of letters of his time in the German-speaking world, was also quite at home among physicists, mathematicians and engineers.

DESIGNING PROGRESS

Although Switzerland made a breakthough in setting up the ETH, the rest of Europe had also begun to seethe with new scientific activity. Luckily, the Swiss succeeded in drawing some of the best and the brightest on the continent to Zürich. In fact, until the outbreak of World War I, at least half the Poly's professors were non-Swiss. Most were Germans whose careers were somehow blocked in the German states. But when the founding of the German Empire under Bismarck and Kaiser Wilhelm I increased the number of academic positions in the unified Germany, German academics found new careers and opportunities there. It became harder for the Poly to attract and keep outstanding talent from abroad.

In addition, 20 years after the ETH's founding, the increasing lack of space began to cause difficulties. The Canton began to chafe at the financial burden of the constant need for new buildings. Zürich rightly feared, given the internal dynamics of the Poly, that enormous expenditures would soon be necessary for purposes not foreseen at the beginning, and the good burghers of the host city no longer wanted to foot the bill.

At the beginning of the 1880s, students crowded into the main building while the federal government and Canton argued about new building obligations before the Federal Court. A new era of technical and industrial progress had already begun, and pressure on resources coincided with the demand for more teaching space. In 1880, under a private initiative, the first telephone network in Switzerland was built in Zürich. A year later the first training courses in electricity began on a voluntary basis at the Polytechnic. A separate building for physics was on order, and until it was built there were no modern laboratories. The 1883 Polytechnic Yearbook warned this would become a vital issue: "If nothing comes of this then the School will be gradually dragged down from its present position to less auspicious levels. If the building is delayed for years then the most favorable time for developing the School will have passed." A steep decline in foreign students, caused in part by external conditions but also by the cramped quarters, brought overall enrollment down to barely 400. However, the number of auditors in the School of Humanities continued to rise. This was not a bad thing per se, but after all, the Poly had been founded to train scientists and engineers, not to serve merely as an imitator of the University of Zürich next door, which focused on the arts and letters.

An 1883 out-of-court settlement over the obligation to support the Poly's building program eventually released the Canton of Zürich from much of the future burden, but not from its obligation to maintain the buildings it had already constructed. Finally—and now at the federal government's expense—the second round of building could begin. Under the guidance of ETH architecture professors Friedrich Bluntschli and Georg Lasius the new chemistry building was constructed (1884–1886) on Universitätstrasse and the new physics building (1887–1890) on Gloriastrasse. The Swiss Federal Institute for Forest Research, created in 1885 by federal decree after repeated demands from the Forestry Association, was also installed there.

As infrastructure development loomed larger and larger, the governing *Schulrat* and ETH faculty recognized an urgent need to extend the training in the Mechanical Engineering department. It was no longer enough for construction exercises to be limited to graphic representations on paper. For meaningful experiments real materials were needed, and a machine laboratory was required. As soon as the Federal Assembly had approved the funding in 1897, construction work could start. The machine laboratory (1897–1900) and the new art room building formed a whole new complex. The space freed up in the main building as a result was used to extend the library and create a larger reading room. The library now had a stock of around 50,000 volumes. Since the ETH's founding, the versatile astronomer Rudolf Wolf had spent almost 40 years building up the library collection. But it was only in 1921 that a full-time trained specialist took over the library.

Since the revision of the authorizing statutes in 1866, the sixth department of liberal learning had been wholly given over to training teachers in mathematics and the natural sciences, while the "pure" humanities were split off to form a seventh department. Farming organizations had also successfully won the creation in 1878 of the Polytechnic's first affiliated institutions, a seed testing station and an agri-chemical research station. From these modest beginnings, they developed later into independent institutions, severed their links with the ETH and moved to the nearby town of Oerlikon.

Rising entrance standards made it necessary to extend the length of courses in the specialist schools. The number of professors doubled during the first 50 years. Since student numbers increased many times and the Polytechnic was reluctant to make long-term financial commitments, more private lecturers were admitted—we might call them "adjunct professors" today. Many more tutors were engaged to cope with the increased teaching load. New laboratories and institutes came along, which remained within the structure of the Polytechnic. The fourth revision of the statutes in 1899 turned the military science section into a separate, eighth department. Its origins go back to a decision of the Federal Council in 1877 creating the Military School. This was long overdue, particularly in light of the fact that members of the Federal Council had insisted in the military reorganization of 1874 that the Polytechnic should provide officer training in military science.

THE GOLDEN AGE OF SWISS ENGINEERING

This period of the ETH story is one of its most exciting. The span of 1855–1905 was the "golden age" of Swiss engineering; many of the ETH's most remarkable achievements took place during this period. The school owes much of its fame to its civil and mechanical engineers, individuals who in their day were not merely admired but almost idolized. They were the phenomenal minds who created visible "monuments"—bridges, tunnels, highways, power systems—which actually made people's lives easier, their sense of human progress grander, and elevated Swiss national pride. It was a form of celebrity fundamentally different from today's trendy worship of rock stars, film actors and television personalities. The names of many of these Swiss master builders are hardly recognized at all in the U.S.—where they also changed the physical landscape— but they are not lost in Switzerland. They are the real legacy of the ETH.

Civil or construction engineering (CE) provided the toughest challenges and the field for the ETH's most visible accomplishments (the Swiss term for construction engineer is *Bauingenieur*). Mechanical engineering (ME) was also prominent; and, as the science of electricity began to reveal its secrets during this period, the ETH was at the forefront with one of the earliest departments of electrical engineering (EE).

Unlike some technical institutes, which had a tendency to over-specialize, the ETH civil engineering faculty maintained broad coverage of the subject matter through its long-standing tradition of having just four full professors. For more than two decades, Professor Karl Culmann oversaw the whole school while maintaining his CE teaching load and student mentoring. In the field of structural analysis and bridge engineering, his "graphical static" technique pioneered new calculation methods using geometric diagrams. Other core CE subjects adapted to Switzerland's particular challenges were road and railway construction and hydraulic engineering (river, canal, and lakeside engineering). After Culmann's death, the transport revolution made the creation of a special chair for road and railway engineering indispensable, and increasing reliance on internal combustion motorization shifted the emphasis from railway to highway engineering.

What is most striking is that the ETH, characterized by men like Culmann, had a distinctly practical orientation. The ETH evolved with the world around it even as it helped shape that world. Thanks to this adaptability, the faculty was responsive to rapid technological change or actually contributed to it, as success or maturity in one field created new possibilities. For example, as hydraulic studies matured, they contributed to the development of the water turbine. Knowledge of turbine technology in turn, combined with thermal engineering, led to the development of advanced steam turbines under the guidance of the ETH's Aurel Stodola, still a highly respected and well-remembered name in Swiss industry.

The ETH's focus on practical adaptation is also evident in structural and bridge engineering, which were still treated as a single teaching unit until the early 1920s. When Arthur Rohn became President of the *Schulrat*, the chair of bridge engineering was divided into two main subjects: steel and solid-structure engineering, the latter reflecting the rapid growth in the use of reinforced concrete. As a result, the Swiss became world leaders in the use of reinforced concrete, which was lighter, cheaper, easier to work with, and especially adaptable to the Swiss aesthetic vision, as a subsequent chapter on world-famous bridge designers will demonstrate.

From 1855 to 1867, Rudolf Clausius—an icon even today at
the ETH—had begun teaching an electrical theory course (beginning with the fourth semester of the syllabus), reflecting the growing importance the Swiss attached to electric power. In 1912, relatively early in the development stage of the EE discipline, the ETH
appointed a professor for theoretical electricity studies *and* electromechanical engineering. In 1923 another chair of electromechanical
engineering was added to cover both of the electrical generation
and distribution schemes—direct current and alternating current—
that had emerged as competitors in this nascent science (seen for
example in this country as the great battle for dominance between
Thomas A. Edison and George Westinghouse). Soon the ETH
boasted the world's few experts in high voltage engineering, which
had been ascendant since the spectacular energy transmissions
between Lauffen (on the Neckar River) and Frankfurt as part of the
1891 Electrotechnical Exhibition. This event influenced the movement to bring electric power to Europe, and thus Switzerland.
Teaching also covered electricity generators and energy management—fields in which the ETH contributed pioneering work—and
in technical physics and electric traction, all of which permanently
altered the technical and economic landscape of Switzerland and
Europe.

THE ELECTRIFICATION OF SWITZERLAND

The sober Swiss typically avoid hyperbole. But the story of the electrification of Switzerland, in which the ETH played a pivotal role,
is a marvel of human inventiveness.

Switzerland's fast-flowing rivers and cataracts had always been
a source of energy, used since antiquity for mills and simple
machines. But primitive applications of waterpower evolved slowly.
It was the discovery of electric power and the potential for convert-
ing one form of energy, moving water, into another, electricity, that
turned everything on its head. Visionary Swiss soon realized that
their nation's water resources—replenished annually with huge
runoffs from the Alps—provided a virtually unlimited and totally

accessible new resource. Electricity could be generated with relatively simple and easily replicated machines, and this new form of energy could then be transported cheaply far from the point of origin—virtually anywhere. Simple water—Switzerland's rushing streams and deep mountain lakes—was turned to gold. The *potential*, at least, was enormous.

But electrification did not happen all at once. The ultimate uses and sheer flexibility of the new power were not even known, and the technology of generation developed in fits and starts. "Modern" electricity was not invented in Switzerland. In fact, in the early days, the Swiss brought in generating technology from abroad. The earliest technologies were borrowed and adapted, usually under license, from foreign inventors and patent holders. Scientists and engineers throughout the industrialized world had little experience with this new technology, however promising it seemed. It was what we now see as the chicken-and-egg technology dilemma. While demand was low and hard to predict, large investment in supply was difficult to justify. Without supply, demand developed slowly.

This was, and remains, a common enough problem that we still see in the evolution of technology. Switzerland's European neighbors had ample waterpower, at least in their Alpine regions, yet they did not electrify their countries or comparable regions in the 19th century. Switzerland, which did not possess vast coal or timber reserves, was different. The Swiss moved ahead faster on hydroelectric power, and part of that initiative came from the involvement of ETH engineers.

The Swiss people had learned about this burgeoning technology at events like the National Exhibition in Zürich in 1883 and the Frankfurt Electrotechnical Exhibition in 1891. They knew they had no coal, but had initially been skeptical of the potential of waterpower to energize the whole country. It is not known exactly who the first genius was to connect the mechanical energy potential of Swiss water with electric energy generation, but the ETH was certainly involved in making the connection. In 1883, H.F. Weber of the ETH reported that "the masses of water rushing out of the Alpine valleys" represented "mechanical work of a nearly infinite quantity." In 1895 ETH professor Johannes Pernet gave a public talk on electricity. To his surprise and consternation, the citizens of Zürich virtually stormed the lecture hall. A crowd four times the size of the lucky ones inside clamored to be let in, and the organizers prevailed upon Pernet to repeat the talk that same evening and twice on succeeding Saturdays. Free tickets were distributed to prevent the turmoil of the first night's lecture, and even then the hunger of the people of Zürich and neighboring towns went unsatisfied.

Public lectures like Pernet's and industrial exhibitions and trade fairs informed a wide number of Swiss about the benefits of the new technology, creating a ready acceptance among them to become consumers and thus investors. This ready acceptance was aided by the spirit of the times in which the marvels of science and technology seemed to open vistas of possibility. The language of the period was exuberant, with constant references to progress, expansion, modernization and the conquest of nature. Combined with the stabilizing nature of Swiss politics, support for electric power became broad-based, accompanied by an almost ideological fervor. Electricity *was the future*, and its promise to transform life in Switzerland's harsh and unyielding terrain seemed wonderful indeed. By 1895 Switzerland had over 70 power plants, almost all financed by small investors or local communities. Other countries, including the United States, did not achieve a comparable level of electric power generation, especially in small towns and rural areas, until the early decades of the 20th century.

A final factor set Switzerland apart: the initial capital costs of ramping up to an electrical culture—generators, lines, lights, trains, factories—were substantial. But in Switzerland, money for this economically and socially complex project did not come from Swiss government funds or subsidies, as was the case, for example, with Rural Electric Associations in the U.S. in the 1930s, a part of the Depression-era New Deal. Nor did the funds come from big financial institutions. The money came instead from tens of thousands of small individual investors, mostly middle-class shareholders or small communities that pooled their modest savings to build their own power plant and distribution grid. In effect, electrification became a popular social movement, in keeping with the Swiss decentralized polity and local autonomy. The Swiss way was unique, and stayed true to its traditions.

THE CONQUEST OF THE ALPS AND THE SWISS ELECTRIC RAILWAY SYSTEM

Once the infrastructure for generating and distributing electricity was built, the new power grid opened new applications, most significantly in transportation. During the mid- to late 19th century, almost all train locomotives were coal-fired and steam-driven. Coal to power those sturdy mountain climbers had to be imported at great expense, since Switzerland had none of its own. Thus, when the Swiss realized the potential of water power to generate electricity to run their trains, they had ample incentive to move ahead quickly. But cheap power was only part of the solution to Switzerland's transportation problem. Electric trains, powerful as they were, still had to run on tracks. And Switzerland's formidable landscape presented a daunting problem to railroad-grade inclines. Cog trains were useful in some instances, but were slow. Chasms and sheer rock faces blocked the way almost at every turn. So the Swiss took up the incredible challenge of building a system of railway tracks in some of the harshest terrain on earth—soaring bridges over water torrents hundreds of feet below, tunnels dug meter by meter through Alpine granite, abutments, fills, roadways hanging from cliffs. It happened very fast; the achievement is remarkable even today. And it taught the Swiss—particularly Swiss engineers from the ETH—how to build. The northern plain was almost child's play, but Swiss road and railroad creations in the Alps remain some of the engineering wonders of the world.

The ETH was there for virtually every rail laid down. The school's *Alpeningenieure*, or Alpine engineers, were young and eager to put their theoretical learning into practice, and soon were taking advantage of a revolution in available construction materials—concrete, steel, and the marvel of *steel-reinforced concrete*. As Swiss historian Dr. David Gugerli has observed, it was "the industrial conquest of nature. Driven on by the human urge to conquer the summits, tracks, steam power, tunnels and cogwheels tamed the Alpine wilderness." Of course, building bridges over rushing rivers was not new to the Swiss. The men of the Poly were following in the footsteps of their countrymen who for centuries had worked to make at least part of the Alps passable to trade. One of central Europe's most famous landmarks was the *Teufelsbrücke,* the Devil's Bridge, which the people of Canton Uri had built over a chasm of the River Reuss as early as the 13th century, opening up access to the Gotthard Pass and allowing profitable commerce to develop between northern Europe and Italy.

There are two explanations why it was called the Devil's Bridge. One is that it was so narrow—about six feet wide with no handrails—that a misstep could send the traveler plunging to his death in the cataract below. But Swiss children learn another and more colorful version. To travelers of the Middle Ages it seemed such an impossible feat to throw an 80-foot arch across this precipitous valley that "only Beelzebub himself could have accomplished it." Folklore holds that the locals did make a pact with the Devil to erect the span and Satan agreed, but only in exchange for the first soul to walk across it. The canny Swiss sealed the bargain, but when the bridge was completed, foiled the Devil by sending across a goat.

In time the Swiss established the *Eisenbahn* (railroad) and *Zahnradbahn* (cog-railway) throughout the country, including over precipitous up-and-down terrain that would otherwise seem impassable by human conveyance. Swiss electric trains, cable cars and cog-rail systems became the widely used technical model for the rest of Europe and even the United States, where the first cog-railway was built at Pike's Peak in Colorado, modeled on the design of ETH engineer Roman Abt.

Three of the "Four Fathers" of the Swiss electric railway were ETH graduates: Emil Huber-Stocker, Hans Behn-Eschenberg, and Anton Schrafl. Huber-Stocker was from Canton Zürich, a descendant of an old Züricher family prominent in the area since the Middle Ages. He earned his mechanical engineering degree from the

ETH in 1886. Behn-Eschenberg, who was graduated from the ETH in 1889 with a diploma in mathematics and physics, was from Stralsund in Prussia. His father became a professor at the ETH after seeking refuge in Switzerland to escape the 1848 revolution in Germany. Anton Schrafl was from Lugano in Canton Ticino and earned his degree from the ETH as *Bauingenieur* in 1896. The fourth "Father," Robert Haab, handled the policy issues and provided liaison with the Swiss Federal Council.

The railway team had to solve unprecedented technical problems. The first was how to generate and distribute enough electricity throughout the country to power the widespread web of railroads. Then they had to transmit the power continuously to a locomotive moving along its track. The electric locomotive had to be as powerful as a coal- or oil-fired machine and with sufficient traction to handle the steep inclines. And they had to accomplish all this while making the system economically viable. They solved these challenges with an admirable result, a testament to the engineering genius produced at the ETH.

THE GREAT ALPINE TUNNELS

As the 1870s began, the ETH was 15 years old and Swiss civil engineering was still in its childhood, if not infancy. But ETH engineers were soon to get the opportunity to cut their teeth on the most formidable national undertakings yet conceived—the great tunnels under the Alps to link Switzerland and Italy—specifically, the St. Gotthard and the Simplon.

The St. Gotthard massif is part of the Lepontine Alps in south central Switzerland, reaching a height of 10,472 feet (3,192 meters) and providing the sources of the Reuss, Rhine, Ticino and Rhone Rivers. This portion of the range and the St. Gotthard Pass that traverses it are believed to be named for Saint Godehard, or Gotthard, an 11th-century bishop who maintained a hospice for travelers crossing the pass, an important link in Europe's north-south trade since the Middle Ages. The St. Gotthard Road, built between 1820 and 1830, provided a means for wagon and animal traffic to transit the massif, and the prosperity that this trade produced convinced the Swiss that a railway passing under the Gotthard through a tunnel would generate even more trade.

The St. Gotthard Tunnel, begun in 1872, challenged Swiss engineers to master a whole range of geological science applications and new techniques of boring, drilling, blasting and shoring. Here Alfred Nobel, a name we will hear much more of later through the Prizes established by his will, touches on our story directly through his new invention, dynamite (from the Greek *dynamis*, meaning power). Patented in 1867 and going into full production only a few years prior to the launching of this immense task, Nobel's new explosive proved invaluable in driving the 10.2-mile (16.4 km) tunnel through the base of the mountain. Upon its completion in February 1880, it was the longest such tunnel in the world. Two years later, the tunnel's railroad was completed, linking Lucerne with Milan, Italy, vastly increasing north-south trade and bringing new revenues to Switzerland. But the accomplishment was not without great human cost. Hundreds of workers were killed during the 10-year construction from cave-ins, flooding, accidents in handling the early heavy and awkward pneumatic drills, and from diseases contracted from the harsh environment.

THE SIMPLON TUNNEL

In 1898 the Swiss began their most ambitious engineering project ever, the 12-and-a-half-mile (20 km) Simplon Tunnel between Brig in Canton Valais and Iselle di Trasquera in Italy's Piedmont. Along with the Gotthard Pass, the Simplon Pass had been a major trade route between northern and southern Europe since the Middle Ages, and had been improved by a road built in 1801 by Napoleon. A tunnel through the mountain would eliminate the miles of twists and switchbacks and allow direct rail traffic between Switzerland and Italy on this vital route of European commerce. The earlier St. Gotthard Tunnel had shown it could be done, at least in theory; but the Simplon would be longer, deeper, and an order of magnitude more difficult because of the complex geology of the site.

One is compelled to admire not only the skills but also the self-confidence of the Swiss engineers who took on such a challenge. ETH graduates like Albert Heim, Switzerland's most renowned geologist and a professor of geology at the ETH, and civil engineer Ferdinand Rothpletz played pivotal roles, as did Charles Andreae, who later held the ETH special chair for road and railway engineering. The Swiss covered their bets by retaining consulting engineers and specialists from Italy, Austria and England.

There was no question that a tunnel through the Simplon would be a great advantage; but could it be done, even with the lessons learned from the St. Gotthard? It would have to go through the heart of a mountain over 2,000 meters high. The rock varied in density. The builders would have to solve the difficult problem of ventilation, to say nothing of the heat they expected to encounter in the heart of the mountain. Cuts would be begun from both ends simultaneously. That meant the miners would have to proceed with enough precision to meet in the middle, under a mile of solid rock. At more than 12 miles in length, Simplon would be the longest railway tunnel in the world.

The Swiss are a careful people. They wanted the tunnel, but the plan—and every variable they could measure—was analyzed minutely before the go-ahead was given. With confidence in their own ETH engineers and the advice of tunnel experts from Italy, Austria and England, the Swiss decided it could be done despite the difficulties they would have to overcome.

Work began on both the Swiss and Italian sides with a bore consisting of two single-shaft tunnels running in parallel at a distance of about 55 feet. Periodic cross galleries were dug between the main shafts for ventilation, for equipment access, and for removal of spoil and debris. Great care was taken to protect the skilled (and courageous) miners, and to reduce the fatigue and discomfort from exposure to Alpine air after working in the heat of the galleries. A large dormitory was built near each entrance, provided with cubicles for dressing and hot showers. At the top of the building steampipes were fixed to dry sweaty work clothes. Each man was given his own private clothesline and padlock to which he affixed his day clothes and personal items, passing them by means of a pulley over the roof and securing them with the padlock. Returning from work he entered the warm building, had his shower, and lowered and retrieved his day clothes. He then hung his wet mining uniform on the hook and pulled it up to the roof until he returned to work, when he found his clothes warm and dry.

Hydraulic drilling allowed the tunnels to be bored three times faster than with earlier equipment, and also created less dust, the primary cause of miners' pulmonary disease. Not a single instance of the malady was reported during the work, and although a well-appointed hospital was provided at each end of the tunnel, the beds were generally empty.

In September 1901, at a distance of two and a half miles from the Italian side, the crews unexpectedly ran into a great subterranean river. This caused serious delays, and for a period of six months the total advance on the Italian end was only 46 meters. The difficulties at this point were so severe that men of less determination might have abandoned the project. Tectonic stresses forced them into close-timbering the shafts on the sides, the top and the floor with the heaviest available baulks, square pitch pine 20 inches thick. When the forces of the living rock crushed these timbers into splinters and completely blocked the gallery with wreckage, steel girders were tried, but they too bent under the stress. It seemed no available material could be found to withstand the enormous pressures, until finally a solution emerged. The engineers formed steel girders into squares, placed them side by side, and filled the inner spaces with concrete. Amazingly, they held and work could proceed. Fortunately the "bad ground" only extended for a distance of about 50 meters, but it cost thousands of francs per meter to overcome the difficulties. To shore up the tunnel permanently and safely, the builders encased the problematic areas in granite masonry over three meters thick.

Meanwhile progress from the Brig (Swiss) side was good, and the miners reached the halfway point on schedule; but then they began to encounter great heat from both rock and deep hot springs. The ambient temperature approached 131°F. Then a fresh difficulty emerged. It was necessary to commence driving downhill to meet the miners coming uphill from Italy. But as the gallery descended the hot springs followed. Soon the miners at the boring machines were standing in a sea of hot water. For a time they kept ahead of it by pumping out the water with centrifugal pumps. At last, with only 300–400 meters remaining to link up, it proved impossible to continue downward.

There was no thought of giving up at that late stage. The miners tried several expedients, including branching tunnels that helped divert and drain off the flow of hot water. Progress could now only be made from the Italian face, but even there the difficulties from hot springs became so severe that for a time one of the shafts had to be abandoned. Access to it could only be obtained by driving the parallel gallery ahead and then returning and to take the hot water flow in the rear. The only way the hot springs could ultimately be tamed was by throwing jets of cold water under high pressure into the source, thus cooling them to a temperature the miners could stand.

The initial breakthrough occurred at 7:00 A.M. on February 24, 1905, when a heavy charge was exploded in the roof of the Italian tunnel, blowing a hole in the floor of the Swiss shaft and releasing the impounded hot water. By continuing the spray of high-pressure cold water, the temperature of the tunnel was brought to a tolerable level. Once the galleries had been driven past these hotspots, the rock faces cooled off rapidly.

It took an additional month for the official link-up. On April 2, 1905, the visitors and officials from the Italian side, traveling in a miner's train, arrived within 250 meters of the *Porte de fer*, the "Iron Door" where the two shafts met in the middle of the mountain, 10 kilometers or more from either entrance. They completed their journey on foot to the junction point, where officials and visitors from the Swiss side had arrived. In a moment replete with drama and emotion, Swiss Colonel E. Locher-Freuler cracked the door and shoved it open. The two parties met and fraternized, embracing one another. The Bishop of Sion, capital of Canton Valais, held a dedication service, invoking Divine blessings on the tunnel, the officials, the workmen and the trains, and commending to God those who had lost their lives in the execution of this great work, some 45 in number. By 1906 the two parallels were finished, fine-tuned to a common grade, shored up, and soon were carrying railway traffic north and south. Thus ended one of the greatest engineering feats of its day—or any day—a triumph of ingenuity and determination.

THE FIRST NOBEL PRIZE

The kudos earned by the ETH for these extraordinary engineering exploits attracted many foreigners to the ETH as faculty and students. The admission of foreigners to any school is always problematic. Besides the basic issue of language differences, school systems and levels of attainment and certification seldom match up perfectly. Moreover, the most gifted applicants are not always those who shine in secondary school environments. Early on, therefore, the ETH *Schulrat* made what proved to be a wise policy decision on admissions that affected not only foreigners but also the Swiss themselves. Graduation from an accredited *Gymnasium*, or secondary school, was not to be a prerequisite for enrollment at the ETH. Promising students could take a qualifying exam and be accepted on that basis. One can only wonder if the Swiss foresaw that this enlightened policy would open the door of higher education to two of the world's greatest scientists and the ETH's best-known graduates, whose achievements became a byword in the adventure of modern science. Those two men were Wilhelm Conrad Röntgen and Albert Einstein, the latter to be discussed in the next chapter. Röntgen, who was graduated from the ETH in 1869, won the first Nobel Prize (in Physics) for his discovery of the x-ray. But he had had a problem in school.

Röntgen was born in the Rhineland to a German father and Dutch mother. When he was three the family moved to his mother's homeland, where young Röntgen completed most of his secondary education. One must say most because he was not allowed to graduate from his technical school in Utrecht when he refused to inform on a schoolmate who had lampooned a teacher. Without a recognized *Abitur,* or high school diploma, he could not enroll in a German university as he hoped. But there was the Poly in Zurich. Its growing reputation and waiver of a high school diploma drew him there, and he enrolled in 1865 after passing the entrance exam.

Röntgen studied mechanical engineering, and also came under the tutelage of ETH physics professor August Kundt, a German and a leading light in his field at the time. Kundt had studied mathematics and physics at Leipzig University in Germany and had pioneered in many fields—optics, acoustics and the behavior of gases. In 1868 he joined the faculty of the ETH, and during his short stay there attracted the loyal following of numbers of students, including Röntgen. Two years later Kundt accepted an offer from the University of Würzburg. Röntgen earned his Ph.D. degree from the ETH in 1869 based on a dissertation on the "Problems of Thermodynamics" and followed Kundt to Würzburg as his assistant.

Röntgen hoped to habilitate under Kundt, that is, to gain his own credentials for an academic career. But Teutonic rigidity is not easily overcome, and Würzburg, which was later to bask in his reflected glory, denied Röntgen's request to habilitate because the Ph.D. from the ETH had been granted without a prior *Abitur.*

Like so many pilgrims of modern science, Röntgen changed schools. He went to Strasbourg, recently seized from the French after Napoleon III's disastrous defeat at the hand of Bismarck in 1870. The University of Strasbourg was now under German management, but the faculty retained the privilege of deciding its own criteria for habilitation. There Röntgen obtained his academic credentials, and no doubt with a sense of triumph, returned to Würzburg where he assumed August Kundt's chair of physics in 1888. There he practiced the precise, careful experimental physics he had learned from his old mentor, and won the esteem of his colleagues and superiors. In 1894 he became the Rector of the University of Würzburg, in which post he served for a year before returning to his first love, research.

As a reward for his administrative service, the university gave Röntgen free rein to conduct his experiments. He was interested in the phenomenon of rays emitted by certain substances. Scientists of the era were beginning to suspect the existence of what later came to be called radioactivity, the effects of which at the time they could detect but not observe directly.

Röntgen had taken note of an experiment by Phillip Lenard (who later received the Nobel Prize for Physics in 1905). Lenard had made an enclosed glass discharge tube and replaced a bit of the glass wall with a thin aluminum window, allowing the invisible energy generated—the rays—to pass out of the tube into the laboratory. Röntgen used this cathode tube in his experiments in the phenomena of rays and in November 1895 made his momentous discovery. He observed that a detecting screen lying on a table far beyond the range of the cathode rays studied by Lenard was energized or made fluorescent by a type of ray that he dubbed "x-ray" because it defied classification into the known categories.

After making this critical observation—a kind of vision into the invisible—Röntgen holed up in his laboratory to explore the properties of his new form of rays. One was the ability to pass through matter of differing densities at differing rates of absorption, allowing him to photograph the bones in a human hand. The reserved German quickly realized useful applications of his discovery and engaged in a bit of unlikely showmanship to popularize it, circulating x-ray pictures of the human hand, among others, which he claimed was his wife's. The mystery of the x-ray, and especially its obvious usefulness in medicine, fascinated physicists, physicians and the general public. They were equally fascinated by Röntgen's refusal to patent his x-ray machine or to accept any royalties or emolument from its discovery except for the academic prizes, medals and memberships he received, including the first Nobel Prize, awarded in 1901.

In 1900 Röntgen accepted a more elevated position as Professor of Experimental Physics and Director of the physics institute at the prestigious University of Munich. He died in 1923, perhaps embittered over controversies and allegations surrounding the x-ray—for example, that he had pirated Lenard's work or that an assistant and not he had first noticed the effects of the x-ray in the laboratory in

1895. But his name is immortalized by the great benefit he unselfishly conferred on mankind, and by the term "roentgen," which is the basic measurement of x-ray or gamma radiation.

These heroes of science—who at one time or another passed through and were encouraged by the ETH—include some of the greatest innovators of the 19th century, perhaps of any century. Practical men—builders, inventors, engineers and physicists—their names are no longer widely known, but their accomplishments endure. Unlike the ruins of Greek temples, which stand as mute testimony to the intellectual glory of Greece, the bridges, roads, tunnels and machines of these pioneers continue to benefit their country and the wider world.

CHAPTER SIX

A Quantum Leap
1905–1955

The process of development into a full-fledged technical university culminated in the early 1900s when the Polytechnic was
given the right to award the title of doctor in engineering sciences,
natural sciences and mathematics, just as polytechnics in Germany
and Austria were already doing. To reflect the Poly's elevated
stature and at the same time raise the bar for technical education in
general, the Swiss decided by federal decree in June 1911 to rename
the institution. The Polytechnic School became the *Eidgenössische
Technische Hochschule*, the Swiss Federal Institute of Technology.
At the same time the title of Director was changed to Rector.

A discussion of a foreign country and its linguistic idioms presents occasional problems in translation. In German *hoch* means
"high" or "upper," and *Schule* is "school." Thus a literal translation would render this in English as "high school." However, as
mentioned earlier, a *Hochschule* is not the same as a "high school"
in the United States, that is, a secondary school. A *Hochschule* is
akin to a university in terms of the level of learning but different
from the traditional university in significant ways. To avoid confu-
sion in the use of these terms, this account uses *Hochschule* or its
rough contextual equivalent, "institute."

The most comprehensive reorganization since the ETH's creation in 1855 coincided with a third physical expansion. In 1911
the Federal Assembly authorized a loan of nearly 12 million Swiss
francs to finance the construction of much-needed new buildings

and the renovation and extension of the Hauptgebäude, the school's main building designed by the celebrated Gottfried Semper. The project resulted in a sad but necessary reminder that even our icons are subject to error. The work on the historic main building added two wings and the cupola, completed in 1919, that now dominates the city's skyline. However, it took ten years instead of the estimated three to complete the conversion and repairs because, as architect Gustav Gull reported with chagrin, "During the renovation of the Semper building, serious design flaws became apparent which jeopardized the whole building project. The cost of correcting these faults was enormous." The surprise was all the more unpleasant because of the high regard held for Semper as an architect. He had left Zürich to design other famous buildings in Europe. It turned out that during initial construction Semper had been forced to accommodate the demands of Zürich's state building inspector, whose main concern was to keep down costs. It is a common tale but true, as anyone knows who has ever been involved in public construction—bureaucratic power is often the trump card.

BURGEONING RESEARCH

In addition to training specialists and ensuring that the course of study met high academic standards, the institute also had a third task, mandated in the Statutes of April 1924—scientific research. Today federal support for scientific research is managed by the Swiss National Science Foundation (SNSF), generally referred to as the Swiss National Fund, which supports countrywide research in universities and industry and fosters the development of new science talent. Founded in 1952, the SNSF represents all segments of the scientific community, the cantons and the federal government, and it attempts to harmonize and rationalize the funding of research projects.

However, before the creation of the Swiss National Fund, engineering and scientific research eligible for state funding mostly centered on the work done by the ETH and affiliated institutes. This does not mean that the authorities and institutional directors were primarily responsible for the development of this role; quite the contrary. In many cases, it was industry and professional associations that put external pressure on the ETH to establish new chairs, research institutes or laboratories. Since there was a lack of funding for new research commitments, the ETH received considerable support from industrial concerns and private patrons. "It behooves the Institute to directly serve industry," observed President of the *Schulrat* Hans Pallmann in 1955, expressing the emphasis on practical benefits that had guided the ETH from its inception. In addition to "pure" research, the ETH was expected to engage in applied research that would enhance industrial and commercial productivity and thereby benefit the whole nation, but—and this is crucial—without compromising the quality or level of classroom instruction.

Training students in research also benefited from the fact that Swiss research policy was independent and not determined by the pattern of other countries, where scientific research was also making great strides. For comparison, in Germany there was the world-famous Kaiser Wilhelm Society for the Promotion of Science, established in Berlin in 1911. Its personnel were also dedicated to advancing research, particularly in certain natural sciences, but they had no teaching commitments and could devote their full attention to the laboratory. This financially robust body, which changed its name to the Max Planck Institute in 1948, deprived the ETH of two of its leading scientists, the chemist Richard Willstätter and Albert Einstein.

The United Kingdom created a special ministerial department for industrial and scientific research, France appointed an under-secretary of state for scientific research in 1937, and of course the United States was also beginning to invest in research as the 20th century progressed. In Switzerland, state and industry cooperation in research found its initial focal point at the ETH. Close collaboration between all institutions involved in research, first applied to the ETH, was only extended and consolidated relatively late nationwide. In the winter semester of 1954–1955, the ETH encompassed some 40 institutes, 10 laboratories, and seven collections open to the public, all involved in teaching and research. Then there were the associated agriculture and forestry research sites. The Management Science Institute, the Institute of Economic Research and the Department of Industrial Research at the Institute for Technical Physics, set up in the inter-war years to concentrate on tackling the crisis of unemployment, all had their own sources of funding. The ETH itself was fortunate enough to receive generous donations and support from its alumni.

The new emphasis on research also benefited from the ETH's expanding its international horizons after World War I. Previously, Swiss educational exchange programs had been focused primarily on neighbors France and Germany. But in the inter-war years the ETH and other Swiss universities began to take part in student exchanges with the U.S., beginning with an Institute of International Education program in 1926. Subsequent arrangements were made with institutions in other countries, but it was only after 1945 that student and research exchanges really gained momentum due to the postwar political situation, which provided a broad platform for international scientific exchanges.

A MATURING ACADEMIC STRUCTURE

The ETH statutes of April 1924 established the institute's 12 departments that remain the present-day structure, despite marginal changes in the years since. For the first time a distinction was made between ordinary and associate professors, giving greater value to the existing auxiliary teaching positions. (*Ordinarius* is translated "ordinary," but means full professor; the German word does not carry the sense of "lacking distinction" that it does in English.) From then on, the ordinary professors were responsible for electing the Rector. New chairs were established for textile production technology and aerodynamics. Professorships for structural aeronautical engineering and aircraft construction were established in 1937, giving rise to hopes that this incredibly promising sector could be developed further in Switzerland. In 1935, electrical engineering became a separate department, as ETH notable Rudolf Clausius had wanted from the beginning.

A new department in natural and earth sciences was added. The School of Natural Sciences comprised four branches: botany and zoology, physical chemistry, geographical geology and mineral geology. The Swiss valued their forests, and the ETH became one of the most highly respected forestry teaching and research institutes in the world.

During the two world wars, agriculture became a high priority out of sheer necessity. The Swiss had to make the most efficient use of the rich agricultural lands of the northern Plateau, especially since the country was surrounded by the Axis powers during World War II and needed to be as independent of food imports as possible. The ETH Agriculture School's scientific research was effective in increasing yields, contributing not only to the wartime economy but also to the Swiss people's determination—and ability—to maintain their neutrality and independence.

THE ROLE OF THE HUMANITIES

During the early years, international experts in higher education considered the creation of this sixth school as a dubious experiment. In fact, many educators in Europe at large regarded the School of Humanities as an anomaly that ran counter to the accepted contemporary view of the specific character of a polytechnic. Although in 19th-century Zürich it was not always possible to overcome the prevailing antagonism between the Cantonal University and the Polytechnic, the Poly followed the spirit of Stapfer's founding ideas, and thanks to the far-sightedness of its founders, led the way in bridging the gap between science and the humanities. Skeptics had viewed the Poly's move into the humanities as a suspect remnant of the failed federal university, which would have been the second of the two planned all-Swiss *Hochschulen.* Yet this move proved to be the first stage of a development that other polytechnic schools followed and would introduce later.

The ETH completely reworked the approach to "general studies," with the aim of creating an awareness of the overall intellectual environment for science, and to complement subject-specific studies, which by their very nature were based on specialization. Though determined to broaden its students' horizons and improve their general education, however, the ETH chose not to make subjects compulsory or impose examinations, as can be seen from the modest requirements in the 1924 ETH statutes requiring all students to attend at least one course per semester on general subjects from the philosophy and political science section. This forum of lectures had the additional benefit of attracting famous foreign professors who provided an introduction to literature in all three national Swiss languages (before the legalizing of Romansch as a fourth language). This brought to realization the early hopes for the *federal* institute in promoting mutual understanding of the country's different cultural and linguistic traditions.

The founders had provided for two law teaching posts, one for constitutional law and another for civil and commercial law. Its importance in professional life meant that most faculties made law a compulsory subject. Although in the past the ETH had provided a forum for individual lectures on philosophy, educational theory and psychology, it was only in 1881 that a chair was created for these subjects.

THE IMPACT OF CARL JUNG

The legendary Carl Gustav Jung lectured on psychology at the ETH from 1922 to 1941. He was appointed honorary professor in 1935 and was one of the institute's most popular lecturers. He presided over full, enthusiastic classes throughout his tenure in Zürich.

For a time Jung was the disciple, confidant and heir apparent of Sigmund Freud, founder of the therapeutic system that Freud termed psychoanalysis. Freud, a Viennese, and Jung, a Swiss, became the two greatest names in the history of psychology and the art and science of psychotherapy. Arguably they are two of the most influential thinkers of modern times. It speaks volumes for the ETH that a school founded to train Swiss practical scientists and engineers to unlock the secrets of the physical world should also boast Carl Jung, a peerless explorer of the mysteries of the human psyche.

Jung was born in 1875 in Kesswil on the shore of Lake Constance in the Canton of St. Gallen. His father was a Protestant pastor, and his highly literate family encouraged his intellectual pursuits. An odd legend existed in the family that Jung's grandfather was the illegitimate son of Johann Wolfgang von Goethe. This presumed connection with Goethe and the German poet's immortal *Faust* influenced Jung deeply toward a romantic yearning for knowledge—knowledge or *gnosis* in the deepest sense. In 1900 he earned a medical degree at the University of Basel and began his professional career at the Burghöltzli, Zürich's psychiatric clinic and insane asylum, where he worked until 1909.

By this time Sigmund Freud had published his first major work, *The Interpretation of Dreams,* and to a mixture of wide acclaim and skepticism had established a practice in psychoanalysis in Vienna. It was inevitable that Jung would learn of him and that the two men would meet, which they did in 1907. Jung's work at the Burghöltzli on schizophrenia and on emotional disorders that came to be called "complexes" led to the publication of *The Psychology of Dementia Praecox.* This work in turn came to Freud's attention. Kindred spirits for a while at least, the two men talked for 13 hours straight at their first meeting. Jung fell into the orbit of the older and more famous man, traveled with Freud to the United States in 1909 to participate in his lectures, and for three years regarded Freud as both friend and mentor.

Jung's break with Freud, a seismic event in the history of psychology, came in 1913. Reluctantly, Jung began to have sharp doubts about what he believed was Freud's undue emphasis on sexuality as the dominant factor in the unconscious. Jung believed it was simplistic to ascribe all, or virtually all, psychological problems to repressed sexuality. While the power of sex was undeniably a factor in the unconscious, Jung believed the psychotherapist had to explore other and deeper issues.

In his view we are all wounded in our psyche, some more grievously than others, if by nothing more than the alienation that afflicts a person when he leaves childhood behind and suddenly must confront a difficult world no longer centered on him and his needs. Jung's studies and observations persuaded him of the validity of his own theories, which he systematized under the name of analytical psychology—today often called "depth psychology."

He concluded that neurosis was the suffering of a soul that had not reconciled itself to its external reality, that had not discovered its meaning. It was necessary to follow an inner quest into one's own psyche to confront one's demons and to become whole. The symbols presented by dream and myth were both clues to the nature of one's disorder and guideposts to a successful inner quest. These symbols were common to all mankind and visible in the dreams, myths and lore of all cultures. Jung called them "archetypes."

Jung also rejected Freud's theory that human psychological development is essentially complete after the first six years of life. He held that personal development is a lifelong process and emphasized that conflicts established in infancy are often not resolved until adulthood. As Dante wrote in *The Inferno*, midway in life's journey men and women may suddenly find themselves, as it were, in a darkened wood, having lost their way. This is the moment of real crisis, in midlife, when some begin to search for inner truth and seek to achieve a state of positive self-assertion and identity integration, a state Jung called individuation. Confrontation with and integration of one's own "shadow," or fragmented and false self, is necessary for the individuation process to succeed.

Jung concluded further, based on the ubiquity of common archetypal symbols in all cultures, that they existed in a kind of "collective unconscious" of mankind. In *Symbols of Transformation* (1912), he posited that the correct interpretation of the symbols manifested in the patient was the key to recovery. This work precipitated the final and irrevocable break with Freud, for in seeking knowledge about archetypes, Jung delved deeply into mythology, Eastern religions, mysticism, alchemy and even extra-terrestrial visitation, most of which Freud regarded as mere superstition.

Although many psychiatrists today still follow some form of Freudian analysis, Freud's ideas began to lose adherents by the late 20th century, while Jung has enjoyed a recent ascendancy over his former mentor. Jungian-based practice is now as common as

Freudian. For better or worse, many of Jung's concepts—or at least a post-modern interpretation of them—have influenced some of contemporary literature's most important works, as well as the New Age movement, a resurgence in mysticism, occultism and even belief in UFOs.

This short treatment cannot do justice to the fullness and complexity of the ideas of either man. Whether psychoanalysis as practiced by either Freud or Jung should be considered reliable today is an open question; but it can be said that both men will be respected as philosophers long after their validity in science or medicine is considered obsolete. Jung outlived Freud by 22 years, passing away in 1961 in Küsnacht in the Canton of Zürich. His last words reportedly were "Let's have a really good red wine tonight."

ACADEMIC HONORS

While Jung was famous in his day and brought international repute to the ETH in the field of psychology, there was then no formal recognition in his field in the form of international awards. In more established fields prestigious honors were bestowed in the form of the Nobel Prize, established by Swedish chemical engineer Alfred Nobel. For the ETH, the first half of the 20th century was a time of extraordinary academic honors won by people who had been students, lecturers or professors at the institute. Counting those who shared the award with others, 21 men associated with the ETH in physics and chemistry have won the Nobel Prize, including two chemists who won the award for medicine. The stand-outs include the first Nobelist, Röntgen—for discovery of the x-ray—and perhaps the best known, Einstein—the "Man of the Century," who revolutionized the way we think about the physical world.

This is an extraordinary achievement for a single school in a small country, and contrasts favorably with institutions in neighboring Germany, France or Italy. Twenty-one Nobel Prizes during a 104-year span average to roughly one every five years. Of the 100 Nobel Prizes awarded in chemistry since the inception of the Prize, counting both shared and individual awards, the men of the ETH—

a single institution—have won an astounding 12 percent. In physics, the proportion is less because the tendency in recent years has been to give multiple awards each year. In most years since the 1940s there have been three winners annually in each category, and the total number of awards in physics since 1901 is 175. Men of the ETH have won nine, or five percent of the total—still an impressive share. And while there are some extraordinary names on the list— Max Planck, Marie and Pierre Curie, Walter Heisenberg, Niels Bohr, Enrico Fermi—few if any became household names like ETH graduates Conrad Röntgen and Albert Einstein.

THE CHEMISTRY NOBEL PRIZES

The Chemistry Department was granted the right to award the doctorate in a federal decree of March 1909. The first doctorate was awarded to the chemist Jean Piccard, the twin brother of the hot-air balloonist, deep-sea explorer and ETH physicist Auguste Piccard. During the first 60 years of the department's existence five graduates were awarded the Nobel Prize for Chemistry, although not always during their time in Zürich.

Alfred Werner, born in 1866 in Alsace, showed an aptitude for chemistry and later enrolled at the ETH, where he received a Diploma in Technical Chemistry in 1889. He lectured at the University of Zürich, became a Swiss citizen in 1895, and at the same time became a full professor at the University, turning down prestigious offers from Vienna and Würzburg in preference for his adopted city. He conducted groundbreaking work on valences in atoms, the attractive force that permits chemical bonding. He questioned the belief that this affinity is exerted from the center of the atom and acts uniformly on all parts of the surface of the atom. The Nobel Prize in 1913 was given for his "coordination theory," codifying his observations of modified valences and successfully depicting predictable variable valences in the molecular composition of certain compounds.

Richard Willstätter, a Professor of General Chemistry at the ETH from 1905 to 1912, was distinguished for his research into plant pigments, especially chlorophyll, and won the Nobel in 1915. Willstätter, who was born in Karlsruhe, moved back to Germany but ceased conducting scientific research in response to that country's growing anti-semitism. In 1938 he fled to Switzerland, one step ahead of the Gestapo, and lived out his remaining days in a village near Locarno.

German affairs played an even more poignant role in the career of Prussian-born Fritz Haber, who taught at the ETH under Professor of Chemistry Georg Lunge in the early 1890s. A German patriot, Haber offered his services to Kaiser Wilhelm II during the Great War and in 1918 was awarded the Nobel Prize for his synthesis of ammonia from its constituent elements. More significantly, his breakthroughs, including a method to isolate nitric acid, allowed the Germans to negate the Allied blockade by synthesizing explosives and poison gas without raw materials. Haber, considered by many to be "the father of chemical warfare," was a tragic figure whose wife, also a chemist, committed suicide, distraught by the consequences of science in modern warfare.

Maintaining his fierce loyalty to his country, Haber spent years after the Treaty of Versailles attempting to extract gold from seawater in order to help Germany cope with its war reparations. Then Hitler took over in 1933, and Haber found that his being Jewish counted more to the new government than his past service. He was forced to leave his beloved country, going first to England. Unhappy there, supposedly because of the weather, the last journey of his life was made in 1934 to Switzerland, but he died upon reaching Basel, broken in both body and spirit.

Dutch-born Peter J.W. Debye, a scientific "man for all seasons," was a professor at the ETH from 1920 to 1927 and was awarded the 1936 Nobel in Chemistry for his research on molecular structures, notably his experiments on x-rays and electron interference in gases. In 1940 he joined Cornell University in the U.S., going on to become head of its Chemistry Department. Debye was followed by Vienna-born Richard Kuhn, a former classmate of Wolfgang Pauli, who became Professor for General and Analytical Chemistry at the ETH in the late 1920s. Kuhn was awarded the 1938 Nobel Prize for his research on vitamins, especially the biochemically vital vitamin B2, known as riboflavin.

The institute's roster of famous chemists continued with Leopold Ruzicka, a Croatian by birth and the last to hold the ETH chair as Professor of General Chemistry (also of inorganic and organic chemistry). Ruzicka had trouble with the entry requirements at the ETH, learning to his dismay that the exam included not only chemistry but also descriptive geometry, for which he had little aptitude. He enrolled instead at the Karlsruhe Polytechnic in Germany, where he studied under ETH graduate Hermann Staudinger, who would later win his own Nobel. In 1912 he ended up at the ETH as Professor of Chemistry and became a Swiss citizen in 1917. He pioneered research in toxic organic compounds he named pyrethrins, and later he synthesized androsterone and testosterone, for which he won the Nobel in 1939.

ETH chemist Thadeus Reichstein was part of the team that discovered cortisone, and he shared the 1950 Nobel Prize in Medicine with two Americans. He taught at the ETH for a short time as an associate professor and went on to chart new territory as the head of the Pharmaceutical Institute in Basel, which is now considered the international headquarters of this industry so important to Switzerland and the world. Reichstein was also the first scientist to artificially synthesize vitamin C, or ascorbic acid, making this health-giving substance widely available for the benefit of the world. Studies have shown that this most useful of all the vitamins (not truly a vitamin but a metabolic compound derived from certain sugar molecules) is required in over 400 chemical reactions in the body for them to occur efficiently.

Hermann Staudinger, who lectured at the ETH from 1912 to 1926, received the 1953 Chemistry award for his fundamental work in the field of macromolecular chemistry. His discoveries laid the foundations for the expansion of the plastics industry.

THE PHYSICS NOBEL PRIZES

The extraordinary flowering of Nobel laureates connected with the ETH during this period also occurred in physics, especially theoretical and sub-atomic physics. Mathematics and physics provided the stage for the remaining Nobel laureates, thanks in part to outstanding teachers like Paul Scherrer, who both achieved acclaim in his field and taught several Nobel winners.

Wilhelm Conrad Röntgen was the first ETH Nobelist for his discovery of the x-ray, as discussed earlier. After him came Charles-Edouard Guillaume, who won the Physics Prize in 1920. Discovering anomalies in nickel-steel alloys, Guillaume was able to develop a means of precise molecular measurement. Then came the 1921 Physics award to Albert Einstein, based on his earlier work on the photoelectric effect. First a student at the ETH, Einstein became a temporary instructor in the teacher training school, then lectured in theoretical physics at the ETH for a short time, between 1912 and 1914. He will be discussed further below.

Otto Stern won the 1943 Nobel for Physics based on his findings in directional properties of particles in magnetic fields. Stern was on the ETH faculty and later immigrated to the United States, where he lived when the Prize was awarded for work done earlier in Europe. Wolfgang Pauli, who also merits further discussion, developed the famous exclusion principle that became a cornerstone of quantum mechanics and earned him the Nobel Prize for Physics in 1945. Felix Bloch was the 1952 Nobel winner in Physics for pioneering what later became phased-array radar, the foundation of today's air traffic control system and modern military air-defense radar.

THE ETH AND MODERN PHYSICS

The year 2005 was not only the 150th anniversary of the ETH but also happened to be the 100th anniversary of the *annus mirabilis*— the remarkable year—when a young ETH graduate, a minor civil servant working in the Swiss patent office in Bern, published four papers that represented a quantum leap forward in man's understanding of the fundamental nature of reality. That young man was Albert Einstein. Of course, in the early 1900s no one used the term "quantum leap." Though now common in the language, it did not exist prior to 1905 because until then no one knew what "quantum" meant. Since we use this term so freely today, we ought to know what it meant when it was coined. Today the layman typically uses it to describe a large or significant movement. Technically it comes from the "quantum jump" of a particle—an electron, for example—that moves abruptly from one discrete energy state to another, as described in quantum mechanics.

Einstein is the principal author of the revolutionary changes in man's perception of the physical universe in the early 20th century, most notably through his "special relativity theory," which he later expanded and refined to include a "general relativity theory." Relativity theory has radically altered our notions of space and time, and in particular of *movement* in space and time. Einstein also contributed significantly to quantum theory, which deals with the atomic and sub-atomic structure of the universe and depicts a physical realm governed not by strict, predictable laws, as Newton proposed, but characterized seemingly by pure chance, at least in part. Modern physics thus stands in contrast to the "determinism" of classic or Newtonian physics, although Newton's laws are still applicable to explain everyday phenomena and enable us to do practical things, like driving a car or constructing a building.

In light of today's controversies about certain other theories (beyond the scope of this book to evaluate), it must be pointed out that a "theory" in the scientific sense is not an untested hypothesis or opinion. A scientific theory has been subjected to rigorous verification and falsification techniques and is thus a reasonably established explanation to account for a set of known facts or observed phenomena.

Like Röntgen, Einstein did not earn an *Abitur* during his first attempt in secondary school. A notoriously poor student, he had a creative, restless mind and found it excruciatingly boring to sit under a drillmaster—that is, a schoolmaster—in a rigidly structured schoolroom for 50 minutes digesting a prescribed piece of the syllabus. He departed his home in Munich, Germany without his *Gymnasium* diploma.

He took advantage of the ETH's entrance examination process, although in 1894 he failed it the first time and had to prep for two years in languages and other subjects at a secondary school in Aarau. This time he did earn a *Matura*, passed the exam and enrolled at the Poly, which he did first with a view to becoming a school teacher. He received his basic science education and was graduated from the ETH in 1900. Becoming a Swiss citizen in 1901, he moved to the federal capital of Bern and became a clerk in the Swiss patent office, where his work examining patents for electro-magnetic devices may have helped form his ideas in physics, which he continued to develop in the company of close friends.

EINSTEIN AND THE INFLUENCE OF MICHELE BESSO

Einstein's ideas on physics began a revolution in how we look at reality. One cannot give all the credit to Einstein, however. Others were thinking similar thoughts at the same time, and once Einstein opened the door, they quickly followed. Those other pioneers are well known: Max Planck, Niels Bohr and Walter Heisenberg, to name a few. But Einstein was influenced and aided by another ETH man, now virtually unknown.

An account of the ETH would not be complete without a few words about Einstein's great friend Michele Besso, an ETH gradu-ate and engineer of Italian extraction. He was a lifelong friend and a near intellectual peer with whom Albert Einstein carried on a 52-year correspondence on theoretical physics as well as personal mat-ters. At the end of his 1905 paper on special relativity, Einstein gave only one acknowledgment: "In conclusion I wish to say that in working at the problem here dealt with I have had the loyal assis-tance of my friend and colleague M. Besso, and that I am indebted to him for several valuable suggestions."

Born in Riesbach, Switzerland, in 1873, Besso was six years older than Einstein. His family was Jewish and had migrated to a country with well-established conditions of religious freedom. Besso was an excellent student, especially in mathematics, and attended the ETH five years before Einstein enrolled. Their com-mon Jewish heritage, the ETH connection, and a love of music brought them together. Einstein often played violin at the home of a friend where he and Besso met, and they soon became close. Einstein introduced Besso to his future wife and later secured a patent job for his colleague in Bern where he was employed. For five years the families were close friends in Bern. The two men walked to work together daily, discussing physics and other topics. When Einstein moved back to Zürich to lecture at the ETH, their discussions ended, but the famous correspondence commenced. Besso later left the patent office, but returned there until his retirement in 1938. At one point in 1926 he was in danger of losing his job until the now-famous Nobelist Einstein intervened on his behalf. Besso's letter to Einstein a few years later gives Besso's view of their long friendship:

> For a long time, I have been thinking of how many . . . ties . . . bind the two of us together. I owe to you my wife and, along with her, my son and grandson; I owe to you my job, and with that the tranquility of a sanctuary protecting me from people, as well as the financial security for hard times. I owe to you the scientific synthesis that without such a friendship one would never have acquired—at least, not without expending all one's personal forces—and you know even better than I do what an immense sense of extra-personal order comes with such knowledge. On my side, I was your public in 1904 and 1905; in helping you to edit your communications on the quanta I deprived you of a part of your glory.

Besso died near Geneva in 1955, only a few months before Einstein. Upon his death Einstein wrote to Besso's sister and son, expressing his feelings about their friendship in a manner that also bespeaks Einstein's generosity and humanity:

> The gift of leading a harmonious life is rarely joined to such a keen intelligence, especially to the degree one found in him. . . . Our friendship was born when I was a student in Zürich, where we met regularly at musical evenings. He, the

older and wiser, was there to stimulate us. The circle of his interests appeared truly without boundaries. Nevertheless, it was his critical philosophical preoccupations that seemed most characteristic of him. Later it was the patent office that brought us together. Our conversations as we returned from the office had an incomparable charm—it was as if human contingencies did not exist at all. . . . [I]n quitting this strange world he has once again preceded me by a little. That doesn't mean anything. For those of us who believe in physics, this separation between past, present, and future is only an illusion, however tenacious.

EINSTEIN'S REVOLUTION

In 1902, while working in Bern, Einstein and two friends started the "Olympia Academy," which held regular evening meetings over the next three years for discussion of philosophy and physics. (This was before Besso's arrival; he was not part of the original three.) In 1905 the group broke up, but the three friends continued to correspond. In a letter to one of them, Conrad Habicht, in the spring of 1905, Einstein described his research for the year, a program that laid the foundations of 20th-century physics. Einstein wrote:

I promise you four papers. . . . The first . . . deals with radiation and energy characteristics of light and is very revolutionary. The second work is a determination of the true size of the atom from the diffusion and viscosity of dilute solutions of neutral substances. The third proves that assuming the molecular theory of heat, bodies whose dimensions are of the order of 1/1000 mm and are suspended in fluids, should experience measurable disordered motion, which is produced by thermal motion. It is the motion of small inert particles that has been observed by physiologists, and called by them "Brown's molecular motion" [now termed Brownian Motion]. The fourth paper exists in first draft and is an electrodynamics of moving bodies employing a

modification of the doctrine of space and time; the purely
kinematical part of this work will certainly interest you.

What is striking about this list—apart from the fact that it was
compiled by a totally unknown 26-year-old physicist—is that the
first paper announced the inception of the light quantum, Einstein's
resolution of questions first broached by Max Planck in 1900. The
fourth and last paper announced his invention of the theory of relativity. These theories are the most revolutionary development in
the history of physics, and arguably in the history of science.

Einstein wrote later about his insights in that remarkable year:
"A storm broke loose in my mind." He saw with almost poetic
vision that matter and energy are relative and interchangeable. The
mass of an object increases with its velocity, which he expressed in
the famous equation $e=mc^2$ (energy equals mass multiplied by the
square of the speed of light). This has profound practical implications, because it proves that a tiny amount of matter can produce
stupendous amounts of energy. This principle underlies nuclear
energy, among other applications.

The authors and refiners of quantum theory, who along with
Einstein include such notables as Niels Bohr, Werner Heisenberg
and Wolfgang Pauli, remarked on the seeming "absurdity" or non-
commonsensical aspects of the sub-atomic world it depicted. In
application, the equations of quantum mechanics have a practical
value, explaining the behavior of sub-atomic particles in nuclear
reactors, of electrons in computers and television tubes, the movement of laser light in fiber-optic cables, "solid-state" technology,
superconductivity, and much else of real usefulness. Yet, from the
perspective of logical positivism, quantum mechanics seems to
make no sense.

Among the "absurdities" are the following propositions:

• There are no such things as "things." Objects are ghostly,
   with no definite properties (such as position or mass) until
   they are measured. The properties exist in a twilight state
   of "super position" until then.

- All particles are waves, and waves are particles, appearing as one sort or another depending on what sort of measurement is being performed.
- A particle moving between two points travels all possible paths between them simultaneously.

In later years Walter Heisenberg recalled that "an intensive study of all questions concerning the interpretation of quantum theory in Copenhagen finally led to a complete and, as many physicists believe, satisfactory clarification of the situation." He was referring in part to his famous "uncertainty principle," which attempted to reconcile the presumed absurdities and imponderables. In 1927 he posited that we cannot simultaneously measure both the position and velocity (or momentum, strictly speaking) of a sub-atomic particle with precision. If we measure one of those quantities more precisely, the value of the other one necessarily becomes less certain. It was not a solution all could easily accept. Many physicists, confronted with the implications of the quantum theory, agonized in near despair that nature could be as absurd as it seemed in these atomic experiments.

Einstein was not an atheist and rejected the purely philosophical implications of quantum theory, the uncertainty principle, and the Copenhagen interpretation of quantum mechanics that completely ruled out any determined predictability or Newtonian "clockwork" in the universe. His famous dictum that "God does not play dice with the universe" shows that Einstein believed there was still a hidden order or undiscovered set of variables behind the seeming unpredictability of quantum mechanics. Toward the end of his life he wrote:

> We are in the position of a little child entering a huge library filled with books in many different languages. The child knows someone must have written those books. It does not know how. It does not understand the languages in which they are written. The child dimly suspects a mysterious order in the arrangement of the books but does not know what it is.

THE METAMORPHOSIS OF WOLGANG PAULI

Perhaps the reader had not expected to encounter a mystery in the story of a technical university, but it is a matter of great curiosity that people at the ETH are clearly reluctant to talk about the relations between the school and one of their most illustrious professors, a man whom many called "the conscience of Physics." This man was Wolfgang Pauli.

Pauli and Walter Heisenberg expanded on the implications of Einstein's light quantum and refined the theory of quantum mechanics. Pauli became a full Professor of Physics at the ETH, where he remained until 1940, when he took a leave of absence in the United States. There he taught at Princeton University though he retained his position at the ETH. In 1925 he proposed his "exclusion principle," one of the foundation stones of quantum theory, positing a limit to the number of electrons present in each quantum state of atoms and molecules. In 1933 he proposed a solution to the puzzle of seemingly excess energy in the beta decay of a neutron, and postulated the existence of what was later called the neutrino. The neutrino is an elementary particle associated with what came to be known as the "weak force," one of the four fundamental forces or energy fields in nature, in which "sub-particles" are exchanged as the mechanism of the force (the other three are gravity, the "color force" and electromagnetism). As noted earlier, he won the 1945 Nobel Prize in Physics for his exclusion principle.

In the beginning Pauli was close to Heisenberg and Niels Bohr and was one of the "Copenhagen trio." But in later years Pauli began to encounter doubts similar to those that had troubled Einstein, specifically about the Copenhagen view that there must be a division between the interior world and the outer physical world. Pauli began to feel it was wrong to separate the human from the physical sphere. That led him to also conclude it was wrong to separate science from religion, or psychology from physics. At the end of his life (he died in 1958 at the age of 58) he had become increasingly religious. This was the culmination of a journey he had begun with another illustrious ETH man discussed earlier, Carl Jung.

In 1937 Pauli was a world-famous physicist and had already done the work that would earn his Nobel in 1945. But he was also a deeply troubled man. His mother had taken her own life after discovering his father's infidelity. Pauli went through a brief marriage to a cabaret singer, drank heavily and quarreled frequently, sometimes in public. The world-famous Dr. Carl Jung was at the ETH. Who better to go to for counsel? The two men established a regular routine, and while Pauli did not undergo formal psychoanalysis, he did share over 400 dreams that disturbed his sleep and his waking life, dreams Jung interpreted and later used in his seminal works, *Psychology and Alchemy* and *The Analysis of Dreams.*

Thus bloomed an extraordinary friendship, an intellectual conjunction between psychologist and physicist, between two men who were among the world's leading practitioners of their respective disciplines, with enormous influence on each other. Exchanging insights into their respective fields, they found surprising common ground between Jung's "depth psychology" and quantum physics. The relationship influenced Jungian psychology, and many of Jung's ideas shaped how Pauli saw the underlying reality of the physical world. They discovered the correlatives between analytical psychology and particle physics, and each transformed the other's view of the universe.

Pauli was "a man with two souls, like Goethe," according to Jung. He and Pauli balanced each other, and both shared a theory of "wholeness" in mind and matter. Both glimpsed that mind and matter were joint manifestations of a deeper archetypal reality. This was what the ancients called the *unus mundus,* the First Cause or unifying principle that scientists (and proto-scientists or alchemists before them) had sought that would encompass and explain the random events and "meaningful coincidences," or "synchronicity" in Jung's term, that punctuate human existence.

Prominent among Jung's archetypal symbols was the Mandala (Sanskrit for circle; also connection or community). A circle incorporating a square, it also assumed personal significance to Pauli. To him, as to Jung, it represented a metaphysical reality. Pauli's corresponding symbol was his "great vision," *die Weltuhr,* where psyche and matter meet in a metaphysical domain. In the realm of quantum physics, there existed the element of the unexpected, the seemingly irrational. Matter at its deepest roots could only be described as a metaphysical reality—the ineffable. From Niels Bohr, Pauli had grasped that paradoxes are the *sine qua non* for understanding underlying reality. Both Jung and Pauli concluded that phenomena exist which cannot be explained rationally and that the world cannot be apprehended fully by pure reason alone. This was held to be true in physics and true in psychology, and was the foundation of Pauli's approach to what he called the "moral problem" in physics. By this he meant that positing a basis for modern man on "pure rationalism" left man incomplete and fragmented. He believed psyche and matter are linked by a "metaphysical bridge suspended over an abyss." Pauli wanted a holistic view of nature like the early alchemists, and this led him to explore the "psychophysical problem" with Jung—areas and issues neglected, or intentionally avoided, by modern science. They tried ambitiously from their different vantage points to forge a unified framework that covered the seemingly infinite complexities of quantum physics and human psychology.

Something happened to sour relations between the ETH and Pauli around the end of the 1930s. Today people at the ETH will concede this, but there are no clear explanations. Why did Pauli leave Zürich, where he held a prestigious professorship, was surrounded by adoring students and enjoyed—presumably—a congenial life in Switzerland? Did he go to America for fear of a Nazi invasion of Switzerland and subsequent persecution as a Jew? This is certainly a possibility. The Nazis did not attack Switzerland in World War II, although they drew up plans to do so and were extremely threatening. The Swiss themselves expected to be invaded, particularly in May 1940 and March 1943, and prepared to resist accordingly.

Perhaps the answer to the mystery lies in Pauli's close relationship with Carl Jung. It is certain his links with Jung brought about a metamorphosis from "pure" scientist—a position of total rationalism—to something approaching that of mystic. One cannot help but suspect that this transformation worried, then antagonized, the institute, with its emphasis upon rigorous science standards in its teaching and research. Perhaps the disenchantment was mutual. Whatever may have happened between Pauli and the ETH, he does not go unhonored today. There is a street named for him on campus, and the ETH has named the physics portion of the prestigious annual lectures that rotate between math, chemistry and physics "The Pauli Lectures."

Philipp Albert Stapfer envisioned a Swiss national university as early as 1798.

Famous architect Gottfried Semper designed the ETH's main building.

This 1880 postcard depicts the ETH overlooking the city of Zürich and the Limmat River.

Gustav Gull designed the dome atop the ETH's main building. It is shown here under construction around 1918.

The city of Zürich as seen from the ETH Terrace. In the center background stands the Grossmünster Church, said to have been originally founded by Charlemagne.

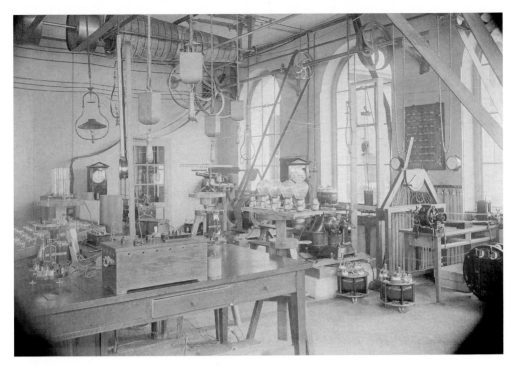

A laboratory in the ETH's Institute of Physics around 1882.

A lecture hall in the ETH's Institute of Chemistry, 1896.

Wilhelm Röntgen, winner of the
Nobel Prize for Physics, 1901.

Fritz Haber, winner of the Nobel Prize
for Chemistry, 1918.

Alfred Werner, winner of the Nobel
Prize for Chemistry, 1913.

Charles-Edouard Guillaume, winner of
the Nobel Prize for Physics, 1920.

Richard Willstätter, winner of the
Nobel Prize for Chemistry, 1915.

Peter J.W. Debye, winner of the Nobel
Prize for Chemistry, 1936.

Albert Einstein, winner of the Nobel Prize for Physics, 1921. He is shown here as a 19-year-old in 1898, his first year at the ETH.

Wolfgang Pauli, winner of the Nobel Prize for Physics, 1945.

ETH Professor Paul Scherrer taught a generation of physicists. His name lives on at the Paul Scherrer Institute.

Richard Kuhn, winner of the Nobel
Prize for Chemistry, 1938.

Tadeus Reichstein, winner of the
Nobel Prize for Medicine, 1950.

Leopold Ruzicka, winner of the Nobel
Prize for Chemistry, 1939.

Hermann Staudinger, winner of the
Nobel Prize for Chemistry, 1953.

Otto Stern, winner of the Nobel Prize
for Physics, 1942.

Vladimir Prelog, winner of the Nobel
Prize for Chemistry, 1975.

An early picture of the entrance to the
St. Gotthard Tunnel.

ETH Professor Albert Heim was one of
Switzerland's most renowned geologists.

Professor Albert Heim (seated, third from left), leading a geological excursion to a
glacier in July 1904.

Othmar Ammann moved to the U.S. after graduating from the ETH. He became America's most successful builder of bridges.

At right is New York's George Washington Bridge, designed by and with construction supervised by Ammann. At the time of its construction in 1927, it was nearly twice the length of any other suspension bridge.

Robert Maillart took on the challenge of Switzerland's difficult Alpine terrain while creating bridges of great beauty.

Maillart's Salginatobelbrücke, 1930, is a dramatic example of how Swiss designers and structural engineers achieved the seemingly impossible.

Christian Menn used revolutionary techniques to build bridges in both Switzerland and the United States. Shown here is the Ganterbrücke in 1983.

Werner Arber, winner of the Nobel
Prize for Medicine, 1978.

Karl Alexander Müller, winner of the
Nobel Prize for Physics, 1987.

Heinrich Rohrer, winner of the Nobel
Prize for Physics, 1986.

Richard Ernst, winner of the Nobel
Prize for Chemistry, 1991.

George Bednorz, winner of the Nobel
Prize for Physics, 1987.

Kurt Wüthrich, winner of the Nobel
Prize for Chemistry, 2002.

Felix Bloch, winner of the Nobel Prize for Physics in 1952, became the first Director-General of CERN, Europe's largest nuclear research facility, in 1955.

An aerial view of the CERN research facility outside Geneva.

Inside CERN's 27-kilometer-long tunnel that houses a Large Hadron Collider, designed to lead to new discoveries in the field of particle physics.

The Philadelphia Savings Fund Society building was designed in 1932 by ETH graduate William Edmond Lescaze.

Among the many designs of Aldo Rossi, who taught architecture at the ETH in the early 1970s, is the Teatro del Mondo in Venice, Italy, 1979.

The central hall of the ETH's main building in Zürich.

A panoramic view of Zürich as seen from the ETH Terrace.

The central plaza at the Hönggerberg campus.

Though Switzerland has relatively little crime, these ETH students are engaging in an exercise class called "Body Combat."

An ETH rowing team on the Limmat River, which flows through Zürich below the ETH Terrace.

At the ETH, as at other universities, the suits and ties of yesteryear have been replaced by more casual student attire.

Hands-on laboratory skills remain an important part of an ETH science education.

An auditorium at the Hönggerberg campus.

An aerial view of the Hönggerberg campus.

The dome in the heart of the ETH Zentrum.

CHAPTER SEVEN

The Revolution in Structural Engineering

The Nobel Prize is not awarded for the engineering disciplines, even though engineers and builders have enriched our everyday lives as much as chemists and physicists. If there were a Nobel for engineering, no doubt ETH graduates would be as prominent among the winners as they have been in chemistry and physics, for the Swiss in general and ETH graduates in particular spearheaded a revolution in structural design and construction, especially in bridges and the basic transportation infrastructure that undergirds modern civilization.

OTHMAR AMMANN, AMERICA'S GREATEST BRIDGE BUILDER

Americans are often surprised to learn about the ETH, its academic record and its international reputation. This is not entirely due to America's regrettable but indisputable insularity. It is also in part because the Swiss prefer to let their accomplishments speak for themselves. No one captures this Swiss characteristic better than ETH graduate Othmar H. Ammann. Of the great Swiss structural engineers of modern times, he leads the list. He should be of particular interest to Americans—even celebrated by them—for there was no greater bridge builder in our country than Ammann, who, after being graduated from the ETH, immigrated to the United States in 1904.

Darl Rastorfer, a leading authority on Ammann, wrote in *Six Bridges, the Legacy of Othmar H. Ammann*:

During a long life of uninterrupted practice, Othmar H. Ammann designed and built a series of long-span bridges that altered the course of engineering history and transformed the face of New York. He also wrote some of the finest technical papers ever written in his field and founded two public departments of civil engineering and two private consulting firms. This highly accomplished man was surprisingly self-effacing. When thrown in the spotlight of fame, his response was to maintain the quiet, ordered lifestyle he had adopted during the lean years of his early career: never stay late at the office; be home in time for dinner; relax and then work some more in the evenings and on weekends; garden, hike and listen to symphonic music for recreation. His focus rarely strayed from family, home, and the design of the world's longest bridges.

Ammann was born in 1879 in the village of Feuerthalen in the Canton of Zürich, on the south bank of the Rhine directly across from Schaffhausen. He entered the ETH in 1898, studied under legendary civil engineering professor Wilhelm Ritter, and was graduated in 1902.

Inspired by another ETH professor, Karl Emil Hilgard, Ammann arrived in New York in May 1904 with the intention of gaining practical experience in the design and construction of big steel bridges. Hilgard had worked in the U.S. for several years as a bridge designer for the Northern Pacific Railroad and persuaded his protégé that the bustling, rapidly expanding young country offered opportunities normally open only to "graybeards" in Europe. He intended to stay for only a few years. Ammann had a girlfriend back in Zürich, who later became his wife. And anyway, why would anyone want to permanently leave such a congenial place as Switzerland?

Within two weeks of his arrival in New York Ammann landed

a job with a leading consulting engineer, an independent firm providing advice and support to governments and construction companies on difficult projects. The quiet, unassuming young engineer was remarkably competent and well trained. A self-starter, he could solve any problem he was given with only a modicum of supervision, and he proved to be especially adept in the neglected area of construction technology.

Ammann went from one consulting job to another, rising through the ranks along with the increasing scope and difficulty of each new project. In the summer of 1905 he found the time to travel to Zürich and marry his sweetheart, Lilly Wehrli. Upon his return to the U.S. he faced his greatest challenge, along with Frederic Kunz of Philadelphia.

Kunz, one of a handful of experts on long-span steel bridges, had been hired by the Canadian government to investigate the collapse of the Quebec Bridge over the St. Lawrence River, one of the notorious bridge failures of the early 20th century. Ammann met Kunz around this time, assisted in the investigation, and gained his first exposure to, and fascination with, the challenges of long-span design. Through Kunz the Ammanns met the famous Austrian-American bridge builder Gustav Lindenthal, who offered the young Swiss a position on the biggest project of its type at the time, the Hell Gate Bridge in New York. It involved two and a half miles of spans, including viaducts, trestles, two short-span bridges and the Hell Gate Arch, its most conspicuous segment. When it opened in 1917, it was the longest-spanning arch in the world. The elegant arch, supported by graceful steel trusses, not only was a visual landmark but also was immensely efficient, carrying 75,000 pounds per linear foot, an unprecedented capacity for that time.

The tall, portly and gregarious Lindenthal had taken a liking to the short and reserved Ammann, and they got along famously until duty called Ammann away from the Hell Gate Project in midstride. Ammann had met with a group of Swiss expatriates in New York on August 1, 1914, to celebrate Swiss National Day, commemorating the founding of the Swiss Confederation in the Rütli Meadow in 1291. Before the day was over the Swiss learned the fateful news that war was about to embroil Europe. Kaiser Wilhelm had deployed troops right across the Rhine from Switzerland and threatened Basel. Ammann was still a Swiss citizen, an army reserve officer, and moreover had immediate family in Basel. He took the first passage he could arrange home to command a company stationed in the St. Gotthard Pass.

Though a strong sense of civic and familial duty had called Ammann away, Lindenthal was displeased with the abrupt departure of his capable assistant who had kept the Hell Gate Project running so smoothly. When it became clear the Great War would not engulf Switzerland, he was released from military duty and sailed back to New York a few months later. But the damage had been done to his relationship with Lindenthal. With Lindenthal, Ammann never regained a position of full trust or one with the challenges he sought in bridge design, now his first love. He had remained in the United States far longer than he ever intended, and now considered a return to Switzerland. However, in 1923 a new opportunity intervened—literally the opportunity of a lifetime, the challenge for which he had been preparing and training for the past 20 years.

Since the completion in 1883 of the Brooklyn Bridge, the most audacious engineering achievement of its day, the City of New York had contemplated a similar span uptown, crossing the Hudson River to link the island of Manhattan with New Jersey and relieve traffic congestion at the ferryboat landings. Lindenthal's design for the Hudson River crossing was a gargantuan suspension bridge with 28 traffic lanes and an initial estimated cost of $100 million. Moreover, its planned location at West 57th Street would displace hundreds of businesses and tens of thousands of residents. As opposition to the design hardened, Ammann became convinced, even as he worked to help sell the scheme for Lindenthal, that it was excessive in scale and cost. When he shared his reservations, hoping to save what now appeared a doomed project, Lindenthal rebuked him soundly. It was a harsh reminder that the rupture in the relationship from 1914 had never healed.

Ammann now faced a serious dilemma. Should he continue

with a man who no longer trusted him fully, in the pursuit of a design in which he no longer believed? Should he at long last return home with his family and find a career in Switzerland? Or, despite the anguish it would cause, should he break with his mentor, go out on his own, and even dare to compete with him? An idea of his own for a Hudson River bridge had been brewing in his imagination, a revolutionary idea in fact, yet one that was, in his words, "eminently doable."

Ammann made the tough decision, one that changed his life, the science of structural engineering, and the face of New York forever. In February 1924 he went public with his proposal for the Hudson River project. While highly respected, he had never sought the limelight and had always worked in the shadow of better-known men. Now, at the age of 44, he unexpectedly stood poised to revolutionize his profession.

The projected costs for Lindenthal's structure had grown to a staggering $500 million, while Ammann estimated his costs at $40 million. He planned to locate his bridge at the more sparsely populated northern end of Manhattan and adjacent Bergen County in New Jersey, avoiding the uprooting of people and businesses in midtown, not to mention Lindenthal's added costs of approaches and interchanges on high-value real estate. But it was his restrained design, positively elegant in comparison to his erstwhile mentor's overblown plan, that won the day. In 1925, the New York Port Authority chose Ammann's design, to the bitter chagrin of Lindenthal. Soon thereafter Ammann was hired to superintend the project, now called the George Washington Bridge. No doubt with a twinge of regret for his native Switzerland, to which he had long planned to return, Ammann became a U.S. citizen.

Construction of the bridge at 179th Street began in the fall of 1927, with more than 100,000 miles of steel cable strung across the river. Though not the behemoth Lindenthal had planned, the new Hudson River bridge was still monumental. With a 3,500-foot main span, nearly twice that of the next largest suspension bridge in existence, its slender deck was to arch gracefully more than 200 feet above the Hudson. At more than 600 feet, its two great towers would stand nearly 50 feet taller than the Washington Monument. Each of its four cables could support more than 90,000 tons, 10 times more than each cable of the Roebling-designed Brooklyn Bridge.

For his design, Ammann owed as much to material advances since 1883 as he did to his own ingenuity. Improved steel ensured that when drawn to only 0.196 inch in diameter, each of the 26,474 wires that made up one cable had a strength of at least 240,000 pounds per square inch, more than one and a half times that of the cable wires in the Brooklyn Bridge. Better "spinning" machinery allowed the wires to be hung from the towers 16 times faster than in 1883. Engineers had learned from the behavior of Ammann's ingenious model to compress the wires together into their final, three-foot-diameter cylindrical form.

The suspended road deck—which is why they are called suspension bridges—is the most critical and most vulnerable part of the structure. Many forces act on this long horizontally suspended plane, primarily traffic and wind. They can cause the deck to sway from side to side and oscillate up and down. If the forces acting on it are too strong, the deck can lose its structural integrity and collapse. This was no theoretical fear; many such bridges had failed catastrophically in Europe. And of course there was the notoriety of the Quebec Bridge collapse. Nineteenth-century engineers stabilized their bridges with heavy steel guy wires running from the suspension towers to the road deck, or from both tower and ground to the deck. Later engineers added deep steel trusses along the sides to stiffen the roadbed. Until the George Washington Bridge, modern suspension bridges were stiffened with such trusses and beams to limit motion in traffic and wind, made more critical when a bridge's length was great relative to its width and depth, as with the George Washington Bridge. But stiffening trusses gave bridges thicker, less attractive decks and added to the cost.

Ammann perfected a technique based on what was called the "deflection theory." He intuitively grasped, and then validated by calculation, that the sheer weight of his span, increasing with each linear foot, along with its necessarily heavy support cables, would by themselves provide sufficient stiffness. This approach produced a design more revolutionary for its length because it no longer needed the heavy trusses common to suspension bridges. The George Washington's resulting slender profile, both from the side as well as from above, excited Ammann's aesthetic sensibilities, as it did many astonished engineers of the time, not to mention the public.

However, much later, in 1940, the extremes of Ammann's innovation were dramatically demonstrated in the wind-driven collapse of the aptly nicknamed "Galloping Gertie," otherwise known as the Tacoma Narrows Bridge. After his investigation of that famous failure, which had been captured on film for the nation to see, Ammann said wryly, "Its smaller weight and extreme narrowness has drastically revealed that this practice has gone too far."

A suspension bridge is truly a work of sculpture because it is based on the natural curve of a cord strung between two points. Ammann declared, "It is a crime to build an ugly bridge." He was not only a master engineer but also an artist who tried to capture the pleasing curves found in nature, in contrast to the massive stone blocks of earlier bridges. Today, when low cost seems to be the primary consideration in public works, Ammann's wisdom resonates: "In fact, an engineer designing a bridge is justified in making a more expensive design for beauty's sake. After all, many people will have to look at the bridge for the rest of their lives. Few of us appreciate eyesores, even if we should save a little money by building them."

In the depths of the Great Depression, Ammann completed the bridge six months ahead of schedule, "fulfilling a dream of three quarters of a century," gushed *The New York Times*. On October 24, 1931, in front of thousands of spectators, New York Governor (and soon to be U.S. President) Franklin Roosevelt and New Jersey Governor Morgan Larson opened the bridge. In tribute to his mentor, typical of Ammann's generous spirit, the Swiss engineer drove with Gustav Lindenthal onto the bridge that the older man had spent his lifetime fruitlessly dreaming of.

After opening the new bridge in 1931, a scant four years after construction began, and—to the wonderment of local authorities—under budget as well as ahead of schedule, Ammann was now Chief

Engineer for the New York Port Authority. He went on to design and oversee numerous other bridges and tunnels that make New York City accessible (although some residents today might find that a relative term). He built the Triborough Bridge that connects Manhattan with the Bronx and Queens, the Little Hell Gate Bridge connecting Randall's and Ward's Islands, the Lincoln Tunnel from West 39th Street to New Jersey, the Bronx-Whitestone Bridge over the East River, the Throgs Neck Bridge between Queens and the Throgs Neck Peninsula in the Bronx and, perhaps his crowning glory, the Verrazano Narrows Bridge between Brooklyn and Staten Island.

One of the finest engineering achievements on record, the Verrazano's towers holding the suspension cables are as high as a 70-story building. Each tower was assembled with 10,000 steel cells, fastened with six million rivets and two million bolts. The Empire State Building contains some 365,000 tons of steel as compared to 1,265,000 tons contained in the bridge. Like Greece's Parthenon, whose columns were made slightly convex to present the most pleasing appearance—a technique called *entasis*—the bridge towers are tapered from top to bottom. The two towers are plumb, but the curvature of the earth means the tops are one and five-eighth inches farther apart than the base. Since metal expands in hot weather, the roadway at the center of the span rises or falls by as much as 12 feet during a temperature change of 100^0F.

Ammann also found the time—how is hard to imagine with such a list of projects, any one of which would represent a lifetime's achievement—to consult on the Golden Gate Bridge in San Francisco, which astounded the world with a narrower and yet even longer span. If such gracefully thin and relatively light bridges were sometimes disconcertingly flexible in a breeze (as drivers and engineers noted), they were also lovely to look at.

By the early 1960s, when the George Washington's lower deck was added, as specified in his original plan, Ammann had eclipsed his mentor Lindenthal. His other stunning creation, the Bayonne Bridge connecting Staten Island and New Jersey, was the world's largest steel arch bridge for more than four decades, more than 600 feet longer than the previous record holder, Lindenthal's Hell Gate Bridge.

In retirement Ammann liked to gaze through a telescope from his high-rise Manhattan apartment at a new sight some 12 miles away, his Verrazano Narrows suspension bridge. As if in tribute to the engineering prowess that made Ammann's George Washington Bridge great, this equally slender, graceful span would not be surpassed in length for another 17 years. The Romans, themselves great builders, said, *Si vis monumentum, circumspice* ("If you seek his monument, look around you"). The George Washington, Bayonne, Triborough, Whitestone, Throgs Neck and Verrazano Narrows Bridges are Ammann's monuments; like the city's skyscrapers, they were literally invented in New York. These six structures set the standard for long-span suspension bridges. All such bridges in the foreseeable future, until some entirely new concept not now imaginable comes along, will be an adaptation of them and will owe a debt to a small unassuming Swiss engineer from the ETH.

In 1964, the year before Ammann's death, President Lyndon Johnson awarded him the National Medal for Science. Although he had become a naturalized citizen of the United States in 1925, Ammann never lost his love for Switzerland, and Switzerland never ceased to lay claim to Ammann. In 1930 he received an honorary doctorate as *Bauingenieur* from his alma mater, and in 1979 the Swiss government issued a commemorative stamp in his honor.

ROBERT MAILLART

While Othmar Ammann was perfecting his craft and creating sculptures in steel in the United States, a contemporary, Robert Maillart, was doing the same in Switzerland. However, Maillart built his ethereal structures in the new medium of reinforced concrete, a major contribution to the revolution in structural engineering. He became the first engineer to depart from masonry in favor of the new, strong, relatively inexpensive, and highly versatile construction material.

Concrete itself was not new. It is a building material made of crushed stone or sand mixed with water and cement. Cement is a binding agent usually composed of pulverized limestone that "sets up," or hardens, the mixture as it dries. The Romans had mastered the use of concrete in ancient times. However, while concrete can carry compression well, it will crack under lateral pressure unless reinforced with steel or iron. Robert Maillart did not invent reinforced concrete any more than Othmar Ammann invented the steel-frame suspension bridge. But, like Ammann, he took a technique he encountered as a young ETH graduate and perfected it in the art and science of bridge construction in Switzerland.

Maillart was descended from a family of Belgian origins with a history of artistic talent, a predisposition that later made its mark on his career. His family of Belgian émigrés settled near Geneva in the 1850s, and Maillart's grandfather became a Swiss citizen. His father died when Maillart was two, leaving him and five siblings to be raised by his mother in Bern, where he studied at the *Gymnasium* and excelled in mathematics and drawing.

In 1890 he qualified for entry to the ETH, where he came under the influence of Wilhelm Ritter, also one of Othmar Ammann's mentors. Ritter was a full Professor of Civil Engineering and Director of the "Poly" from 1887 to 1891. He was famous for the practical dimension in his engineering training, with its emphasis on graphic analysis and lectures using wooden models for illustration. Thanks to Ritter, and before Ritter the ETH's first CE professor, Karl Culmann, and the architect Gottfried Semper, the civil engineering curriculum at the ETH was the most visually oriented of any engineering school of the time. It was no happenstance that two of its most illustrious graduates studied under the same faculty and went on to create the most visually imposing as well as technically advanced bridges of the 20th century.

When Maillart earned his degree in 1894, the ETH did not teach a course in reinforced concrete, and little use was made of the material in Switzerland. French and German engineers had begun to experiment with it and improve on the discovery that an inner skeleton or framework of iron or steel rods would allow the hardened concrete to bear heavy lateral loads. Young Maillart grasped both the practical and aesthetic potential of this exciting new material. Because it was mixed as a fluid, it could be formed into arches and beams—into almost any shape desired. It required less maintenance than steel, which had to be painted periodically to prevent corrosion. It could be mixed and formed on the spot, which meant that much of the money needed for the project could be used to hire local labor and be plowed back into the community the bridge would serve, a key advantage to the frugal and then relatively poor Swiss.

After graduating from the ETH, Maillart spent several years in apprenticeship, so to speak, practicing the basics of his profession on routine projects while continuing to study the use of reinforced concrete, envisioning how to exploit its aesthetic and practical value, and foreseeing it would provide the medium to depart from masonry as a standard construction material. In 1896 he completed his first solo project, an arched railroad viaduct in which he used blocks of reinforced concrete. Though modest in scale, this early effort foreshadowed Maillart's characteristic combining of technical skill with a strong, clean visual impact. Soon afterward he was hired by the *Tiefbauamt*, the heavy construction division of Canton Zürich's public works department, and given the opportunity to submit a design for a new bridge over the River Sihl, one of two rivers flowing through the city along with the bigger and better known Limmat. His design for the Stauffacher Bridge, an elegantly simple, low-rise single arch, was selected and completed in 1899, bringing him more renown and newer opportunities.

Marrying Maria Ronconi from Bologna, Italy, Maillart settled down in Zürich, set up his own design and consulting firm, and proceeded to make engineering history. He changed the face of Switzerland with economically, technically and aesthetically innovative designs much in the same way Ammann forever altered the landscape of New York.

For the next 40 years, until his death in 1940, Maillart designed and built—or supervised the building of—47 bridges across the length and breadth of Switzerland. The array of projects in which he participated, like Ammann's *oeuvre*, is astounding not just for technical and aesthetic brilliance but also for the sheer scope and number of structures. These Swiss engineers not only built great bridges but also were so extraordinarily productive that they built *many* of them.

Maillart's approach was anything but "one-type-fits-all." An innovator, he employed a variety of techniques depending on the terrain, traffic requirements and degree of technical challenge: hingeless arches, arches with expansion hinges, the continuous hollow-box concrete beam (which he invented), hollow-box cantilever beams, and deck-stiffened arches. His bridges carried roads or railways across deep Alpine gorges as well as wide rivers. And in almost every case there was something original and distinctly "Maillartian": that unique combination of economy, technical brilliance and visual elegance—the perfect marriage of form and function.

Of course, the engineer is not a sculptor and does not have the freedom to choose any form that strikes his fancy. Considering the wild terrain of the Alps, it's a wonder certain bridges were built at all—man overcoming the most capricious whims of nature. But Maillart showed that utilitarian structure has both a rational and visual or aesthetic basis. Achieving the proper balance between the two is the essence of engineering *design*; and when either is suppressed, the process ceases to be true design and becomes mere analysis and drafting. Maillart's genius—and Ammann's, too, in his own medium of steel—was a manifestation of the technical imagination, something fostered at the ETH. It was the ability to see that the physical form, structure and dimensions of an edifice, while governed to a large extent by the math, could transcend calculation because a designer was at work rather than a mere analyst. Analysis and calculation were the servants of design and not its master.

David Billington, a professor of civil engineering at Princeton University and a prolific author on engineering subjects, is a leading authority on both Othmar Ammann and Robert Maillart. In his study *Robert Maillart's Bridges* he captures the essence of the Swiss-led revolution in structural engineering perhaps better than anyone else in his description of Maillart's masterpiece: the 1930 Salignatobel crossing in Canton Graubünden near Chur. High up in the Rhaetian Alps across a distant valley, the span seems to spring out of the living rock, for the face of the ravine on either side carries the load, eliminating the need for the usual stone abutments to anchor it.

> After one curve a small white form appears through the trees. After a few more curves it comes into full view—a bridge, connecting two mountains over a wild ravine. To laymen its form is unclear at first and then distinguishable as a bridge. To knowledgeable engineers, however, it is not only immediately clear, it is also the reason for the pilgrimage. Here is one of the most beautiful examples of pure twentieth-century structure. But it is also complex and, even to the skilled engineer, an object of mystery and wonder.

CHRISTIAN MENN

Following the trail blazed by Maillart, ETH engineer Christian Menn has carried the structural revolution into contemporary times by incorporating into his predecessor's designs a promising new advance in reinforced concrete known as *prestressed* concrete. In this technique the concrete structural member is precast and formed with internal stresses that are the opposite of, or countervailing to, the stress loads it will have to bear when incorporated into the final structure. One means of achieving this is to introduce the reinforcing steel rods or cables under tension inside the concrete load-bearing member.

Christian Menn was born in 1927 in Canton Bern, entered the ETH in 1946, and two years later began coursework under Pierre Lardy, a professor of engineering specializing in bridge construction in masonry and concrete. Following graduation, he performed his Swiss military service but contracted tuberculosis in 1951, forcing him to spend 14 months in a sanatorium. That time was not wasted. While a patient he passed his time in intense theoretical

5

146

studies on the structural analysis of the spiral staircases in the hospital. Upon his recovery he accepted an offer to assist Professor Lardy, with whom he spent the next three years (1953–1956) at the ETH. Along with two other students, he served as a teaching assistant in Lardy's engineering courses and helped the professor with his research and consulting. In addition, he completed his dissertation and in 1956 received the doctoral degree with Lardy as his principal advisor.

Menn's earliest bridges were relatively long-span, deck-stiffened arches in the tradition of Maillart, but eventually the revolutionary material of prestressed concrete began to open up new visions of design. He saw that precast, prestressed members could actually replace the arch itself. The deck of his bridge could then become the main supporting member without the arch. Moreover, during construction, no expensive scaffolding would be needed for the arch, nor would the external wooden formwork—in essence, a mold—in which to pour and shape the concrete, as was the normal practice.

The 1962 Reichenau Bridge over the Rhine (which begins in the Alps) in Canton Graubünden is an early example of Menn's technique. It is an arch of relatively low rise, ostensibly owing much in its design to Maillart. But with prestressing, Menn was able to build a longer span and use new forms. In this case he came up with a deck-stiffened arch spanning 98 meters (328 feet), with a wide, prestressed concrete deck slab cantilevering laterally from both sides of a single box. (A cantilever is a beam or load-bearing slab that is anchored or supported at one end and carries the load at the other end or distributes it along the unsupported portion.)

The 1975 Felsenau Bridge over the Aare River north of Bern is a later and more impressive example of the simplicity and elegance possible with the skilled application of prestressed concrete. It eliminates the traditional arch and carries the roadbed over a curved hollow-box beam, creating a structure of exceptional lightness—a stripped-down form of transparency that satisfies all three of Menn's main criteria for design—efficiency, economy, and aesthetics. An uncommon feature of the Felsenau design is the single box for a wide roadway. Previously, prestressed segmental bridges had two boxes, one for each half of the bridge. The single box with wide cantilever slabs requires less material than two boxes.

Unlike Robert Maillart, Christian Menn has not confined his talents to his home country. In 1991 Menn addressed an architectural technology conference at Harvard University as the guest of Spiro Pollalis, Professor of Design Technology and Management at the Graduate School of Design, who was teaching a course titled "Bridges: Structural Order and Form." Menn arrived in Boston at a time when the "Big Dig" transportation project was beginning to spark controversy (which continues to this day over cost, performance and quality-control issues). Part of the Boston master plan was a new highway bridge across the Charles River between Boston and Charlestown to replace the decrepit "High Bridge." The initial plans had come under heavy criticism during the early 1990s, and the entire Big Dig project was in jeopardy. "Scheme Z," as the plan for the new Charles River crossing was called, was a sprawling design of 16 traffic lanes feeding into and out of a series of loop ramps climbing a hundred feet over the water. It was unsightly, expensive, and generated heated opposition on both sides of the Charles, in Boston, Cambridge, and Charlestown. Residents characterized the scheme as "the ugliest monster that anyone had ever seen," according to architect Charles Redmon, a member of the Bridge Design Review Committee (BDRC). "I don't think anyone could find anywhere in the states a larger, more ungainly spaghetti mess of a roadway."

It was during the Harvard conference that Menn first thought of submitting his own bridge design, a rudimentary version of which he sketched while he and his host Professor Pollalis drank tea in the reading room of the Harvard Faculty Club. Menn proposed a sleek, modern cable-stayed bridge with 10 traffic lanes. He had begun to explore this new concept with the Ganter Bridge (1980) in the Swiss Alpine Canton Valais. This bridge traverses a deep valley with a cable-stayed, prestressed cantilever construction. The term "cable-stay" refers to the new method of attaching diagonal steel cables under tension from the horizontal deck carrying the roadway. The cables attach to a high central tower or towers, usually concrete. The vertical (gravity) load of the deck is transmitted through the cables to the towers and into the foundation as compression force.

The design for the Charles River structure was well received, and Pollalis soon realized it presented the region with the ideal opportunity to build a "signature bridge." Professor Pollalis observed: "Bridges are very public and there is a certain feeling and sentiment when you cross a bridge and when you see a bridge. We knew that . . . and one of the reasons I really wanted a nice bridge for Boston was because I knew it would become the symbol of the city."

The Harvard engineer traveled to Switzerland to confer with Menn and invited his Swiss colleague back to Harvard's Design School for a second meeting with BDRC members. The commissioners liked what they saw and heard. Menn persuaded the Board that bridges need to be clean and simple. BDRC member Redmon recalled: "He worked on a couple of strategies . . . and we came back around and said, 'Can we reduce the number of lanes so that we could produce a bridge that would be quite elegant?' That's the way the process began." Amid the groundswell of local support for the new plan, Scheme Z was scrapped and Menn was hired as a consultant for the building team.

"For me it was a great honor that I could elaborate the concept for the Charles River bridge," Menn said. "It was the biggest adventure in my professional life—not only because it is an interesting and original bridge, but I think also because it is in a very interesting, academic city. . . . I feel that designing a bridge in such a city is absolutely fantastic. . . . This is the most important bridge I have ever designed. The bridge is very, very complicated because there are a lot of complicating boundary conditions. For instance, the bridge is very wide and the clearance beneath is very severe," Menn explained. "I tried to find a solution which could satisfy all of these boundary conditions and from there I came to this concept. Successful design of a perfect structure can never be performed only on the basis of general rules concerning structural system, dimensions and proportions alone, as long as the design lacks in originality and individuality."

The bridge was named for Leonard P. Zakim, a civil rights activist and executive director of the New England office of the Anti-Defamation League of B'nai B'rith who died in 1999. It also honors the defenders of Bunker Hill on Charlestown's heights above Boston, the site of the first major battle between the American colonists and the British in 1775.

The structure is the first hybrid cable-stay bridge in the United States, with both steel and concrete in its design. Steel girders and beams frame the main span of the bridge. The north and south spans were cast in place with prestressed concrete. Two additional northbound lanes, from the North End and Sumner Tunnel to northbound I-93, are cantilevered on steel beams from the eight-lane main span.

There are two towers to hold the cables, the spires of which evoke the nearby Bunker Hill Monument. They differ in height (322 feet and 295 feet, respectively) to allow transition of the roadway from the I-93 Central Artery Tunnel, the downtown part of Boston's Big Dig, to the elevated section of the I-93 Northern expressway. The "pitch," or transition grade, between the new Central Artery ("Liberty") Tunnel and the bridge is as much as five percent. However, motorists do not notice the change in elevation; the tops of both towers are 266 feet above the roadway.

The hollow concrete towers were cast in place with walls only one to four inches thick. Steel boxes were drilled into the spires to fasten the cables into the towers. To prevent the additional weight of the cantilevered roadway section from throwing the entire bridge off-balance, the cables were shifted three inches off-center. To support the towers, workers sank eight-foot-diameter steel shafts into bedrock below the river.

Completed in five years, the bridge is 1,457 feet in total length, with a main span of 795 feet. The bridge was near completion in May 2002 when it was opened to pedestrian traffic. In March 2003, the Zakim Bridge opened to northbound I-93 traffic for the first time, coinciding with the partial completion of the new Central Artery ("Liberty") Tunnel. The southbound lanes of the bridge and the southbound tunnel opened to traffic in December 2003.

These are the technical and historical details. But they say little about the stunning visual impact of the ingenious design. The multiple steel cables splay out from the two towers in a vision—from a distance—like gossamer butterfly wings. Or, as others have suggested, the bridge evokes the image of a mammoth sailing ship cruising serenely up the Charles River. Although beauty may lie in the eye of the beholder, Christian Menn's bridge is quickly becoming Boston's most striking architectural landmark.

THE ETH'S LEGACY IN ENGINEERING DESIGN

A bridge may seem to be simply a matter of crossing from one side of an obstacle to the other. But truly great bridges are not as common as one might suppose, if greatness is measured by a harmonious balance between the utility of the structure and the simplicity and/or elegance of the form—and, not by any means least, economy.

Why are there not more great bridges, and why are a disproportionate number of the great ones found in Switzerland? The answer is one of the ETH's many legacies. It is a regrettable feature of modern technical education that schools often suppress the highest qualities of the human mind—intuition, vision, creativity—overwhelming them with the abstract and the impersonal, with pre-set formulas and mathematical calculation. Too many schools equate analysis with design; and to be sure, no responsible engineer would attempt a bridge without being sure of the math. But there is far more to a great bridge or any public structure than mathematics; analysis is only an aid to design. Designs born out of the aesthetic vision of the architect and artist, combined with the solid technical grounding of the man with the slide rule and calculator, are the best that can be accomplished.

At the ETH, an internationally respected faculty—men like Culmann and Ritter and Lardy—understood this. They in turn sent out into the world students like Ammann and Maillart and Menn, who shared a similar approach, yet found their individualistic vision in steel and concrete. In doing so they made contributions to structural engineering that have never been equaled, and which have conferred indelible economic and aesthetic benefits on the modern world.

CHAPTER EIGHT

The ETH and
Swiss National Defense

Just as the ETH has been a formative influence in Switzerland's economic development, the institute has also contributed significantly to the country's defense and security. For some 125 years, the ETH's military school, known formally as the Military Academy at the ETH Zürich (*Militärakademie an der ETH Zürich*) and by the acronym MILAK-ETH, has trained professional officers who provide the nucleus of the armed forces' leadership.

A "who's who" of senior Swiss officers, past and present, shows a disproportionate number—about 30 percent—have been ETH graduates or faculty. While many of them have commanded or served as staff officers in combat formations, they have clearly dominated the technical-military specialties, for example engineering, cartography, signals and communications, artillery, air defense and aviation. Construction engineers trained at the ETH were prominent in the planning and construction of the *Réduit National*, the Alpine fortress network that played a pivotal role in deterring a Nazi invasion of Switzerland in World War II.

It almost always comes as a shock for Americans to learn that neutral Switzerland—home of such worldwide humanitarian organizations as the International Committee of the Red Cross and the Global Fund—has produced some of the finest soldiers in Europe. A prominent U.S. Senator is reported to have said during hearings in 1997 related to Swiss conduct during World War II, "Does Switzerland have an army?" Yet, as we have previously dis-

153

cussed, Switzerland has a proud, centuries-old military tradition. In fact, there is a wry old Swiss maxim that captures the essence of the country's national defense: "Switzerland does not have an army; Switzerland *is* an army."

This saying is based on the principle of "the nation-in-arms," under which all able-bodied men of military age served in the defense force, keeping rifle, ammunition and equipment at home and, like America's colonial Minutemen, were ready to mobilize on short notice. From the beginning of the Confederation to the present, the Swiss Army has been a popular force of citizen-soldiers—in essence, a militia, although in the West that term usually bespeaks a lack of training and professionalism that is not the case in Switzerland.

The old maxim is not quite as true today as it was in the past, especially now that the Cold War has ended and there are no clear threats to Swiss or European security. Consequently, the Swiss have reduced the size of their military establishment, just as other European nations and the United States have done, and by about the same proportions. The Swiss militia army has fallen from around 600,000 at the height of the Cold War to around 200,000 today. However, Switzerland's policy of compulsory military service remains unchanged; it is both constitutionally mandated and deeply woven into the fabric of Swiss society. Since requiring the service of all men of traditional military age would produce a force much larger than now needed, the Swiss have solved the problem by narrowing the age of those liable for service. Instead of all able-bodied men from 19 to 55, as in the past, those from age 20 to 30 make up the bulk of the force, with a cadre of about 1,000 full-time officers who are expected to perform dual duty in peacetime as commanders of the militia's operational units and to serve as general staff, technical specialists and trainers. ETH-trained officers are the nucleus of this full-time cadre.

ARMED NEUTRALITY

By the late Middle Ages the Swiss began to realize that their multi-lingual, multi-cultural polity could not survive if they took sides in the innumerable wars of their European neighbors. Injecting Europe's external quarrels into the delicate balance between the linguistic communities the Swiss had achieved with such effort would only rip the country apart. As a result, the Swiss settled upon a policy of political neutrality. It was staunchly supported by virtually all Swiss and formally recognized by the European powers at the 1815 Congress of Vienna after the final fall of Napoleon.

However, neutrality should not be confused with defenselessness or lack of military aptitude. On the contrary, for several hundred years the hardy reputation and combat skills of the Swiss fighting man had led neighboring princes to employ them in the thousands as contract soldiers. Switzerland made sure the martial qualities of its people were maintained and organized to put teeth in Switzerland's guiding foreign policy principle—a well-armed neutrality.

The ETH plays a prominent role in Swiss national defense in three areas most worthy of focus in this story: professional officer training, the effectiveness of the national militia-based force, and deterrence through military preparedness, factors which together make Swiss neutrality credible and sustainable.

MILAK, THE MILITARY ACADEMY AT THE ETH ZÜRICH

The vast majority of Swiss officers are part-time citizen-soldiers and receive much of their military training in their units—that is, on-the-job. However, any effective army, and especially a national militia force, needs a nucleus of highly trained full-time professionals. The complexities of modern warfare demand it. Training that professional nucleus is the mission of the Military Academy at the ETH.

In October 1877, the Swiss Federal Council decided to establish a military division at the Polytechnic with the following subjects: History of Warfare, Strategy, Tactics, Military Organization and Administration, Engineering, Weapons (including ballistics) and Fortifications Theory. General Ulrich Wille (1848–1925), one of the notables in Swiss military history, served as commander-in-chief of

Swiss forces during World War I. Prior to his elevation to that post, he was an influential and energetic promoter of the new educational concept of professional officer training at the ETH. He became a lecturer at the Department of Military Sciences in 1903, and from 1909 to 1913 was also head of the department.

Thus the Military Academy at the ETH has a lengthy history; professional officers of the Swiss armed forces began attending courses in military science at the ETH in 1878. The Swiss recognized that a link between their military and the federal university would provide the richest possible environment in which to educate military officers. A formal military science course lasting two to three semesters was added after World War I, a conflict which the Swiss managed to avoid, but which also reminded them they needed to put some teeth into their policy of political neutrality with a more modern military capability. Today the MILAK strives to provide the Swiss armed forces with professional officers with the requisite academic background and practical skills to function as dynamic leaders, trainers and educators. They serve as the army's up-to-date experts on a wide variety of essential military subjects.

The MILAK is administratively a distinct entity with a separate location in the town of Wädenswil, on the shores of Lake Zürich, about 20 minutes from downtown Zürich and the ETH. At the same time it is an integral part of the institute. It employs the same professors and is based on the ETH's professional officer course under the auspices of the Department of Humanities, Social and Political Sciences. Through the ETH, the MILAK conducts a three-year bachelor-level Professional Officer Program that leads to an ETH Bachelor of Arts Degree in Public Affairs.

The Professional Officer Program for young lieutenants is similar to the basic academic education an American officer-candidate receives at the U.S. Service Academies or through ROTC (Reserve Officers Training Corps) at an accredited university or college. In form and structure, MILAK-ETH resembles the U.S. ROTC in that it is part of an independent academic institution, and academic courses are integrated with practical military and field training.

It would be a mistake, however, to draw too close a parallel.

ROTC is a mass program, operating on thousands of American colleges and universities, and typically a single ROTC unit at a major university includes more students than the entire MILAK. Because the Swiss military is comparatively small, the need for full-time officers is correspondingly small. Also, Switzerland's foreign policy of neutrality and non-intervention abroad reduces the need for a large officer corps and for officer training on the scale of Sandhurst in the United Kingdom, Saint Cyr in France or U.S. academies like West Point. The Professional Officer Program on average enrolls only 25 new cadets per entering class, or a total of 120 in the 2003–2004 school year. But despite their small numbers, MILAK graduates are vital to Swiss national defense, for they represent the cadre of academically trained and militarily proficient officers any modern force needs to be effective in today's complex world.

MILAK also provides a one-year Diploma Course for those officers who are already university graduates, and conducts supplementary training for senior officers at various stages in their career, in what could be described as "continuing military education." The content of coursework at all levels consists of such essential topics as military leadership and communication, strategic studies, military history, military sociology, psychology and pedagogy. Built around these formal academic courses is the technical and practical field training every officer needs to be proficient in his military duties. In effect, then, the MILAK acts as the nexus between the classroom and the field. It integrates the academic part of the officer's *education* with the military components of his *training*.

SWISS DEFENSE, DETERRENCE, AND THE ROLE OF THE NATIONAL MILITIA

The question logically demands to be answered: what kind of military force does this educational system produce, of which the ETH is an indispensable component? How effective is it, in the context of Swiss defense policy and strategy? "Militia" is not a favorable term in the U.S., partly because of the poor combat record of hastily formed militias as compared to regular forces in America's early wars, and more recently because of fringe political groups that have adopted the term "militia" to describe their organizations. Can a national militia truly constitute a quality force?

Armies do not spring up or exist in a social and cultural vacuum. Cultural, political, and demographic factors often determine the kind of military organization a given society will produce. For example, today's United States employs a force of well-paid volunteer professionals, highly trained and technologically sophisticated, and suitable for heavy power projection. It is a military reflecting the values of this country, its wealth and its strategic requirements. Conversely, military organizations and practices can influence or shape how a society evolves. In ancient Greece, for example, the principal type of warfare between city-states was the clash of heavily armed infantry soldiers, or *hoplites*, who made up the *phalanx*, a tight mass of spearmen. As military historian Victor Davis Hansen has described, "The sheer terror of hoplite battle, the courage needed to stare at a wall of spears, and the urgency for group solidarity in the confines of the phalanx gave positive momentum to ideas of civic responsibility and egalitarianism . . . in ancient Athens and other city-states, helping form the emotional and spiritual substructure of Greek culture and politics."

Nearly 2,000 years separate the *polis* of ancient Greece and the early Swiss Confederation; yet, there were remarkable similarities between the Greek phalanx and the massed pikemen of the *Eidgenossenschaft* that time and again routed the armies of the Habsburgs and Duke Charles of Burgundy in the Middle Ages. In medieval Europe through the 16th century, the phalanx was known by various names and assumed various tactical forms—the *schiltron*, or the Spanish *tercio*, for example. But it was still a tightly packed, well-disciplined body of spearmen, capable of moving across the battlefield like a terrifying hedgehog with steel-tipped spires, and it could defeat mounted, armored knights who were formerly supreme on the battlefield.

The Swiss became masters at this form of warfare with their *Haufen* (in German, "heap" or "mass"), a phalanx of pikemen supported on either side by "sleeves" of light-armed skirmishers, crossbowmen, and later, by *harquebusiers*—soldiers armed with an early form of musket. These troops accompanied the *Haufen,* opened the action, then retreated behind the pikemen as the latter came to close quarters with the enemy. Hence, 16th- and early 17th-century battles were usually decided by "push of pike," as the old saying went.

Paradoxically, the phalanx, whether ancient Greek or more recently Swiss, was not the soulless, machine-like assemblage it might have appeared as it moved inexorably across the battlefield. It was a highly personal form of fighting. As suggested above, it demanded an unusual combination of courage, initiative and discipline for a man to function effectively in the phalanx. But it was not the discipline of the lash; it was the self-discipline that flowed from solidarity with neighbors from the same canton who stood shoulder-to-shoulder in formation. The Swiss command structure was informal. Since the Swiss had no royalty, it was organized around natural leaders or men with long experience of battle. There was little of the rigid hierarchy and class structure of other European armies; each Swiss soldier was a valued part of the whole and had "standing."

Centuries of this type of battle and constant training for it between wars produced a Swiss militiaman who was not only rugged and brave but also independent. Thus evolved in the Swiss militia a distinctive type of individualistic soldier with the ability to act on his own initiative, fiercely loyal to his trusted tactical leader —usually a friend or neighbor, but who also resisted distant, arbitrary, impersonal authority. These traits, combined with the Swiss political tradition in which power was exercised from the bottom up and not from the top down, produced the only radically democratic system of national defense in all Europe.

Now come forward from the era of massed pikemen to the advent of firearms on the battlefield. The Swiss made the transition perhaps better than any other nation. Once an army of fearsome pikemen, the Swiss became an army of even more fearsome riflemen. Marksmanship, in fact, became the Swiss national sport. Shooting societies sprang up in every town and village, in part to assuage the anguish of Napoleon's conquest in 1798 and to make sure it never happened again. These local clubs were organized into a national body officially supported by cantonal and central governments: the Swiss Shooting Federation (*Schweizerischer Schützenverein*, or SSV), whose stated aim was to "cultivate an art beautiful in itself and of the highest importance for the defense of the confederation." Shooting matches and festivals were held all over the country, and marksmanship assumed an almost mystical significance as an act of nationalism, the tangible expression of the nation-in-arms, peaceable and officially neutral, but determined to fight any invader who would threaten Swiss territory and independence.

This all seems quaint to us today, when the military does not place great emphasis on individual marksmanship. To be sure, even in Switzerland rifle shooting is not quite the desideratum it once was. Even so, tens of thousands of Swiss still participate in annual shooting matches all over the country. One can get a sense of the value placed on precision marksmanship at the annual *Knabenschiessen*, Canton Zürich's festival that takes place every September in picturesque Albisgütli, in the shadow of the Uetliberg hills. *Knabenschiessen* is German for "Boys' Shoot," although girls also participate and sometimes win. It is a three-day event, replete with rides, food and all the trappings of a carnival, but built around the serious purpose of determining the best marksmen with the service rifles provided by the Swiss Army. The winner gets to pick his trophy from a rich selection of prizes, and also wins the approbation of a community that still takes sharpshooting seriously.

Most modern militaries put their faith in heavy firepower—high-volume automatic weapons, armor, tube and rocket artillery, and air-delivered, precision-guided bombs and missiles. The U.S. Marine Corps still adheres to the motto "Every Marine is a rifleman" and has retained some emphasis in its training on individual marksmanship. In contrast, the average U.S. Army trainee fires no more than 80–100 rounds to qualify as a so-called rifleman, and at targets typically under 100 meters. Notable exceptions are the Army and Marine Corps scout-snipers, who train to shoot accurately to 1,000 meters and even beyond. But the snipers are a tiny elite corps. Accurate shooting beyond 100 meters, once the goal and task of every infantryman, is now the specialty of a select few.

In World War II, individual shooting was a little better in the U.S. Army than now; the legacy of famed marksmen like Alvin York, a hero of World War I, was still fresh. Yet, the American infantry soldier of 1941–1945 was an indifferent rifleman, at best. Even the vaunted German Army trained its soldiers to shoot well only out to 100 meters, relying instead on the shock and heavy firepower of the armored *Blitzkrieg* and the close air support of the Luftwaffe. Swiss soldiers, on the other hand, trained to shoot accurately to a standard of 300 meters, and most could hit targets well beyond that. The Germans were well aware of the quality of the Swiss rifleman, and one visitor from across the Rhine observed, "No Swiss, but a stranger dare say it, that this militia was worth half a dozen standing armies."

These then are the foundations of Swiss national defense: a militia of tough, brave and well-motivated soldiers; a Constitution mandating compulsory service and which also made the army's weapons and equipment uniform among the cantons, creating a truly national force; and, as firearms came to dominate modern warfare, a nation of highly skilled marksmen, among the best in the world. Beginning in the 1870s one could add to this mix the new ETH and its military academy, which ensured the introduction of skilled military engineers and modern technology into the force, along with a solid nucleus of trained professional officers.

The militia pattern ought to be familiar to Americans, at least to those schooled in our own military history, for it is how U.S. defense was once organized. From the mid-1600s to the late 1700s, immediately prior to ratification of the Constitution, each colony had a militia consisting of every able-bodied male, typically from 16 to 55 years old. Service was compulsory and, as with today's Swiss, each member was required to keep his weapons at home and ready to use—a suitable musket or rifle, ammunition, a bayonet, tomahawk or sword, and other accoutrements necessary to outfit an infantry or cavalry soldier. Local governments, or very often the militia units themselves, kept a supply of surplus arms to provide to individuals too poor to purchase them on their own. As the community in arms, the militia of every colony and, later, independent state provided security for what the Second Amendment to the U.S. Constitution calls "a free State"—free not only from attacks and insurrections but also a check against violations of the laws by public officials, known commonly to colonial Americans as "usurpation" or "tyranny."

SWISS NEUTRALITY AND NATIONAL DEFENSE

The argument is sometimes made that the Swiss Army has never been put to the test of modern mechanized battle. Consequently, no one can say with certainty that its military system is effective. Doubters question whether the Swiss method of defense holds any lessons for others, especially for a superpower like the United States, currently engaged in a global war and with military forces operating in over a hundred countries. However, the doubters should heed the famous observation of Sun Tzu (400 B.C.), Chinese author of *The Art of War*, a classic studied by every army in the world: "To fight and conquer in all your battles is not supreme excellence; supreme excellence consists in breaking the enemy's resistance without fighting."

The effectiveness of the "nation-in-arms" concept and the Swiss Army was demonstrated during history's most demanding test, World War II. From 1940 to the end of 1944, Switzerland faced not merely belligerents in a general European war, but was totally surrounded and constantly threatened by one of the most aggressive totalitarian regimes in history. A dozen nations had proven the ineffectiveness of their militaries by falling rapidly to German arms; even great powers suffered setbacks at the hands of the Wehrmacht. Yet, Switzerland deterred the Nazis' will to invade despite numerous invasion plans drawn up by the German high command. Indeed, Switzerland's experience in World War II is a case study in the deterrent power of a highly trained and quickly mobilized national militia.

THE ROOTS OF SWISS NEUTRALITY

As the reader is well aware by now—and it bears repeating in this particular context—Swiss neutrality is not opportunistic or of recent vintage. It was not conceived suddenly to appease the Nazi threat. It has been the principal feature of Swiss foreign policy since 1515, when the Swiss took a beating at the hands of the French King Francis I at Marignano, near Milan, Italy. This unprecedented defeat—made possible by French artillery finally ending the supremacy of the pikemen—made the Swiss reflect, and they soon realized they must remain aloof from the wars that continued to ravage Europe. Otherwise, the Confederation would surely disintegrate. The cantons, differing in language, religion and economic interests, had entered into a confederation so that each could better safeguard its liberty from encroachments by foreign powers. They could only maintain the alliance by staying out of external conflicts. If they had chosen sides, for example, in the Thirty Years' War (1618–1648) that raged between Catholic and Protestant states over Europe, their unity would almost certainly have shattered. Thus, the policy of neutrality evolved to maintain the harmony of the Confederation. The Swiss would still be ready to fight, but would no longer rampage outside their borders, joining the cause of foreign princes or religious or economic interests.

The benefits to Switzerland were enormous—peace with neighboring states (and, in turn to them, peace with the Swiss), and internal peace and harmony. Freedom from the ravages of wars and invasion produced the stability that allowed Switzerland to cultivate the manifold talents of its people and to develop the country. Far from seeing neutrality as weakness, the Swiss grew to regard scrupulously minding their own business as a positive—good for them and good for their neighbors.

SWISS DEFENSE IN WORLD WAR II AND
LE RÉDUIT NATIONAL

After the fall of France in 1940, Switzerland faced a dangerous, almost insurmountable strategic situation, and the most difficult

period in its history began. The Swiss were now completely surrounded and could be attacked simultaneously from all sides by the
Axis Powers without hope of support from the Allies. Facing this
dire strategic threat, the high command made a decision striking in
its boldness. In the event of a German invasion, they decided to concentrate Swiss forces in the mountainous center of the country
around the entrances to the Alpine valleys. The strategic concept
was that controlling the mountain passes and railroad tunnels that
would likely be the object of an invader would itself deter an attack.
If the Nazis invaded, the Swiss were prepared to destroy the St.
Gotthard and Simplon tunnels and railroads, removing the easiest
means of passage between Germany and its Italian ally. They would
hold out as long as they could in the mountains, making the
Germans pay a high price in blood. Projected casualties and antici-
pated failure to gain strategic objectives before the Swiss destroyed
them would be too high a price for the Germans to pay.

This new defense concept was known throughout the country
as the National Redoubt, or by its French name, *Réduit National*.
A redoubt is normally an enclosed defensive bastion or fortification.
The word comes from the Latin *reducere*, one meaning of which is
to lead back or withdraw. A redoubt thus implies a defensive position into which a military force falls back from its forward deploy-
ments or withdraws into. In this case the term can be misleading,
for the Swiss National Redoubt was not a pinpoint location like
Fort Eben Emaul in Belgium or the fortified strongpoints of France's
Maginot Line. It was a huge perimeter of linked positions of various types covering nearly the whole of the central Alps, extending
from Sargans near the Austrian border to St. Maurice, a few miles
from France, and from Lake Lucerne in the north to the St. Gotthard, close to the Italian border in the Canton of Ticino.

A quick glance at the map reveals this startling fact: in their
determination to deter an attack by mounting an invincible defense
in the Redoubt, the Swiss were prepared to give up the northern
plain, where most of their cities, population, agriculture and manufacturing were located. André Siegfried, a member of the French
Academy, known for his travels on all continents, wrote about

Switzerland shortly after the war when memories were still fresh. In evaluating the National Redoubt he wrote:

> It cannot be said too often that such a concept was inspired by great heroism, and the way in which the Swiss government and the country as a whole accepted it without recrimination and without hesitation was admirable; because it involved, in the event of an invasion, the abandonment of the Swiss plateau and the families of the defenders to the mercies of the invader. The very soul of Switzerland fell back on its original hearth. In the whole history of war there are not many examples of such courage.

Modern military analysts question whether Swiss militiamen armed primarily with bolt-action rifles constituted a credible deterrent in the 1940s' age of mechanized warfare. This attitude underestimates the value of long-range precision marksmanship, especially in favorable terrain—a landscape providing good cover and concealment to riflemen, good fields of fire, and which obstructs movement by large mechanized formations. Swiss Alpine terrain is excellent for this kind of warfare, and the Swiss took good advantage of it.

As the danger increased, the Swiss reinforced their Alpine fortress and extended it to become a tremendously strong defense system. ETH-trained engineers of all types played a vital role in constructing this ingenious system of bunkers, gun emplacements, observation posts, and covered sites for rifle teams. It made maximum use of the mountainous terrain, established interlocking fields of fire, provided excellent observation of likely avenues of approach, and offered protection for gun crews and rifle units. There was also impregnable protection from aerial bombs and artillery for men, munitions and supplies, thanks to the Swiss' unequaled experience in tunneling in the Alps. Stocks were laid in to last the underground garrisons for several months. The Germans themselves estimated it could take as many as 21 divisions to subdue the country. It is unlikely that even a force of that size could have taken the Redoubt, and certainly not before the defenders destroyed the Simplon and St. Gotthard rail tunnels.

CHAMPIONS OF *LA DÉFENSE SPIRITUELLE*: KARL MEYER AND JEAN RUDOLF VON SALIS

During World War II there was another national redoubt even more decisive than the one in the Swiss mountains. That was the one in Swiss hearts—the love of liberty and its accompanying spirit of resistance. Switzerland's press and radio contributed substantially to this "spiritual defense," or *défense spirituelle* in French. In addition to shoring up the moral and intellectual defense of the country, Swiss print and broadcast journalism was also highly valued by the Allies and the resistance movements in Nazi-occupied territories. Between 1939 and 1945, Nazi Propaganda Minister Josef Goebbels delivered 169 denunciations of the Swiss press to the Federal Council, even threatening to kill Swiss journalists and scatter their ashes in Siberia. The Swiss government never answered and remained calm.

One would expect ETH graduates in the armed forces to play a critical role in Swiss military preparedness in the critical days of World War II, when Switzerland stood surrounded and under daily threat of invasion; and they did. But what is unexpected, and all the more remarkable, is the role ETH men played in *la défense spirituelle*. Two of Switzerland's leading champions in arousing and sustaining defiance of German and Italian threats were professors Karl Meyer and Jean Rudolf von Salis of the ETH.

Karl Meyer, born in Lucerne in 1885, studied history at the University of Zürich, and in 1920 was appointed lecturer in history and later *Ordinarius* (full professor) at both the ETH and his alma mater. He became nationally known as a leading expert on Switzerland's founding and early history, and authored two influential books, *The Origins of the Confederation* and *The Struggle for Freedom of the Confederate Founders*. Both these works appeared in 1941, when Nazi Germany had overrun all of continental Europe and much of the Soviet Union and North Africa as well. The German war machine seemed invincible, and the pressure from across the Rhine for the Swiss to accommodate the New Order was intense. At a most critical moment in Switzerland's history, Meyer's books touched the deepest wellsprings of Swiss patriotism, reminding the country that they had faced great dangers in the past and had prevailed, thanks to their spirit of resistance.

Through these works, his teaching, journal articles, and his public lectures, Karl Meyer helped to dampen any thought of surrender or compromise, reinvigorating the determination to preserve Switzerland's neutrality and independence. Meyer's words had a particular impact among his fellow German-speaking Swiss, to the fury of the Nazis. They claimed to represent the aspirations of all German speakers in Europe, and yet in Germanic Switzerland, with only a few minor exceptions, the people had nothing but contempt for the brutality, despotism and crudeness of Hitler's regime. The utter rejection of Hitler by German-speaking Swiss, who were arguably even more anti-Nazi than the rest of the country, gave the lie to the Third Reich's claim of legitimacy among all Germanic peoples and cultures. Moreover, the attitude of the German-Swiss was absolutely crucial to the resistance of the nation as a whole. With over 70 percent of the population, if the German-Swiss had succumbed to Hitler's threats and blandishments, it would have been impossible for the rest of Switzerland to resist.

Meyer's ETH colleague Jean Rudolf von Salis was born in Bern in 1901 to one of the leading families of that city. The bi-lingual von Salis was equally at home in French and German, and his name is often given in its French form, Jean-Rodolphe de Salis.

He studied first to be a journalist in Berlin and Paris, where he also acquired his history credentials and became a professor of history at the ETH in 1935. When war broke out in 1939, von Salis was given the task of reorganizing the federal press service. A universal scholar and a man of humane and liberal sympathies, he detested totalitarianism in whatever form it appeared, whether in Nazi Germany, Fascist Italy or Communist Russia. He began a regular radio broadcast to counter the lies and threats of Nazi propaganda minister Josef Goebbels. A man with a powerful vision of liberty, von Salis, in his *Voix du Pays* ("Voice of the Nation") broadcast and his articles in French, shored up the spirits of *Suisse Romande* even as his compatriot Karl Meyer stiffened the courage and will to resist of German-speaking Swiss.

These illustrious professors of the ETH were not the only sources of encouragement for the Swiss during the dark days of the Third Reich, when it seemed no one could resist the German onslaught. Swiss determination to defend their independence was widespread and flowed from many sources, not least of which was the army itself, personified in the steadfastness of its commander-in-chief, General Henri Guisan. Nevertheless, Karl Meyer and Jean Rudolf von Salis contributed significantly to the determination to resist at all costs. Both are remembered as heroes of *la défense spirituelle*.

PART III
THE ETH IN THE MODERN AGE

CHAPTER NINE

The Acceleration of Science 1955–2005

In 1955, the ETH celebrated its first hundred years, and both the institution and Swiss people could reflect on a spectacular record of success. Created as an experiment by Swiss risk-takers during the onset of the industrial age, the school had gone on to educate and employ some of the most famous names in the history of science. Their achievments had been impressive indeed.

The centennial year 1955 also marked one of those transition periods when the world stood on the cusp of a new era. The first half of the 20th century, with its progress in so many areas, had been torn apart by two devastating world wars and a global economic depression; but now, at least in the West, people thought that at last a freer and more hopeful world was possible. By 1955, Europe had begun to emerge from the destruction of World War II. The Germans called their recovery the *Wirtschaftwunder* ("economic miracle") because the country bounced back so quickly during the 1950s. America's Marshall Plan encouraged a focus on purely economic growth, and U.S. forces maintained a protective defense umbrella for the entire continent.

Though Switzerland escaped, with a few exceptions, bombing and shelling, it was poor and exhausted after the war. Surrounded by Axis powers, their trade routes blockaded at sea, their resources going to a massive defense buildup, the Swiss had been forced to plow their yards and parks for potato gardens, acquire a taste for hare (since all other meat was rationed) and live in the cold since the supply of imported coal, the day's primary heating fuel, was all but cut off. Education and research were not at the top of Switzerland's priorities.

After the war defense spending did not go away. When the Iron Curtain dropped and the reality of the Cold War replaced initial postwar optimism, the Swiss both continued their neutrality and retained their military in a state of readiness. Their disdain of Communism was just as clear and deep as their disdain of the Nazis. On principle, however, Switzerland stayed out of NATO, the UN, and the European Economic Community. Research went on at the ETH, but there was little money to fund the larger laboratory installations that science increasingly required.

Meanwhile across the Atlantic, the United States—alone among the great powers—emerged from the war with its infrastructure not only intact but immeasurably strengthened. The "arsenal of democracy" had become the world's economic powerhouse and, with the influx of European science refugees, rapidly was becoming the center of postwar research activity as well. The projects that had been undertaken at secret wartime locations flowed over into new university and corporate labs.

American universities came alive, as did an intellectually hungry generation of soldiers returned from the war. In 1944 the U.S. Congress passed the "G.I. Bill," which allowed millions of former soldiers to attend college with government-funded tuition. This was a brilliant stroke for the U.S., because not only had the country moved from a Depression-wracked, largely rural populace to a burgeoning manufacturing economy, but the government had used its increased tax base to propel millions of young men into higher education. America's colleges and universities, whose enrollments had fallen drastically during the Depression and the war, now had an influx of fully-funded students. Wartime projects had turned out a harvest of new technologies which could be turned to civilian uses. Rebounding consumer demand, a treasure chest of new electronics, and an ongoing commitment to research lifted an entire generation into prosperity. American higher education took off.

The ETH did not lay dormant, but took on more of a purely

Swiss character during these years. Since its founding, the ETH had an international, but primarily German, faculty. Even its student body had a large number of non-Swiss. During and after the war that recruitment strategy fell apart. The best German scientists had either fled to the United States or were tainted by their wartime associations. Eastern Europeans were now trapped behind the Iron Curtain. But the Swiss at the ETH, superbly educated in chemistry, physics and mathematics before the war, remained keenly aware of the most important frontiers of scientific knowledge. Within a short time, extremely bright individuals began to lay long-term foundations for what was to be an ETH and a Swiss renaissance. One of this small group of thinkers was Vladimir Prelog, a Balkan refugee who had managed to get to Switzerland during the war.

An organic chemist by training, Prelog was born in Sarajevo. He studied at the Czechoslovakian Institute of Technology in Prague and, in 1935, accepted appointment at the University of Zagreb in Croatia. When German tanks rolled into Zagreb in 1941, Prelog was able to make his way to Switzerland, where he became a professor at the ETH. In the decades following the war, Vladimir Prelog was one of those rare individuals able to assess the new world of science. More importantly, he came up with—and convinced others of—concrete strategies that would allow his ETH to establish a leadership position in the new sciences. As for his own research, Prelog, together with John Comforth of Britain, would go on to win a Nobel Prize in chemistry in 1975.

Indeed, in the path of Einstein, the ETH continued to produce geniuses on the frontiers, researchers in fundamental ideas, who had broad impact across the whole of science, and ultimately across the whole of society. Typical was Karl Alexander Müller. Born in 1927 in Basel, he entered the ETH at the age of 19 to study nuclear physics. It was the first year after Hiroshima, and he later called it the "atom bomb semester," because his physics class in 1946 was three times larger than it had been the year before. Müller eventually won a Nobel Prize for breakthroughs in superconductivity.

It is a sad fact that our modern wars, as numbing and destructive as they have been, have also accelerated the development of technology—both increasing the potential for good and putting the potential for evil deeds on a whole new scale. World War II brought stunning advances in rocket technology, radar, sonar, medicine, chemistry, communications and optics, not to mention organizational techniques and the mass processing of information. The ultimate breakthrough, of course, was the unleashing of the power of the atom according to theories first put forward by ETH-trained Albert Einstein.

The year 1955 was a turning point. West Germany joined NATO, prompting the Soviet Union to form its own military alliance, the Warsaw Pact. Nuclear strategy was now part of the equation, and Switzerland, the source of so much theory and application in atomic physics, remained both neutral and at the geographic center between the two blocs. But as the threat of long-range bombers and missiles became every day more real, the positive side of atomic energy also came into focus. In 1955 a consortium of European nations established a research institute in nuclear physics. And Switzerland—the sole nation in Europe that had withheld its participation in foreign wars for 500 years—was chosen to host the endeavor.

THE ETH AND CERN

At Geneva on June 10, 1955, an ETH physicist named Felix Bloch presided over the Foundation Stone Ceremony of an organization called CERN, a new experiment in international scientific cooperation. Decided upon by eleven European governments the previous September, it would be the first joint European nuclear research facility. The ETH's Dr. Bloch was named its Director General.

One aspect of the ETH that constantly amazes foreigners is the shrewd balance the school has achieved between purely theoretical knowledge and real-world applications. Of course, the ETH started as a practical school for the Swiss nation. But in today's world, that balance is well demonstrated in the school's productive relationship with CERN, today one of the world's leading research institutions—in fact, *the* leading institution in sub-atomic physics. CERN is an acronym for the French version of the European Organization for Nuclear Research (*Conseil Européenne pour la Recherche Nucléaire*), and among other superlatives, boasts the world's largest particle physics center.

At CERN's facility just outside Geneva, physicists come to explore what matter is made of and what forces hold it together. The institution is in essence a platform for the tools necessary to nuclear researchers, including nuclear accelerators that bring atomic and sub-atomic particles to nearly the speed of light, and detectors to make the particles visible.

Today this first European joint venture includes 20 member states. It is one of the world's premier sites for the search for fundamental knowledge at the sub-atomic level. Almost as a sideline, it was CERN which, in conjunction with the U.S. Advanced Projects Research Agency, developed the World Wide Web, originally designed to speed information sharing among physicists working in different universities and institutes around the world.

Though international in scope, CERN is still a decidedly Swiss operation, and its heart is brilliant people. The first Director General, a physicist of the new atomic generation, Felix Bloch, was born in Zürich in 1905 and graduated from the ETH, worked in both Europe and the United States, and went on to win the 1952 Nobel Prize in Physics. At the ETH, Bloch started out in engineering, but soon switched to physics. He attended courses by Chemistry Nobelist Peter Debye and other notables through whom he became acquainted with the new theories of quantum mechanics, and he continued his studies in theoretical physics with Walter Heisenberg at the University of Leipzig, where he earned a Ph.D. in 1928 with a dissertation dealing with the quantum mechanics of electrons in crystals and developing the theory of metallic conduction. Thereafter, this international Swiss took various assistantships and fellowships, primarily in Germany, which gave him the opportunity to work with Pauli, Heisenberg, Bohr, and Fermi, and to undertake theoretical studies of solid-state electronics as well as of the stopping power of charged particles.

Following Hitler's ascension to power, Bloch left Germany in

1933, and a year later he accepted a position at Stanford University in Palo Alto, California. There, working with a simple neutron source, he determined that a direct proof for the magnetic moment of the free neutrons could be obtained through the observation of scattering in iron. In 1936, he published a paper in which the details of the phenomenon were worked out and in which he described how it could lead to the production and observation of polarized neutron beams. The further development of these ideas led him in 1939 to an experiment at the cyclotron at UC Berkeley, in which the magnetic moment of the neutron was determined within an accuracy of about one percent.

During the years of World War II, Bloch was also engaged in the early stages of the work on atomic energy at Stanford University and Los Alamos, and later in countermeasures against radar at Harvard University. Through this work he became acquainted with the modern developments in electronics which, in conjunction with his earlier work on the magnetic moment of the neutron, opened the door to a new approach toward the investigation of nuclear moments.

In 1954, Bloch took a leave of absence from Stanford and returned to Switzerland to serve for one year as the first Director General of CERN in Geneva. Brilliant minds like those of Felix Bloch set the tone for physics at the ETH. There is no more elite club.

CERN's breakthroughs are many and legendary. One of the first achievements of CERN's first accelerator in the 1950s—a 600 mega-volt proton Synchro-Cyclotron—was the long-awaited confirmation of the decay of a pion into an electron and a neutrino. Needless to say, the existence of the neutrino had been predicted by ETH physicist Wolfgang Pauli in a 1930 hypothesis.

Today CERN houses the world's largest particle physics laboratory, though it may recently have become even more famous from author Dan Brown's best-selling novel, *Angels & Demons*. (CERN's current website has a playful true-or-false section concerning the novel's suggestion that it is trying to rule the world.) CERN's most significant upcoming project is a Large Hadron Collider (LHC), due to come on-line in 2007. This device will probe deeper into matter than ever before possible.

BREAKTHROUGHS IN MICRO-IMAGING

During the postwar era, researchers at the ETH Zürich began to explore new fields of research that could hardly have been imagined even a decade earlier. The first was the area of medical micro-imaging—with the electron microscope and, later, nuclear magnetic resonance (NMR) imaging devices. With the cold cathode electron microscope, the Swiss took an entirely new path, with attempts by private firms tied to ETH labs as early as 1940. With their background in chemistry and pharmacology, the Swiss were in an excellent position to turn the advances in electronics and experimental techniques to the purposes of basic science.

Hans-Heinrich Günthard took the initiative in these efforts. A Professor of Physical Chemistry at the ETH, Günthard and Nobel Prize winner Leopold Ruzicka convinced the administration to use inventions made in the U.S. during the war to advance chemical research at the ETH. The first devices—infrared- and nuclear resonance spectrometers—were assembled by Günthard and his co-workers at the Zürich campus at the beginning of the 1950s.

Working closely with U.S. labs and spin-off firms, Günthard and ETH doctoral candidate Richard Ernst—later a Nobel Prize winner—together with Weston Anderson were able to increase the sensitivity of the NMR spectrometer by a factor of 100 in 1964.

In the mid-1970s, NMR specialists worked with ETH Professor of Biophysics Kurt Wüthrich to achieve a decisive breakthrough whereby two-dimensional Fourier Transformations could be applied to NMR spectroscopy. For the first time, the structure of proteins and nucleic acids could be observed in isolation and the biochemical processes as well as the molecular interactions of enzymes and genetic information systems could be studied in detail. Richard Ernst won the Nobel Prize for his work in this area in 1991, and Kurt Wüthrich in 2002. The first NMR imaging system was set up in 1986 at the Children's Hospital in Zürich.

Today advanced bio-imaging has been targeted as one of the ETH's key strategic goals, and the school is building infrastructure so that researchers throughout the ETH complex will be able to take advantage of the latest tools and techniques in this field.

THE FIRST COMPUTERS AT THE ETH

Another area where the ETH excelled was in the early development of programming machines and the computer. In their successful breaking of the German and Japanese communications codes, England and the United States had made great strides in both theory and practice—finding patterns in enormous amounts of encrypted data with mathematical analysis and machine-automated processing.

The extensive mathematical calculations necessary to create the first atomic bomb would also not have been possible without new math processing machines put in place at Los Alamos. Soon after the war, with the development of the vacuum tube, this processing moved to an electronic platform, and the first real electronic computers were constructed. Many of the world's leading physicists and mathematicians were involved in these developments, and they immediately recognized the revolutionary implications of automated calculations for complex problems for the sciences generally.

The Swiss may not have had immense resources, but they stayed on top of the science—the mathematics and physics upon which these new machines were being built. And since the Swiss were superb designers of precision tools, there seemed to be a natural marriage between theory and the technologies required for rapid progress in this new field.

As early as 1948, the ETH set up a new seminar on applied mathematics with the task of making "programmable processing" available at the school. Two years later, in 1950, Konrad Zuses' Z4 Relaiscomputer was up and running at the ETH. By 1957, the ERMETH research computer, completely built at the ETH, was installed. The ETH even had a computer with a graphic interface five years before the American Macintosh. The school's Institute for

Informatik developed the so-called Lilith computer at the Zürich campus between 1978 and 1980. Lilith could be controlled via a graphic, windows-type technology and a mouse, and was used at the ETH until 1990. Unfortunately, the attempt at commercialization—one of the first tries at lab-to-market development—was unsuccessful. But programming languages designed by 1959 ETH graduate Niklaus Wirth, including Pascal (1968–1972) and Modula, and later Oberon (1989), served in some respects as models for today's widely used Java (1995) and C+ languages.

Computers did not change the sciences at the ETH overnight, but as researchers in different disciplines were able to study the machines, they started coming up with exciting applications. The pace of developments increased, and there was a lively interchange between Swiss scientists and their European and American counterparts—in effect, the rapid globalization of a new technology.

Funding was key. The Cold War evolved into a competition in technology based on the arms race between the Soviet Union and the West. Although the Swiss were neutral, they were by no means oblivious to the technology challenge. As early as 1952, the Swiss government saw the need, and a National Fund for Science (similar to the National Science Foundation in the U.S.) was established. A similar measure, proposed 10 years earlier, had met with cantonal opposition and been rejected. The ETH and universities throughout Switzerland were helped by the new fund. The ETH's core missions—teaching and academic research—continued to receive a federal appropriation, with supplemental funding for specific labs and cooperative projects coming from Swiss industry. The new National Fund gave the ETH money for strategic projects that went beyond core missions, especially those for which there was little hope of private sector funding.

SPUTNIK AND THE RESEARCH COUNTEROFFENSIVE

In 1957 the entire Western world got a wake-up call when the Soviet Union successfully launched the first earth-orbiting satellite. Was Soviet technology actually outperforming Western technology?

The lesson seemed to be that a massive nationally organized and funded science program was capable of producing results that the independent and uncoordinated organizations of the West could not. Whether one could call it panic or a new resolve, Western nations all took a new look at their science programs and education and decided that these areas were too important not to be aided and organized by the state.

For their part, Europeans, and the Swiss in particular, recognized a "technological gap" not only with the Soviet Union but with the rapidly changing U.S. They set out to catch up. By 1970, so ran one of the European plans of 1961, funding of science by Western European nations was to increase by 100 percent. Thus began the reformation crusade—ongoing today—to restructure existing European universities and to establish wholly new centers devoted to emerging fields of science.

During the 1960s, virtually every Western nation was pouring money into the sciences. There was also a new level of cooperation between government, technology-based corporations and university labs. This was the period when the whole theoretical and technological inheritance from 1905 through World War II began to be harvested. Virtually every existing scientific field began to blossom, and whole new areas of science began to be mapped out. It was the great research counteroffensive which fundamentally changed the world—and eventually played a major role in bringing down the Soviet Union.

The ETH also blossomed in the 1960s. The school rapidly became more international, instituted closer cooperation with U.S. universities, and was once more able to attract some of the world's best young scientists. Moreover, the planners at the ETH began to lay out strategic initiatives which would restructure the school to take advantage of the possibilities in the new sciences. In 1961, the first steps were taken to build a new science campus at Hönggerberg. In 1963, the School Council established a Research Center for Molecular Biology in Zürich, drawing on resources from both the ETH and the University of Zürich. An additional Institute for Molecular Biology was set up in Geneva that same year.

The initiatives in the emerging field of Molecular Biology were undertaken under the leadership of Professor Vladimir Prelog, who, as we have noted, arrived at the ETH in 1941. Prelog almost singlehandedly created the structure which resulted in Switzerland's leadership position in biology and life sciences. In fact it was his famous tract "What Is Microbiology" that convinced the School Council of the potential of the field. Prelog modestly discounted his leadership role as head of the ETH Organic Chemistry Lab. Reflecting on his career after becoming a Nobel laureate, he stated, "In becoming director of the Laboratory I reached, according to Peter's Principle, the level of my incompetence, and I tried hard for several years to step down." His wish was finally fulfilled by a system of rotating directors that allowed him to devote more of his personal time to research.

In 1964, the introduction of the electron microscope—a complex development involving both U.S. and Swiss scientists—allowed ETH researchers to study the structure and functions of live cells with astonishing clarity. This effort bore commercial fruit several years later when the Swiss firm Balzers AG was able to produce a successful version of the ETH-developed electron microscope. In 1965 the Federal Council requested that the ETH set up its own Institute for Molecular Biology and Biophysics. They also appropriated a 444 million Swiss franc credit for the school's further expansion.

The development of new areas of research and interdisciplinary initiatives put increasing pressure on the existing organization of the ETH. In 1969, the *Ecole Polytechnique Universitaire de Lausanne* was converted into a Federal Technical School (known henceforth as the EPFL) parallel to the ETH Zürich. It almost seemed as if too much was happening too fast . . . and it was.

THE 1969 REFERENDUM

Swiss students were slow in coming into the activist movements prominent in the late 1960s in both the United States and the rest of Europe. However, eventually the antiwar movement in the U.S., the huge demonstrations in Grosvenor Square, London, and the liberations of May 1968 in France caused Swiss students to question authority and power arrangements in their own country—in Swiss universities and Swiss society.

The "sixties," besides being a decade of fundamental change in science, were also the time of a wave of resistance to what was seen as the establishment—the government, corporations and universities. In 1964, the man who was to become the President of the Swiss Science and Technology Council, Max Imboden, diagnosed Switzerland as being in the throes of what he referred to as a "Helvetic Malaise." He argued that political questions were all too frequently represented as merely technological constraints, that the social elite lacked the will to play an active role, and that the country was drastically in need of reform. This judgment was not limited to the ETH, but the ETH provided a flashpoint.

In 1969, students were accusing the ETH of being elitist, of serving the interests of the rich and powerful rather than the interests of all the Swiss people. There were demonstrations, riots and "liberations" as student activists sought to make the ETH and its science somehow accountable to the public, and to force the members of the academic establishment to articulate their political stance. Students demanded a voice in the governance of the school and representation on policymaking bodies.

In a classic example of poor timing, all this upheaval came just at the point when a basic revision of the ETH-Law, the regulations governing the ETH, was brought forward. By the 1960s, with the alterations in the terrain of science, the ETH was desperately in need of organizational and funding changes. But the new law seemed to be an egregious example of the students—and Swiss society—not being consulted or even informed about what was happening at the ETH.

The federal government's position on the ETH depended in large part on how funding of the ETH would impact funding for the cantonal universities. In 1962 the Federal Council had commissioned a panel of experts to determine whether the cantons were in a position to finance their universities with their own funds. The expert report in 1964 concluded that the resources of the cantons alone were insufficient, and recommended that the federal government prepare an integrated model for financing the universities at the national level. Based on the report, the federal government in 1966 began to provide significant contributions to the cantonal universities. In 1968, there followed a development plan that would place these appropriations on a secure legal basis and deal with questions of organization and fund apportionment. That's where the trouble started.

The new ETH-Law became a lightning rod to student opposition, and the ETH student organization—the VSETH—took the extraordinary step of initiating a nationwide referendum on the issue. Such a referendum required 30,000 signatures. Students boarded trains and buses, canvassed railway stations and went door to door, widely surpassing the required 30,000 names. The ETH-Law was subjected to a referendum and on June 1, 1969, the public turned down the revision decisively by a vote of almost two to one.

The whole restructuring of the ETH went into limbo. There were inquiry commissions, consultations, endless meetings on the nature of responsibility of science in society, but very little was actually accomplished from an organizational perspective. The ETH went on and the structure changed on its own without institutional guidelines. Much was simply put on hold.

The referendum vote, however, represented a fundamental turn in the attitudes of Swiss students. Prior to that year, for the most part, the Swiss student organizations were seen as protecting the interests of Swiss—as opposed to foreign—students. They were culturally conservative and tended to push the administration to hold the line on non-Swiss admissions and hiring. With the 1969 move to the left, the student organizations became international—at times to the point of seeming, to the older generation, anti-Swiss. Students linked their interests to their own generation and contemporary worldwide concerns. Their political posture often reflected a radical rejection of the world of their parents. Their attitudes were based on anti-Vietnam War sentiment, solidarity with the developing world, the campaign against nuclear energy and nascent environmental concerns. In any case, the change was significant. When, for instance in 1974, the Swiss government attempted to restrict the number of foreigners coming into Switzerland, there was massive opposition from students. There was an anti-Western, anti-establishment and even anti-technology feeling in the air.

Ironically, for all the ruckus, the number of foreign students at the ETH, which earlier had been as high as 60 percent, since 1963 has hovered at around 20 percent until quite recently. At least that's the case at the undergraduate level. Only in the recent decade has there been a coordinated attempt to recruit students abroad. At the graduate level, the percentage of non-Swiss professors and postgraduate students is conspicuously higher, since it has been, at least since Prelog, an essential strategy of critical growth departments to seek out the best young talent—wherever it can be found.

The turmoil of the late 1960s continued into a more general questioning of the direction and use of science itself and the apportioning of scientific resources. The new world was *terra incognita*. Everything was changing. The prosperity of the West stood in stark contrast to the distress of the undeveloped world. These conflicts and questions, obscured for a time within the shadows of the Cold War, were to emerge later and with greater urgency after the collapse of the Communist threat.

A FLOURISHING OF NEW DISCIPLINES

The turmoil of the 1960s, once feared to be a permanent state of affairs, began to abate nearly as quickly as it had begun, as the various disintegrations frightened even young people into preferring a more stable environment for their future. One might add that once the sixties generation began to have children of their own they by no means wished the same sort of cultural anarchy on their offspring.

Though the era left a permanent stamp on Western culture, the world began to get back to business. For the ETH this meant, among other achievements, a return to collecting Nobel Prizes, a total of seven between 1975 and 2002.

Vladimir Prelog's 1975 award, which we have previously noted, was followed by a Nobel Prize in Medicine for Werner Arbor, a Swiss citizen who entered the ETH in 1949 and studied under the great Paul Scherrer. Dr. Arbor became a Nobel laureate for his work in molecular genetics, including the discovery of enzymes that break down the larger molecules of DNA into identifiable pieces.

In 1986 Heinrich Rohrer, who studied under Wolfgang Pauli, shared the Physics Nobel for his work on electron microscopes, which he and his co-winner termed Scanning Tunneling Microscopy. Their invention permits imaging of matter as small as 100 Angstroms. The following year, Karl Alexander Müller of Basel—who enrolled in the ETH during the "atom bomb semester"—shared the prize with a younger German colleague, Georg Bednorz, who earned his Ph.D. in Physics from the ETH. They won the 1987 Nobel for breakthrough work in the important new field of superconductivity, especially in nonferrous ceramic materials.

Richard Ernst was the 1991 Chemistry Nobelist for pioneering work in the use of nuclear magnetic resonance spectroscopy as a highly precise measuring method. Ernst, whose ancestors had lived around Winterthur since the 15th century, took an interesting route to the field of chemistry. He had originally wished to become a musician, but at age 13 discovered an old box in his attic filled with chemicals collected by a deceased uncle who had been a metallurgical engineer. Young Ernst became fascinated by mixing the chemicals, frequently frightening his parents with accidental explosions and releases of poison gas. In his case the labs of ETH were surely a safer way to funnel his curiosity.

To crown the ETH's achievement in the field of nuclear magnetic resonance, which has resulted, among other things, in the development of the MRI as a medical detection device, ETH Professor Kurt Wüthrich shared the Nobel in 2002 with an American and a Japanese. His contribution was in perfecting the NMR technique and applying it to reveal the three-dimensional structures of biological molecules suspended in solution.

As an illustration of the saying "it's a small world," or at least a small country, it's interesting to note that Dr. Wüthrich's family owned the famous Bären Inn outside of Bern. It was at the Bären at the height of World War II that General Henri Guisan, commander-in-chief of the Swiss Army, held his controversial meeting with the head of SS Foreign Intelligence, Walter Schellenberg. It was at this secret meeting that Guisan affirmed to the Germans in person that Switzerland would defend itself to the death against any invader. At the time, the General could not know if Switzerland would survive the war, much less become a highly prosperous nation and a leader in global science in the latter half of the 20th century. And if he had happened to see a five-year-old playing near the Bären Inn during his famous meeting, he would not of course have recognized the future Dr. Wüthrich, currently the latest in an impressive stream of Nobel laureates from the ETH.

THE PHARMACEUTICAL RENAISSANCE

Switzerland has been a major force in the development of new medicines for over a century. Switzerland's success has been due to its well-established pharmaceutical industry, but this innovative capacity is now being supplemented by a burgeoning biotech industry.

Swiss pharmaceutical multinationals are primarily based in Basel, but they've long had close relationships with ETH labs. The early exchange of research methods and findings during the 19th century focused on chemistry and particularly on dyes, immune antibodies and other physiologically active agents that would react with disease-causing organisms. In 1906, Paul Ehrlich, following more than a decade of research, articulated the concept that synthetic chemicals could selectively kill or immobilize parasites, bacteria and other invasive disease-causing microbes. His ideas would eventually drive a massive industrial research program that continues to the present. Swiss companies—names like Hoffmann-La Roche, Ciba, Geigy, and Sandoz—were the first to turn their knowledge of chemistry into the production of medications on an industrial basis.

ETH chemists and pharmacy researchers were involved from

the start. The breakthroughs are too numerous to name. Vitamin C was the first vitamin to be artificially synthesized in 1935, a process invented by Dr. Tadeusz Reichstein of the ETH. Swiss research labs —both corporate and academic—have made enormous progress in the treatment of illness, including infectious diseases, childhood diseases, some types of cancer, cardiovascular disease, diabetes, mental illness and hepatitis. Today, pioneering developments like the DNA chip tell whether an individual metabolizes a drug faster or more slowly as a result of genetic make-up. The chip provides information that can aid the selection and dosage of a range of medications, and it's been estimated that use of the chip test before treatment could improve overall efficacy by 10–20% and avoid 10–15% of all serious side effects for many common problems.

In the past few years, the pharmaceutical industry, including fertilization for agriculture and flavors for food—has become more important than ever to the Swiss economy, and the Swiss are working hard to maintain their position. The industry employs close to 26,000 people within Switzerland, brings in export earnings, and links the country with burgeoning health care demand all over the world. The internal Swiss market is relatively small, and as a result Swiss companies have concentrated heavily on foreign markets. Today, according to figures from the World Trade Organization, Switzerland is ranked eighth among the world's exporters of chemical and pharmaceutical products—an astonishing fact given the size of the country. Moreover, Novartis and Roche now operate no less than seven large research centers outside Switzerland, these being located in the U.S., Great Britain, Japan and Germany.

The Pharmacy School at the ETH was, at the founding, the first such school in Switzerland, but it was housed within the Chemistry section until 1908. In 1916 a Pharmacy Institute was established, and that organization continued until the restructuring experiments at the ETH in the 1990s. In 1999, Pharmacy became the Department of Applied Biosciences, reflecting the strategic evolution of the traditional "pharmacy" to "pharmaceutical sciences," which had occurred with the appointment of new professors in the area of life sciences during the 1990s. At this time, a separate institute—the Institute for Pharmaceutical Sciences, or IPW—was established. Three years later, in January 2003, autonomous departments were set up at the ETH and the Department of Pharmacy was combined with the existing institutes of chemistry to form a new Department of Chemistry and Applied Biosciences. The new unit brought together the IPW, the Institute for Chemical and Bioengineering Sciences, as well as the Research Laboratories for Inorganic Chemistry (HCI), Organic Chemistry and Physical Chemistry. New research opportunities were coming on line so fast the school has had to scramble to keep up with continually evolving traditional disciplines while accommodating new ones.

Since 2004, the IPW was moved to the new Hönggerberg campus, where it is once more in the same building as the other institutes of the Department of Chemistry and Applied Biosciences, and close to the Institute for Microbiology.

Today the IPW consists of 10 research units with 140 researchers—of which over 90 are doctoral candidates from 10 nations. Approximately 300 students are enrolled in pharmaceutical science programs, and of these roughly 50 each year finish their studies by taking the federal pharmacy exam. The research strategy in the institute today is one of "from concepts to prototypes" overing a broad range of research areas from target identification to the development of novel therapeutics. The IPW maintains close associations with a number of institutes at the ETH, as well as the Functional Genomics Center Zürich, the University of Zürich and, via the Center for Pharmaceutical Sciences, the University of Basel.

The ETH is at the forefront of new imaging techniques both for research and healing. In 2005, a preclinical PET (Positron Emission Tomography) unit was being installed at the new Imaging Center at Hönggerberg, to complement the PET Center already in place at the University Hospital of Zürich. The new HCI building at Hönggerberg had also become the new permanent home of the ETH Pharmacological Collection (the Hartwich Collection) along with the historical collections of the ETH's former Department of Chemistry.

THE ETH AS "THE FUTURE MACHINE"

The ETH family, and the Swiss more generally, often refer to their revered institution as *die Zukunftsmaschine*, literally "the future machine," by which they mean a knowledge system for "incubating the future." This theme is reflected in the 150th Jubilee celebrated in 2005 at the ETH under the name "Welcome Tomorrow." The school is justly proud of its history, but modern science is too complex and unfolds too rapidly for anyone to spend too much time looking backward. The excitement at the ETH in the 21st century is directed not at the past, illustrious as it is, but at how the school will change over the next several decades while maintaining its excellence and returning benefits appropriate to the investment the Swiss have made in the institute. The Swiss financial center, its reinsurance industry and its international pharmacy industry will be well served by the ETH's forward-looking policies.

Long-term planning, however, is an educated guess at best. Any generation can be blindsided by the future. Policies being put in place today will have a foreseeable effect in the coming decades; but beyond that, no one can know for certain what outcomes may ensue. What will be important in 2030 or what changes we humans will encounter then are doubtless already in the air, unperceived. Inevitably, historians will look back on the present and smile—or perhaps frown—and say, "Why, they had no idea!"

Nevertheless, to the extent that planners can chart a path into the future, the ETH is investing in four areas for its development in the 21st century:

1. *Information Sciences*—the key to this century, just as steam was key in the 19th century and electricity was in the 20th. A leading example is the three-dimensional virtual reality and the 3-D community, in which images are de-constructed, digitized and transmitted into a virtual reality. This is one of the most ambitious programs ever undertaken at the ETH, called "Blue-C" and "Red Hell," and located at the Hönggerberg campus.

2. *Life Sciences*—in which fundamental breakthroughs will occur in both medical and technical areas. Life sciences now embrace "systems biology" that quantifies biological systems from a molecular standpoint, and is the base of the ETH's new Master's program in bio-engineering. Further emphasizing the ETH's commitment to this field, in 2005 a developmental biologist was named the new President of ETH Zürich, Professor Ernst Hafen.

3. *Living and Cultural Space*—the shaping of the environment in which we live, or what the Swiss call "*Stadt und Landschaft*," in an increasingly urban and globalized world. This area includes geology and earth science—for example, groundbreaking (so to speak) research on mega-tsunamis (earthquake-induced ocean waves). Every research institution worthy of the name is, or will be, working on ocean-warning systems to prevent or better forewarn of another tragedy like the disaster of the December 2004 tsunami.

4. *Energy*—in a broad sense, including natural resources and what the Swiss refer to as environmental sustainability. An example is laser physics. The ETH was a major contributor to early laser development and will continue to lead in the field.

In addition to these general categories of focus, it may be instructive to note some of the specific projects under way as the ETH helps lead the way during the 21st century:

The Next Generation of Aircraft Turbines. A team of ETH experts in fluid dynamics, led by the young Iranian-American head of the Department of Mechanical and Process Engineering, was making breakthroughs in the design of the next generation of jet turbine engines, which promise to give more power, use less fuel, reduce pollutants and be more reliable than current engines.

Nanopower—New Paths to Energy. ETH engineers, in collaboration with physics researchers from the ETH's Paul Scherrer Institute, have developed a way to create electricity from water. Fuel cells generate pollutant-free electricity by a controlled oxygen-hydrogen reaction based on an efficient solar thermochemical cycle to split water by means of metallic nanoparticles. The process has the potential of achieving an energy conversion efficiency of over 40 percent, pointing the way to lower costs and increased economic competitiveness. The hydrolysis process and associated reactor technology have been patented by ETH and are currently being optimized using computational fluid dynamics and nanoparticle-formation models.

Whole Systems Biology—A New Swiss Network. ETH Zürich and the Universities of Basel and Zürich are cooperating to develop SystemX, a data-intensive systems biology network which aids scientists in the study of complex biological systems using an integrated interdisciplinary approach. SystemX combines resources from biology, physics, mathematics, computational science, chemistry, information technology, biotechnology and nanotechnology groups within a flexible new organization to use state-of-the-art computing and bio-imaging to study complex systems. The Swiss pharmaceutical industry has been a notable innovator in this area for decades.

Earthquake Research—A Joint Swiss–U.S. Project. A group of researchers from the Swiss Seismological Service at the ETH and the U.S. Geological Survey has presented a method that takes the science and art of earthquake prediction a step further. It enables scientists to continuously assess the hazard situation after a major earthquake in California, for example, and predict the risk of further quakes. The Swiss–U.S. research team discovered that—when one has enough recorded data of earlier occurrences—aftershock patterns can be used as tools to assess the probability of further quakes occurring in a given area during the next 24 hours. This is a very relevant field for the large and highly successful Swiss reinsurance industry.

An Atomic Microscope the Size of a Fingernail. In 2004, researchers at the ETH succeeded in putting an atomic microscope with remarkable functionality on a 7–10mm CMOS chip. Besides micro-mechanics to aid measurement, the tiny chipscope includes all the necessary electronics for processing the signal. Such microscopes have long been used to measure strands of DNA or to create tiny transistors. This new device is capable of processing 16 million arithmetic operations per second, so that it can literally "run itself," making positioning adjustments without outside intervention. It is capable of detecting differences in depth as little as one nanometer (a billionth of a meter) and the monitoring of biological processes at an unbelievably small scale.

THE ETH AND NUCLEAR ENERGY

In a tiny wine-growing village at the foot of the Geissberg in Canton Aargau, roughly halfway between Zürich and Basel, lies one of the most advanced research facilities in Europe, indeed in the world. The Paul Scherrer Institute (PSI) is one of the six pillars of today's Greater ETH and is where some of the most fundamental research in Switzerland is undertaken. In a whole series of areas, the PSI stands on the frontier of science in this century.

Dr. Ralph Eichler, current Director of the PSI, cites a few of them: "We are interested in how warm supraconductors work, the existence of a new boson particle called Higgs, or the mechanism of omnipresent friction. For this we have to develop new experimental methods that are then used in other areas of science and technology, at the PSI or elsewhere, such as, for example, determining the structure of proteins or cancer therapy with protons."

Today, the PSI is abuzz with nanotechnology, the new biology, and the future of energy. Many of its projects are pure science, the benefits of which may not be realized for decades. But the PSI is also deeply immersed in studies that are relevant to the contemporary world. One of the most important has been the development of nuclear energy as a source of electricity.

The reader may recall that the Swiss discovered how to harness the power of flowing water to generate electricity in the late 19th century. But even Switzerland's abundant water power proved insufficient to meet its demand for electric power, which has grown at about two percent per year since 1980. As early as the 1960s, Swiss planners realized that their hydroelectric resources would not be able to handle the projected needs. When planners saw that Swiss hydro sources would not be able to meet the demand, they turned initially to the option of coal- and oil-fired plants. But environmental groups and others opposed such plants on the grounds they would compromise the hitherto clean generation of power. As a result, the government provided incentives to utilities to develop nuclear power, and Switzerland began working on the design and development of nuclear reactors almost from the beginning of this emerging technology.

The promise of nuclear power was the driving force in the creation of the ETH's Paul Scherrer Institute. During the 1950s and early 1960s, Scherrer, a popular and influential Professor of Theoretical Physics at the ETH, and Walter Boveri, President of the world-famous Brown Boveri Company located in Baden, Switzerland, founded a company called Reaktor AG which pursued the industrial development of nuclear energy technology. Unfortunately, the prototype reactor was a failure. By 1957, Swiss nuclear research succesfully employed a small (10 megawatt) American-made research reactor until their own Swiss-built research reactor (30 MW) came online in 1960. Still, the Swiss were temporarily balked in their dream of their own reactor that could generate significant amounts of power.

Despite the initial failure, Scherrer and Boveri continued to be closely involved in reactor research and controlled the research center which operated both Swiss research reactors. Their technological acumen and persistence finally paid off, and it was not long before the country's first commercial light-water reactors began operating. Today Switzerland enjoys a total capacity of 3,220 MW of electricity from its five reactors.

In 1960 the Swiss government took over the nuclear research center and in 1988 restructured it as the Paul Scherrer Institute. It has remained a world-class sub-atomic nuclear research center ever since. In recent years, the PSI's expensive, state-of-the-art infrastructure has allowed the institute to delve into a host of related fields involving atomic structures. Today, the PSI is composed of six research labs sharing large-scale facilities. They cover much of what is happening in contemporary research—synchronotron radiation and nano-technology, condensed matter research with neutrons and muons, particles and matter, life sciences, nuclear energy and safety, and general energy. The institute remains a fitting tribute to the ETH's Paul Scherrer, who almost personally shaped the field of nuclear energy in Switzerland.

Despite its obvious benefits, nuclear energy remains a controversial issue in Switzerland. Its opponents have tried to block it by means of a constitutional amendment through referenda, at both the federal and cantonal levels. At the federal level there have been five popular initiatives of this type to date. In 1990, Swiss voters accepted an initiative banning the construction of new nuclear plants for ten years. In 1999, opponents organized two new initiatives. The first one aimed at an extension of the moratorium on new plants until 2010. The other called for the decommissioning of all five Swiss reactors after a service life of 30 years, but both initiatives were rejected in the referendum of May 2003.

Perhaps public opposition was muted in part by progress, including work done at the PSI, in the design of so-called III and IV generation reactors—safer and more reliable than anything now in service. The world market for the design and service of such reactors is commercially huge, especially with global oil shortages and the absence of viable alternative sources of energy, especially in developing countries. The PSI, which is mandated to be forward-looking and market-oriented as part of Switzerland's "re-industrialization," cannot afford to overlook the economic potential of nuclear power. But at the same time, the institute must be sensitive to legitimate concerns of citizens in Switzerland as well as to the demands of media-savvy opposition groups that would readily block whole parts of PSI research. Much of the research is important, not just in the context of nuclear power but for the science-wide breakthroughs which flow from what is now a global and multi-disciplinary field.

Today, nuclear energy remains a politically explosive and polarizing issue all over the world. In that context, the Swiss story is a highly relevant and informative case study in a pivotal application of modern science. So that the value of crucial policy decisions not be lost—either the document trail or memories of participants—an innovative archival project was initiated in 1999 by Professor David Gugerli, head of the Institute for the History of Technology at the ETH Zürich. The research project, named "Nuclear Energy and Society," is an attempt to collect the records of this crucial period in Swiss history, which may offer insights to future generations that find themselves in parallel situations. The archives were begun informally in the 1990s by individuals at the PSI and in the nuclear industry who realized that the private papers of the pioneers of Swiss nuclear development, as well as records of the companies and institutes involved, might easily pass into oblivion. Thus, in a unique attempt to construct a useful historical resource before the record was fragmented or lost, Professor Gugerli sought to organize the collection for future research. The archive will almost certainly become a model for future case studies of the controversies surrounding nuclear power in the decades to come. It is a new marker in the history of science developed by the ETH.

Today nuclear power is but a part of the ETH's Paul Scherrer Institute. But nuclear energy research was the seed that grew into an entire harvest of modern breakthroughs. The scope of research at the PSI today is breathtaking, though much of what is being investigated or discovered in its labs will not be part of our daily lives for 10, 20 or even 50 years. The Paul Scherrer Institute contributes significantly to the ETH's reputation worldwide, and can rightly be called the flagship unit of this remarkable school.

CHAPTER TEN

New Visions of Architecture and Design

The ETH Architecture Department is one of the most prolific and well-known architecture schools in the world. Internationally renowned architects have taught there, and among those who have studied at the ETH can be counted some of the most innovative and influential working architects of our time.

Gottfried Semper (1803–1879), a German architect, art critic and professor of architecture fleeing the uprisings of 1848, was the founder of the Building School at the Federal Polytechnic in Zürich. It was Semper who designed the ETH's main building from 1861 to 1864, which would become the "city crown above Zürich" and at that time the most important building of the young Swiss federal state besides the House of Parliament in Bern. Upon his death in 1879, his students constructed a "Semper Museum," which in time grew to become the extensive Archive for Modern Swiss Architecture, known today as the gta Archive. This bequest and research library, with some 14,000 volumes and brochures, over 3,000 individual plans, and an enormous photograph and picture collection, houses the documentary record of Swiss architecture in the 19th and 20th centuries.

Following in Semper's footsteps was Gustav Gull, a Professor of Architecture at the ETH from 1900 to 1929, who designed the dome atop Semper's main building which now serves as a crowning landmark for all Zürich. Gull also designed the *Landesmuseum*, or National Museum of Switzerland, one of Zürich's most famous

197

attractions (as it stands across the street from the city's train station, it cannot be missed). This impressive building with its tall central tower is inspired by medieval fortress architecture. It manages to capture the power and majesty of the Middle Ages without sinking into caricature, as does, for example, the contemporaneous fairy-tale castle of Neuschwanstein in Bavaria.

New visions, however, based on changes in materials and design, began to transform the world of architecture in the late 19th and early 20th centuries. The ETH would play an important role in spreading the teachings of the Modern movement (the 1920s to 1970s), which brought a radical rejection of traditional ideas of beauty and hierarchies of the pre-industrial eras and promoted a new aesthetic of functionally efficient architecture, stripped of vir-tually all ornament.

This radically iconoclastic cultural shift coincided with the introduction of new materials and new mathematical understand-ing of how those materials could be combined. Ever-evolving instru-ments and techniques for calculating load, stress and compression enabled future-driven architects to strip design down to bare essen-tials. Buildings could be made more structurally efficient, industri-alized and rationalized for what was seen as a new age. Just as in the field of structural engineering, the plasticity of reinforced con-crete, the strength of steel and, eventually, the light-expanding mir-acle of plate glass could be integrated into magnificent sculptural forms placed in new relationships of space and landscape. Often monumental and abstract, the controversial new structures—as a matter of principle—were designed with minimal connection to the inherited traditions of architecture. Many were beautiful. Virtually all were consciously and aggressively innovative.

In Switzerland—and especially among the architecture gradu-ates of the ETH—there was an extraordinarily close connection between architectural design and the breakthroughs in structural engineering. ETH structural and materials engineers created the resources used by the designers. This, in fact, was the Swiss advan-tage: their architectural designs explored and enhanced the intrinsic characteristics of materials. And as good and careful workmen with an appreciation for quality, Swiss architects, just like Swiss engineers, soon took their talents out into the wider world. Their designs were daring, beautiful and efficient—often in a breathtaking combination. They offered entirely new solutions to age-old problems. And often Swiss innovations in design saved costs as well. As we have already seen, New York City's George Washington Bridge, completed in 1931, was a radically new design by Othmar Ammann which not only was more graceful but also cost far less than the massive structure proposed by one of the leading American bridge builders of the day.

Like a latter-day guild, the engineer/designers schooled at the ETH have created structures all around the world. They worked in France, Germany, England and, most of all, in the United States. The best big projects were offered where the money was. Moreover, architects are like artists. They create to be seen, and are drawn to cosmopolitan centers where culture is in ferment and new designs are venerated as dramatic status symbols of progress.

Before the founding of the ETH in 1855, Swiss architecture had evolved as a mix of local and classical streams. The landscapes reflected German, French and Italian predilections, always with unique Swiss embellishments. The most enduring emblems of Switzerland were the Swiss rural farmsteads, which have dotted the hillsides from time immemorial. They are simple, sturdy and well maintained, independent and often isolated in their picturesque settings.

Industrial factory architecture—simple, utilitarian and often ugly—began to intrude in the late 19th century, at the same time that concrete and steel transformed the design of railroads, bridges, roads and tunnels. Still, Switzerland remained a relatively poor country. Its strict, largely Reformation ethos was not attuned to grand gestures of pomp and circumstance. However, led by ETH engineers aggressively seeking out the future, the country's vanguard was soon carried into the maelstrom of modernism. Designers followed close behind, using newly developed technologies to produce the infrastructure for which Switzerland is justly famous.

ETH ARCHITECTURE AFTER WORLD WAR I

Abstraction, clarification, and the desire, particularly after World War I, to replace craft building with rational and industrialized structures rapidly moved into the architectural schools. Tradition was in large part left behind. The "new architecture" was strongly influenced by the stark, egalitarian geometries coursing through Germany and Austria. Yet Switzerland retained a strong appreciation for place, for structural beauty and for the underlying craftsmanship which the Swiss sought to integrate with modern industrial materials processing.

In 1928, the International Congress of Modern Architecture (CIAM) was founded in Switzerland by 24 architects. For nearly 30 years the Congress addressed the great questions of urban living, space and belonging. Their work had a tremendous influence on the shape of cities and towns the world over. Their main claim was that architecture could no longer exist in an isolated state separate from governments and politics, but that economic and social conditions would fundamentally affect the buildings of the future. As society became more industrialized, they said, architects and the construction industry had to rationalize their methods, embrace new technologies and strive for greater efficiency.

One of the founders and members of CIAM was Le Corbusier, one of the best-known and most influential Swiss architects, whose visions brought new rationality, economy and functionalism to homes and cities. Although he did not study at the ETH, he would become crucial in tying the Modern movement to Switzerland and in particular to the ETH through CIAM.

Another strong influence at the ETH was the Bauhaus school of industrial design, founded in Germany in 1919. Although in existence for only nine years, its influence on modern architecture and design had been immense, and many of its famous students and masters gave the Modern movement a philosophical, as well as practical, grounding in the volatile years of the early 20th century.

The aim of the Bauhaus was to heal the schism between the arts and the crafts, proclaiming that the ultimate aim of all creative activity is a building, which meant that students participated right from the start in building projects. Students were taught to be as proficient in artistic fields as in the technology of production. In addition, they often attended classes in photography, theater production, painting and design.

By implementing the Bauhaus introductory course first at the University of Texas in Austin, then at the ETH in Zürich, a special link and continuity was created between Switzerland and the U.S. This enabled the Modern movement to persist, prosper and establish its tradition in teaching methodology throughout the 20th century. Switzerland soon developed a reputation for welcoming innovative design and producing groundbreaking designers, many of whom passed through the ETH.

The impressive list of visiting professors at the ETH has since helped reinforce this path and enrich an already strong belief in the values of modernism: Aldo Van Eyck (b.1918), Kenneth Frampton (b.1928), Aldo Rossi (b.1931), Alberto Campo Baeza (b.1946), Antonio Ortiz Garcia (b.1947), Antonio Cruz Villalón (b.1948), Hans Kohlhoff, now a full professor at the ETH, and many others.

Swiss ETH and other architects were also instrumental in bringing European-inspired modernism to America. One of its earliest appearances was the Philadelphia Savings Fund Society (PSFS) building, completed in 1932, designed by William Edmond Lescaze, a Swiss architect who was graduated from the ETH in 1919 and immigrated to the United States the following year. The building's lack of historical ornament, its smooth and polished stone surfaces and its large planes of glass closely link it with the European Modern movement.

ETH ARCHITECTURE AFTER WORLD WAR II

The great international success of modern Swiss architecture since World War II stands in no relation to the country's small size. Peace, wealth and stability in Switzerland in the 20th century—in contrast to the rest of Europe—created a sense of longevity. Excellent craftsmanship, education and work ethic assured high production standards, and an understated Protestant aesthetic, pragmatism and attention to detail made for an attractive, serene style.

Switzerland escaped the physical devastation of the war. The Swiss came out of the nightmare earlier than the rest of Europe, and Swiss architects were also active in the United States. Cultural and economic exhaustion produced left-leaning governments in France, England and Italy, and with the onset of the Cold War, these were heady intellectual times in all the arts. The old forms seemed disgraced and in ruins. Governments wanted symbols that gave focus and hope. It is hardly surprising that the modernist schools of architecture swept the field with their theories of radical new beginnings and design cleansed of the past.

As economies were rebuilt, a mature and prosperous Europe finally re-emerged. Once more, there was money to be put into grand architecture, and during the 1960s there were enormous opportunities for architects worldwide as the ETH School of Architecture extended its reach.

From the immediate post–World War II era all the way to the 1970s, internationally recognized Swiss architects shaped the education of future generations of ETH students, who in their turn became renowned architects.

Early on, there were Alfred Roth and Bernard Hoesli (of the "Texas Rangers" group), who had worked at Le Corbusier's studio in Paris. In the early 1970s the ETH solidified its international reputation with teachers such as Luigi Snozzi, Dolf Schnebli and especially Aldo Rossi, who worked toward reasserting the autonomy of architecture in an age of commodity forms.

Influenced by these architects were Marie-Claude Bétrix, Santiago Calatrava, Roger Diener, Annette Gigon, Mike Guyer, Jacques Herzog, Pierre de Meuron, Peter Maerkli, Daniele Marques, Christian Sumi and many others.

During the mid-1970s, the ETH came into the international limelight with a new movement that emerged from Italian-speaking Ticino—the *Tendenza*. A group exhibition at the ETH titled "Tendenzen" attracted wide attention to the works of young Ticinesi architects. Mario Botta, Mario Campi and Franco Pessina,

Aurelio Galfetti, Flora Ruchat-Roncati, Luigi Snozzi and Livio Vacchini were the stars—combining Italian ideas of design with the simple traditional architecture of Ticino. The designs often sought to sustain and strengthen old village structures or to revitalize ancient sites with skillfully integrated new additions.

In the 1980s the so-called Analogue Architecture of Fabio Reinhart and Miroslav Sik at the ETH had significant impact. Reinhart's and Sik's approach sought to integrate design with the shapes and textures of local buildings. They were masters of capturing everyday spirit and atmosphere. Many of the younger Canton Grison architects, such as Andrea Deplazes, Dieter Jüngling and Valerio Olgiati, studied with Reinhart and Sik and continued to deepen the Analogue ideal.

CONTEMPORARY ETH ARCHITECTURE

One of the best-known Swiss architecture teams today is the Basel-based firm Herzog & de Meuron, which won the most prestigious of architectural honors, the Pritzker Prize, in 2001. In winning what is considered the profession's Nobel Prize, Herzog & de Meuron were chosen for "significant contributions to humanity and the built environment through the art of architecture." Combining seemingly irreconcilable styles such as minimalism and ornament, they often collaborate with contemporary artists; form and function characterize their work. Jacques Herzog and Pierre de Meuron, both born in 1950, are ETH classmates and graduates, now both professors at the ETH.

Herzog and de Meuron were responsible for two prize-winning projects in London: the redevelopment of the Bankside power station into the Tate Modern, and the design of the Laban Dance Centre. In the United States they created the de Young Museum of Art in San Francisco and the exquisite Dominus Winery in California's Napa Valley. Their current work includes the main stadium for the 2008 Olympics in Beijing. In fact, Swiss teams are currently active all over China providing expertise in restoration and urban planning in that rapidly changing nation.

Over recent decades, Ticino-born architect Mario Botta (b.1943), who at one time was an assistant to Le Corbusier and later to Louis Kahn in the U.S., has made a name for himself internationally with his bold designs. Botta is one of the most important representatives of the Ticino school and often uses the stone bricks typical of his native canton. His work characteristically shows respect for topographical conditions and regional sensibilities, and his designs emphasize craftsmanship and geometric order.

Botta's buildings include several churches, banks and museums in Switzerland and abroad. He designed the Museum of Modern Art in San Francisco and worked on the newly rebuilt La Scala Opera House in Milan. Much of his Swiss work is located in his native canton of Ticino, such as the bus terminal in Lugano. Botta never studied at the ETH but has taught at its sister institution, the Federal Polytechnic School in Lausanne, and a number of universities, and has been honored by many more.

Bernard Tschumi, another Swiss and a contemporary of Botta, is a former Dean of the Columbia Graduate School of Architecture, Planning and Preservation. Tschumi is an internationally renowned Swiss architect, educator and theorist who has exhibited widely in the U.S. and Europe and has published many essays and books.

After graduation from the ETH, he broke away from its teachings and began to explore architecture as a crossover of space, event and movement, developing new theories about forms of cohabitation and city planning. In 2005, he won a competition to design a luxury hotel and apartment tower in Beijing, China. In the U.S., he built the FIU School of Architecture at the Florida International University in Miami, completed in 2003, and he has undertaken the UC Athletic Center of Cincinnati Varsity Village.

The distinguished ETH architect and professor Dolf Schnebli (b.1928) has influenced many contemporary architects coming out of the ETH. He has won several competitions, and has built the Quartier Nord of the Federal Polytechnic School in Lausanne and the Swiss Re America headquarters in North Castle, New York, which was completed in 1996. He taught at Harvard, the Boston Architectural Association and other American universities. His firm s a m architects (Dolf Schnebli, Tobias Amman, Sacha Menz) is largely influenced by classic modernism, and is interested in quality room design, technical execution, ecology, economy and functionality.

One of Schnebli's disciples, Roger Diener, who with his father forms the Basel-based firm Diener & Diener, expanded the Swiss Embassy in Berlin by merging a new structure with a building that dates from the 19th century. Diener & Diener, which counts among its clients the most respected and internationally renowned architecture bureaus in Europe, are mainly interested in understanding the history and characteristics of building material. Among their commissions, they restored the Museum of Modern Art in Rome and the Architecture Museum in Basel.

Christian Sumi, like Diener, born in 1950 and another Schnebli disciple, taught at Harvard University. In 1984 he founded the architectural office Burkhalter + Sumi, which immediately gained recognition far beyond Swiss borders. Among its projects, the refurbishing and extension of the Hotel Zürichberg in 1995 brought the firm international acclaim. Burkhalter + Sumi's work is characterized by innovative use of timber, a sophisticated use of color which subtly reflects the influence of Le Corbusier, and the joining of elements to form convincing spatial sequences. Their buildings radiate clarity and harmony through their uncompromising modernity while simultaneously conveying a mysterious complexity.

The architecture firm Gigon/Guyer (Annette Gigon and Mike Guyer, who were born in 1959 and 1958, respectively) built the Ernst Ludwig Kirchner Museum, created to house the art of the German expressionist painter. The museum, located in the Alpine resort of Davos, is another example of efficient, clean and well-crafted forms using solid local and modern materials.

Foreign architects, such as Santiago Calatrava from Spain, took it upon themselves to pass Swiss graduate exams and learn the language in order to study at the ETH. Calatrava has been commissioned to design the Port Authority's World Trade Center Transportation Hub in New York City. This $2 billion project will feature a spectacular glass-and-steel Grand Point of Arrival that will become a major architectural landmark, welcoming tens of thousands of daily commuters. The station is scheduled to open in late 2009. Calatrava also built the Stadelhofen railway station in Zürich, a library at the University of Zürich, and a large part of the new City of Arts and Sciences of Valencia in Spain.

There are dozens of other contemporary Swiss architects who, in one way or another, passed through the ETH Zürich, including Michele Arnaboldi, Herbert Ehrenbold, Rene Hochueli, Daniele Marques and Ira Piattini. And, as an interesting twist, writer Max Frisch, one of Europe's major literary voices since 1955 (*Stiller, Homo faber*), obtained a diploma in architecture in 1941. Before he changed careers, Frisch designed, among other things, the Zürich Recreation Park.

THE ETH'S DEPARTMENT OF ARCHITECTURE TODAY

Today, the curriculum of the ETH Department of Architecture is closely integrated with complementary disciplines such as urban planning, civil engineering and the environmental sciences. The curriculum of future architects employs advanced computer-aided design (CAD) and imaging and includes instruction in all these areas. A wide cultural perspective is mandatory. There are no longer to be ivory-tower architects designing single structures in isolation. Rather the new program involves creative interaction between art, science and engineering. It sets out to tackle broad problems generated by society. This is a vastly broader mandate than in the past.

The united disciplines housed within this new architecture are charged with producing innovative solutions that face up to what many Swiss consider the most important challenge of our time: guaranteeing what they refer to as a "sustainable environment." Decreasing exploitation of natural resources by making greater use of renewable, recyclable resources; using ecologically compatible building materials, products and components; increasing the energy efficiency of buildings; and improving technologies and construction processes are all issues that are being carefully researched and implemented. The research is wide-ranging and long-term, increasingly multidisciplinary and explicitly international. Today, solutions designed for Shanghai or Caracas complement those designed for Basel or Bern.

THE HÖNGGERBERG CAMPUS

A primary example of the broad urban-planning approach to architecture is the new ETH campus coming together at Hönggerberg just outside of downtown Zürich. The ETH's original building was designed by Gottfried Semper, and the classical structures on the hill overlooking the Limmat River in Zürich still form the heart of the ETH. Science City, the newest development at the Hönggerberg parallel campus, has been created through a major design competition. Kees Christiaanse, a Dutch architect and a professor at the ETH since 2003, has emerged as the winner. The competing plans—which nicely illustrated the whole open-ended problem of designing a "campus for the future"—have been part of an ETH exhibit that attracted much attention when shown in Berlin and Barcelona.

As guiding principles the designs were to embody a sensitivity toward the diverse requirements of the university while creating a campus with a "decidedly European character." The design will also attempt to set new standards in the considerate use of resources—ground, energy and funds.

In terms of the school's diverse, and seemingly contradictory, requirements, Science City is to be a world-class research facility hosting an international faculty and student body of nearly 10,000 without being elitist or appearing remote from the Swiss public, and without undermining or displacing the original campus. Moreover, it should fit into its setting without disrupting local communities or sensitive wildlife environments. It should be modern and corporate-efficient without setting itself up as another alienating corporate headquarters. The project should move quickly, yet be exhaustively planned. And it should be a symbol and showplace for the future of Switzerland without appearing overproud or jarring.

A campus with a "decidedly European character" is another challenge, since many European universities remain housed in picturesque old student towns—Heidelberg, Cambridge, Oxford or Zürich. The point is to avoid cutting the campus off from its surroundings, thereby creating a new ivory tower. There is also to be student and staff housing within the campus to foster a lively and inviting atmosphere around the clock—in effect a comfortable and complete little town where people will be happy to live and work. The watchwords are "multi-faceted, accessible and open."

"Considerate use of resources," besides being a code expression for holding the line on costs, refers to a central tenet of the contemporary ETH and European thought—a sustainable environment. Not always clearly defined, sustainability refers to the widely shared conviction that modern societies and their economies are somehow not "sustainable" but can be made so through managed growth, environmental regulation and whole-process planning. Short-term advantage and freewheeling capitalism must give way to long-term societal benefits. There are many advantages to this broadened view of planning, though it can also slow things down, create layers of bureaucracy and give veto power to small, nonelected groups. But careful deliberation and compromise are the Swiss way, and in many areas have served the Swiss well.

Christiaanse's winning design interprets Science City as a kind of labyrinth. The central area is filled not with a layout of individual buildings, but with a series of inner and outer "interiors," courtyards and atria. These interiors emerge from a staggered arrangement of intertwining spheres, producing intermediate spaces from public to semi-public to private. The theme is "living" and the principle is "constant change." Living quarters are spread throughout the city rather than concentrated, to achieve multiple usage and to create an animated atmosphere. The ground floors, which occupy the very heart of the campus, are transparent and designed for public use. A congress center is efficiently located on top of an underground garage and combines elegantly with other facilities, including a hotel and library, into a public center.

This was the design that, in the opinion of the jury, best satisfied the guidelines set in the competition. The process and construction, proceeding in measured steps, is ongoing. There is broad interest in the project across Europe, and there appears to be no doubt that what happens at Hönggerberg will affect the design of comparable sites at other universities.

CHAPTER ELEVEN

The ETH
Today and Tomorrow

As the ETH was celebrating its 150th anniversary in 2005, it was becoming a global institution, widening its reach to the best students and faculty worldwide. This was and is in keeping with its original vision, for the ETH, unlike many universities in Europe, has always thought globally and from the outset has aimed at unquestioned excellence. Switzerland knew it had to be open to the world; it was too small and too poor not to be. The ETH's posture has reflected this same expansive vision that made the whole of Switzerland a center for world comity, a neutral and welcoming site for conflict resolution, and the host of organizations like the International Committee of the Red Cross, agencies of the UN, the Global Fund and headquarters for many multinational corporations and even American companies in Europe.

The institute's decision to "go global" has many implications for the school and for Switzerland. One is that the ETH continues to draw some of the world's most visionary minds from every corner of the world. In 2005, 58 percent of ETH professors did not hold Swiss passports. But they are men and women who find the ETH an ideal environment for advanced research in both fundamental and applied science. Another dramatic implication is that the doors of the ETH are opening wider to American students.

Is the ETH a realistic option for an American seeking a world-class education in the sciences? Why would an American choose to attend the ETH? Why go away to a foreign country, even one as

211

hospitable as Switzerland, and—horror of horrors!—perhaps have
to learn a new language? In fact, there are a number of persuasive
arguments, trumped only by the fact that most Americans are not
familiar with the school or the benefits it can offer. The lack of
familiarity will change in time, and public recognition will confer
even more value upon a degree from one the world's highest ranked
universities.

Lest there be any doubt of its ranking, *The Times of London's
Higher Education Supplement* of November 2004 surveyed 1,300
leading academics in 88 countries to determine the top-ranked universities in the world. Harvard placed first, as might be expected
with its 40 Nobel winners and its $23 billion endowment. UC
Berkeley, MIT, Caltech and Stanford were in the top ten, followed
by Britain's Oxford and Cambridge. The ETH was 10th overall and
was the highest-ranked university on the European continent. A
study by the Swiss Council for Science and Technology, under the
auspices of the Federal Department of Home Affairs and Federal
Department of Economic Affairs, compiled a "Champions League"
of the most important international scientific institutions. Of the
thousand institutions evaluated and selected worldwide, 14 are located in Switzerland. The ETH leads the list of those 14.

To produce the 10th best university in the world, and the best
in Europe after Oxford and Cambridge, is truly noteworthy for a
nation of only seven million-plus. New York City has more people.
Clearly, the Swiss are making every conceivable effort to maintain
and extend the high quality of the ETH and to make sure that the
ETH serves Switzerland in the 21st century as well as it did in the
19th and 20th centuries.

Gifted U.S. students should consider the ETH. American teachers or guidance counselors—knowing their students are not likely to
have heard of the ETH, much less see it as an academic destina-
tion—should suggest it to their students. Parents who are quaking
at the thought of $100,000 to $120,000 in tuition and fees (not
including cost of living, travel, and incidentals) might want to consider the ETH. There is no "out-of-country" tuition. In 2005 annual tuition was an astonishingly low 1,200 Swiss francs (about $950

in mid-2005). Yes, that's right, 1,200 Swiss francs. Of course, this does not include other costs associated with four years of higher education—lodging, meals, and transportation, which are not insubstantial in Zürich. Also, the costs of travel to and from Europe have to be included in a full cost comparison. Nevertheless, the student who wants a first-rate science education without starting his career facing a decade of debt repayments would be wise to investigate this option.

Parents and students who discern the challenges and complexities of today's world know that the choice of college or university carries enormous importance. In terms of future earnings and career, there is no decision an 18-year-old high school graduate or post-graduate student can make that is more fraught with life-altering consequences. Graduates of the best schools have the best shot at scaling the heights of law, medicine and science and technology. This is why the top schools can get away with charging $30,000 to $35,000 a year and is a key contributing factor to the spiraling increases even at good state-supported universities, which are typically more than double the annual rate of inflation.

THE BOLOGNA REFORMS AND ETH ACADEMIC DEGREES

Once the affordability issue is settled, an American student will naturally ask, what about my degree? Will my degree from the ETH be fully accepted when I come back to the U.S.? Isn't it true there is no direct correlation between a U.S. Bachelor's and Master's degree and the degrees earned at European universities? Yes, but not for much longer. The Bologna Reforms will see to that.

The term comes from a series of meetings in Bologna, Italy, in 1999 among continental Europe's education ministers to harmonize the higher education systems among European countries. Although Switzerland has declined to join the EU, the country has nonetheless embraced EU proposals aimed at setting common standards in education—common pathways, degrees and definitions. This bootstrap movement came together not so long ago in what is known as the Bologna Reforms. Joined by 29 countries, the Bologna agreement lays out a redevelopment plan up and down the line in education, although states still retain considerable flexibility in how they work up to the targets. Switzerland is participating in the plan, sees its benefits, and is in the process of making significant changes in its educational system.

One of the fundamental changes under Bologna is the transition from a "one-cycle" to a "two-cycle" system of degrees. By and large, Europeans have ended their university experience with a single degree which is, depending on the field, more advanced than the typical U.S. Bachelor's degree. It is closer to a U.S. Master's degree. This is in part because European *Gymnasium*, or secondary school, graduates enter the university with more academic content under their belts than their American counterparts. In other words, the last year of the European *Gymnasium* corresponds roughly in content and rigor to the first year of college in the U.S. With their *Maturität* or *Abitur* degree given at about age 19, graduates of European secondary schools are generally more prepared than a U.S. student emerging from a good American high school.

The participants in Bologna are implementing a two-cycle system of Bachelor's and Master's degrees, conforming more closely to the American degree structure. This is not just a question of changing the title on the diploma. It entails a major reworking of the content of the degrees and how completion is determined.

For some countries the Bachelor's can be a so-called terminal degree. Much like Americans, students can leave school with this degree and take up their careers. However, the Swiss have decided to make the Master's level their terminal degree. Students who complete the program will receive a Bachelor's degree (at the ETH a Bachelor of Science degree), usually after three years. At this point, many will go out and work for some period. In fact, planners are hoping they will do so to develop real-world experience. Then they will be encouraged to return to school for a Master's program running an additional one and a half to two years. In a sense, it's like an American student going back for an MBA some time after undergraduate study, but the majority of Swiss students will complete the Bachelor's program and continue on with the Master's.

At the ETH the first Bachelor's degrees were awarded in the fall of 2005, with Master's degrees being awarded one and a half years later. However, it's a complicated business that differs from department to department. In due course, not just the ETH but all Swiss universities will roll over to this new two-cycle degree program. Admission to the best graduate schools is highly selective in the United States; but here once again, the Swiss are holding firm to an egalitarian principle. If you receive a Bachelor's degree from an accredited Swiss university, you will automatically be admitted to any Master's program in the same field. This is virtually the same principle that is applied at the undergraduate level, where any legitimate *Maturität* diploma is a ticket into the ETH. Completing the tough program is naturally another matter.

Admission of foreigners to Swiss Master's programs will be done on an individual, or dossier, basis, with an entrance exam if appropriate. The ETH expects that by 2007 about 50 percent of students at the institute will be in graduate (i.e., Master's or Ph.D.) programs. Thus, the Master's degree will be the most likely portal to the ETH for U.S. students in the near term, although the future should expect to see increasing numbers of Americans as "undergraduates" as well.

The benefits of these changes, beyond the fundamental reworking of degree content, will come in helping the ETH recruit the best students from all over the globe. Their applications can be evaluated and credits transferred with some degree of uniformity. In addition, compatible degree standards will allow Swiss students to move to other schools in Europe, America or Asia, should they desire. The graduate degree programs are only one part of many such moves intended to increase what the Swiss call *Mobilität*—a term often heard around the university and which means a combination of opportunity, career advancement and overall flexibility.

Switzerland has long attracted large numbers of students from abroad to its excellent private secondary schools. Some are well known, as, for instance, the Institut Le Rosey, which was founded in 1880 and continues to educate the children of the world's rich and famous. But there are many others that offer a rigorous, internationally recognized curriculum within Switzerland's cosmopolitan and linguistically diversified culture. Today there are about 80,000 children enrolled in some 260 private schools. Some go on to university within Switzerland and add to the international atmosphere on Swiss campuses, including Zürich's ETH.

As ever, part of the Swiss strategy to maintain the school as one of the world's leading universities is to draw the best students and professors to Zürich. There is even planning under way to allow ETH graduate degrees to be earned by students who use English either as a native or learned language. You will not necessarily have to know German to take an advanced degree in Switzerland. English is sweeping through universities worldwide as the *lingua franca* of research, management, and even personal communication. One ETH professor noted of a French-speaking colleague, "He wouldn't talk German to me, but he would use English." Needless to say, both professors in question were not native English speakers. Today English has become the default language which can be used virtually anywhere. And, as more and more of the world's intellectual elites become fluent, the more entrenched—and useful—English becomes.

One result of the Bologna Declaration has been the introduction of fundamental academic reforms reaching far beyond the adoption of new degree titles. The reform project has gained further momentum, particularly in the departments. Working parties are busy rethinking courses, defining a skills profile for each degree level and reorganizing the content, method and form of the curricula.

At the international level, a result of the conference has been to encourage collaboration with the ETH's partners in the IDEA League, an association of four leading research schools. (The acronym comes from the first letter of the names of the participants: Imperial College London; Delft University, the Netherlands; ETH Zürich; and Aachen Technical University in Germany.) Students will have the flexibility to move among these partner universities; consequently, an American student could potentially be exposed to a broader range of countries and educational experiences than solely Switzerland and the ETH. IDEA League members expect to benefit from the alliance not only by recruiting foreign students but also by using its collective power to attract more funding. This academic liaison parallels similar partnerships at the corporate level. There is a high degree of cooperation and coordination between Swiss and European firms.

While the ETH adjusts and enhances itself in our increasingly interconnected world, in terms of the academic experience one principle remains firm: the ETH is a teaching university. Its faculty ranks high worldwide in research, but the rule remains that "everyone teaches!" It is remarkable, compared for example to U.S. universities, that the top professors also teach introductory undergraduate courses. This exposes new students not just to "TA's" and junior or adjunct faculty, but to the institute's most exceptional people.

THE STUDENT BODY

There is far more to higher education than a degree. U.S. students tend to look at the total university experience and are interested in the social and cultural as well as the purely academic aspects of a school. They want to know what the institutional culture and student body are like, as well as the physical environment. After all, the foremost element in this story—past, present and future—and the *raison d'être* of any university, in the first place, is its students.

During the 2003–2004 academic year, 12,626 students studied at the ETH. Clearly it is not a mammoth institution like some large U.S. state universities that may have upward of 40,000 students. These 12,626 were enrolled at all levels—Diploma (Bachelor's), Master's, and Ph.D. Of these, 2,063, or 16 percent, were in Construction and Geomatics (which includes architecture); 4,206, or 33 percent, in Engineering Sciences (mechanical, electrical, and process engineering, computer sciences, industrial management and manufacturing); 3,695, or 29 percent, in Natural Sciences and Mathematics (including chemistry, biology, physics and math); 2,011, or 16 percent, in Systems-Oriented Natural Sciences (environmental and agricultural engineering, forestry); and 651, or 5 percent, in

Social and Other Sciences (political science, sports sciences, and the professional military officers course). Some 2,525 students, or 20 percent, were from foreign countries. About 20 percent of the total were Ph.D. students involved in research programs. In 2003–2004, 432 students—104 females and 328 males—about 50 percent of whom were Swiss nationals, were awarded their doctorates.

Female enrollments are increasing steadily, and in 2003–2004 women students represented slightly under one-third of the total, compared to 19 percent a decade ago. The ETH, which pioneered the matriculation of women, beginning in its founding year of 1855, still struggles to address its male/female imbalance, especially in engineering. By way of comparison, an average U.S. electrical engineering department will have 20 percent female students (though not primarily American-born); in Germany it will be about 8 percent and in Switzerland about 4 percent. At the ETH there are more females in other departments and more in advanced degree programs. Nevertheless, the challenge of enrolling more females in the technical sciences is an issue pondered on both sides of the Atlantic. In early 2005 Harvard president Lawrence Summers ignited a feminist firestorm when he wondered out loud whether women simply possessed different aptitudes than men. Calls for his resignation (or worse) rang through the land, though the curiosity remains why the male/female imbalance in engineering persists while former ones in fields like law and medicine have recently been erased.

Will American students be truly welcomed at the ETH? Will they be competitive? Will they be adequately prepared? How will U.S. applicants stack up against their Swiss, French, German or Asian counterparts?

A conversation with faculty and staff at almost any American university reveals a high level of ambivalence about the quality of preparation and motivation of U.S. students. This is less the case at elite institutions, including leading science and technology schools like MIT, Stanford, and CalTech. Students matriculating at these schools appear to understand they have been given a life-altering opportunity. But even at those institutions concern lingers about the math and science foundation provided by American secondary education, especially the public schools.

This is far less a concern at the ETH and in Swiss higher education in general. Dr. Konrad Osterwalder, a highly respected physicist and the ETH's Rector (corresponding roughly to the academic dean at a U.S. university) observes that "Swiss students are serious, highly motivated, and arrive here ready to work hard. This is especially true at the ETH, for the school's academic reputation is well known. Swiss students who lack aptitude or solid grounding in the sciences and mathematics are generally wise enough to choose another university." The well-known rigor of the ETH has not discouraged enrollment. On the contrary, the school's data show that the number of degree students at the ETH in Zürich in engineering, mathematics and the basic sciences—physics, chemistry and biology—has continued to rise significantly over the past decade.

Consequently, the ETH continues to attract the best students in Switzerland and continental Europe. Anyone who has earned the *Matura*, the academic-track diploma from a secondary school, is entitled to enroll at any cantonal Swiss university as well as the ETH Zürich and the Ecole Polytechnique Fédérale de Lausanne (EPFL). There is an entrance exam for others—for example, foreign applicants or Swiss who have been graduated from private schools and do not have a diploma from a cantonal secondary school. This entrance exam, as we have seen, has been the traditional route of entry for talented students who lack the credentials of a secondary school diploma. The fact that Albert Einstein, among others, was initially attracted to the ETH on the basis of the entrance exam policy attests to its wisdom.

However, while there is no entry exam—and no SAT—for graduates with a *Maturität*, there is a very stiff ETH exam at the end of the first year that must be passed "*entiere*" for a student to remain. Following the Bologna changes it is called the "Qualification Exam." This exam equalizes the differences between students and their level of preparation and ability, and also differences between cantons. It gives everyone a maximum two-year chance to succeed at the ETH, for they can take it again. If they fail the second time, they are out. In effect, this means that every ETH student is on probation for at least the first year. About 70 percent of original matriculants remain and complete the exam. There is ample incentive for self de-selection, since students who lack scientific aptitude will avoid choosing the ETH in the first place if they know their chance of passing the "First" are slight.

Thus, in answer to the question, will U.S. students be sufficiently prepared and competitive enough to stay at the ETH once they enter, one can only say, "It remains to be seen." While the ETH clearly welcomes U.S. applicants, the school will not give Americans any special dispensation. It seeks only the best, but "best" according to Swiss standards, not U.S. standards, which are not uniform, to say the least. Nevertheless, mature, confident, intelligent and well-prepared Americans should find the ETH a stimulating and congenial environment, one that gives them as fine an education as available anywhere, and that leads to a rewarding career afterward.

STUDENT LIFE

Good secondary education and natural talent help explain why students arrive at the ETH, and if they pass the "First" they can remain. But then what? What is it like to be a student at such a demanding institution? Swiss students at the ETH, and foreign students for that matter, may be serious, well motivated and hardworking but are not fundamentally different from university students everywhere. While they must work hard, they are not academic drones; by no means placid, they appear restive and eager, full of hope, energy and idealism.

Students are students everywhere, and the ETH is no exception. With their egalitarian manners and ragamuffin dress code, Swiss kids look much like their contemporaries in the U.S. Old status hierarchies are increasingly irrelevant. Instant messaging, wireless portability and the virtually instant assembly of like minds have been changing the texture and pace of student life. Within the university, digitalization continues to revolutionize core processes in research, teaching, resource management and social life. Interconnection and communication have been vastly increased far beyond the physical institution. Books, course materials and research are being synthesized out of the electronic ether, and libraries are busy digitalizing their holdings to make them globally accessible and electronically searchable. Yet, books are not quite as archaic at the ETH as the electronics whiz-kids might have us believe. While the electronic infrastructure is impressive and constantly being expanded, students still prefer good textbooks over online documentation and, in the opinion of some students, always will. Even in this electronic age, "nothing beats good old deadwood," and even the engineering students say they prefer a piece of chalk squeaking over a 19th-century blackboard than a fancy Powerpoint presentation.

Everything and everybody are interconnected, and it seems as if the really important research activity is interdisciplinary. Reflecting a world in which no single individual can master the expanse of knowledge in any field, students work more and more in teams and ad hoc groups. Basics must still be mastered—and entering students tend to be extremely well prepared in the foundation disciplines of science—but the new paradigm in teaching is to bring students to problems for which ready-made answers do not exist. They work on problems as a group, communicating with their peers, professors, other schools and outside interest groups with astonishing ease and speed. Perhaps in student life, the dread inevitability of exams and the delirium of young love are the only things that persist unchanged, or almost.

Speaking of exams, Georg Wilckens, an impressive student from Germany in his final years of Electrical Engineering and former head of the *Studentenverein*, or student union, declared in an interview that the biggest headache is the conflict between final exams and vacation schedules. Serious students know they need to prioritize study.

Of course, one shouldn't assume that students don't have their fun while school is in session. A colorful team of Chinese graduate students—all advanced engineers and scientists—competes in the annual Dragon Boat race on the Limmat River through Zürich. The Union of Chinese Students and Scholars in Zürich (CUZ) also maintains a lively website, covering everything from problems in mathematics to recipes for wrapping Swiss sausages in lotus leaves. The ETH has had Chinese students coming through its programs since the early 1980s.

Students have real influence on the school's decision making (especially as it affects student life), exercised through formal structures but more often informally, through personal relationships with faculty and staff. In fact, students appear to have more influence through the inherent power of reason, or suggestion, than through confrontation. In other words, though the culture is Germanic, it is also Swiss and thus not authoritarian. There are numerous support structures for students, including, for example, an office that helps locate housing, and numerous social, professional and sports organizations, as well as superb athletic facilities. In fact, there is a joke among non-Swiss that Switzerland leads the world in club memberships per capita. In the words of young Herr Wilckens, it is an "almost absurdly rich ecosystem. It seems like, in Switzerland, founding a society is one of the things you are supposed to do once in your life."

THE "CAMPUS" AND THE CITY OF ZÜRICH

What would an American—a potential student or an intelligent observer—notice about the ETH today? Standing on the Terrace on the hill above Zürich and the Limmat River, you could say the ETH looks a lot like a typical U.S. university. Everyone is on cell phones or shooting instant messages or documents back and forth over state-of-the-art broadband networks. Everything seems to be on the move, and the energy of the environment is palpable. New initiatives, new interdisciplinary teams and coordinating groups, new strategic plans, new approaches to teaching and new buildings dot the landscape. Dozens of mind-numbing but efficient acronyms cover fundamental organizational shifts. As in the U.S., there seems to be no existing vocabulary from "the old order" to deal with the multitude of paradigm changes. And there are literally scores of new links with research organizations, funding sources and policy planners all around the world.

It cannot be over-emphasized that one of the main benefits in attending the ETH is to experience its host city. Zürich is one of the most splendid cities in the world—relatively small in size and population but large in its global impact, thanks in part to the ETH and the University of Zürich, in part to the influential financial services and other industries that call it home, and in part to its congenial and welcoming ambiance. It features a pleasing mix of the medieval and contemporary, with scores of winding narrow streets overshadowed by ancient buildings, some quaint, some imposing. Yet it is thoroughly modern, immaculate and efficient, with every amenity and convenience the 21st century can provide. The combination can sometimes be disconcerting, as when one approaches a quaint shop that appears to date from the time of Charlemagne, only to find it equipped with "electric eye" sliding doors. Americans used to the freedom of car ownership (SUVs are particularly not recommended on the city's winding streets) will not feel constrained, as public transportation is cheap and ubiquitous. An extensive network of trains, trams and buses will take you within a short walk of almost anywhere you wish to go.

It is a beautiful city of fine restaurants, museums, ancient churches, charming parks and the stunningly beautiful Limmat River and its source, *der Zürichsee*—Lake Zürich, which extends some 40 miles east and south of the city. Snow-capped Alps line the far skyline. The city possesses a free and open (yet reserved) ambiance that once welcomed historic figures and luminaries as diverse as Irish writer and expatriate James Joyce, the Dada artists and even Vladimir Lenin. It was from Zürich, in fact, that Lenin, paid by the Germans, departed in 1917 in a sealed train to St. Petersburg's Finland Station, from whence he launched the Bolshevik Revolution. Though accepting of political dissidents, the Swiss have also been intensely anti-Communist. Had they known of Lenin's destiny, one wonders if they would have induced him to remain, thus sparing the world 70 years of the consequences of his historic train ride.

A student in Zürich seeking cultural and historical enrichment is also a short train ride from Switzerland's other great cities such as Geneva, Bern, Basel and Lucerne, as well as small Alpine villages like Altdorf, the home of William Tell. (Though Tell may be considered a figure of legend, the giant statue of him in Altdorf's square is quite real.) Of course since Switzerland is a small country, southern Germany, western Austria, eastern France and—if one travels over or through the Alps—northern Italy are just short trips away. From Zürich a student is also a mere hour or two from the world's finest Alpine skiing and winter sports resorts.

"SCIENCE CITY" AT HÖNGGERBERG

The ETH is currently in the midst of a high-profile investment in infrastructure, with a visionary expansion of a new campus outside the city and a major development project for central Zürich, weaving the ETH's original campus into a comprehensive development plan for the city.

The spiritual center of the ETH will always be the Zentrum, the campus overlooking downtown Zürich, dominated by the stately main building of Gottfried Semper. However, many of the hard sciences and labs have moved in whole or in part to the new space-age campus on a ridge north of the city and the Limmat River's northern plain, just outside the old village of HönGG. Commonly referred to as the Hönggerberg campus or just the Hönggerberg, its futuristic appearance certainly grabs attention. The lines, like much of the new construction at the ETH and in Zürich generally, are heavily influenced by the Bauhaus school of architecture, for which Zürich is a holy place.

You get there by a 20-minute ride on tram and bus; and in an experience typically Swiss, you pass a working farm and immense cornfield on the way in. The first and most vivid sensation that greets you (depending on the season) is the tangy, earthy odor of goats, cattle and mown hay.

Students have been living and studying for years at the Hönggerberg, but the full conversion of the campus will happen in stages. Some departments will make the move and some won't, but in raw numbers roughly half of the ETH has been relocated there. The Hönggerberg campus will cost about 450 million Swiss francs, of which 150 million will be for research facilities and 250 million for making it a true campus with housing and the amenities of a small city. As always with a project of this magnitude, there have been starts and stops and major cost overruns. Most of the funds are coming from the government, but the transition to the campus is being paid for by private donations and sponsorships. Great effort is being made to address the concerns of people living around the new campus, to make the whole enterprise environmentally friendly and to build in a distinctly European atmosphere.

As noted earler, an architectural design competition ended with the choice of Kees Christiaanse, a Dutch urban planner and now a professor at the ETH. The campus is to be a showplace for Switzerland, Zürich and the ETH. It is a colossal experiment in creating a university "from scratch" and with its ultra-modern facilities is intended to become the brightest jewel in the ETH crown. Needless to say, in Switzerland the creation of the Hönggerberg has sparked a lively debate on the future of the ETH and beyond that on the role of the university in future society. The basic issue was that the ETH Zentrum, steeped in tradition within the beautiful old city, had gotten cramped; the *Bauhaus* of Hönggerberg, thoroughly of the 21st century, is a strategic risk. Yet, to grow significantly, the school had to break from its urban confines. The symbolism of a parallel "break with the past" is obvious, but the ETH will not give up its roots in the city and neither should it, since the experience of Zürich, the Limmat River and the Lake of Zürich will remain a wonderful and deeply human part of the educational experience.

STRATEGIC ISSUES

The ETH is projected to be an engine of economic growth for Switzerland in those areas where planners anticipate a high value-added component, leading to the "re-industrialization" of the country with new industries both based on and creating knowledge. This is an outcome the Swiss think can be highly leveraged and passed on to what will become modular production centers around the world. Related to these main areas of research and development are other broad issues that will affect the school and the contribution it makes to the future.

Physical Location. People will always have to live somewhere, and the ETH will continue to be a physical assemblage of scientists. But almost as certainly, organizational boundaries will change. The world of research will be organized into communications networks rather than physical spaces and will consolidate into research hubs that straddle traditional schools. As support for brilliant intellect grows, the research workspace of any given specialty will be more in cyberspace than physically in Zürich, Shanghai or Cambridge. The construction and maintenance of laboratories and research facilities will become ever more complex, and perhaps, as virtual modeling and simulation take on a larger role, hands-on-the-machine research facilities will become less important. As the ETH recognizes, emphasis shifts not only to brilliant minds but to the right connections, and the almost gravitational pull of better organization. Knowledge is a nomad.

Today e-learning is the exception, not the norm, but the enormous progress in storage, search and retrieval is rendering teaching material into a valuable commodity. Great lectures by great minds will be available, with all the nuance of personal presentation, anywhere in cyberspace. You will be able to go back, fast forward, check references, or follow a divergent line of thought with a freedom that is only hinted at today. Schools will no longer have an exclusive, closed-circuit monopoly on the best teaching. The ETH, for a host of reasons, is leading the way in efforts to open up the school and to make its resources more widely available.

Competition. Though new forms of cooperation will partly offset competition based on physical location, the ETH will still have the task of attracting top talent. Schools have always had a monopoly on teaching the young, but we cannot assume that there is a necessary connection between teaching and research. During the past 50 years, certain corporations have developed vast research centers rivaling the university. As institutions share knowledge—among themselves and with corporate R&D operations—corporations are also building proprietary R&D zones. The huge Phillips research center at Eindhoven in the Netherlands, for example, brings together thousands of scientists, and research is cooperative and shared between participating corporations. In working to improve its interface with corporate culture, the ETH is itself becoming more like a corporation.

With its nearly guaranteed source of funding, is the ETH more flexible, or less, than its corporate counterparts? The ETH enjoys great autonomy in how it spends its funds, but Swiss spending could and probably will be surpassed in the long term by other governments such as China and India, or even by private corporations pooling resources. Moreover, less democratic governments do not have to submit to popular oversight and regular national referenda, as does the Swiss government.

Certainly, as it exists now, the ETH is a boon for corporations since it is a public resource paid for by the state, but that equation might change. Even with government funding, ETH planners worry that corporations might find the ETH too restricted, and begin to shift their research in-house or to countries that feature greater latitude and fewer bureaucratic hurdles in the life sciences, such as China or India. This could easily come to pass if EU measures—largely followed by Switzerland—begin to restrict research in sensitive areas like synthetic biology. There is already a considerable uproar across Europe about genetically modified foods, genetic manipulations in medicine and the potential of cloning. Coupled with pervasive environmental regulation, an increasingly hostile product liability atmosphere, and draconian measures protecting privacy, the EU—and Switzerland—could find their "market" for research damped down. In effect, the same conditions limiting production in Europe could begin to restrict research activities as well.

This is by no means certain, but is a possibility any forward-looking institution like the ETH must consider.

Academic Freedom. Academic freedom was a reaction to centuries of sectarian conflict and religious persecution. Though precious, in the context of human history it is an artifact of a particular time and culture. In the ideological wars of the 20th century, academic freedom was more candle than sun. Authoritarian regimes overturned it as suited their purpose. The conviction that science should be guided by a set of moral values is still strong today, and we are naive if we think that even the so-called hard sciences are free from controversy. Governments control the purse strings, and Western governments are popular and political. Thus, it may be an act of faith to say that the public will continue to support science whatever it may be.

The ETH may thus be faced with a very difficult balancing act. Science, especially applied science, with its manifest gifts to society, has to date enjoyed substantial freedom. But we are venturing into uncharted waters as we approach the life sciences and the challenges and risks of biological intervention. In its public campaigns, the ETH is in the forefront of those saying we must "speed up" science to help Switzerland and broader mankind, but there are also many competing voices whose message is "slow down" to consider moral questions such science raises.

Intellectual Property. One of the cornerstones of the ETH's strategy for the future is to "make knowledge pay," or, in management talk, to derive a stream of revenues from its investment in the production of knowledge. For the ETH it is a matter of capturing for itself a larger share of the benefits its research produces. It can thereby supplement, or at least diversify, its base of federal funding. The federal government, for its part, seems content for the time being to derive the benefits of its investment in the ETH from the increased tax base of a thriving economy.

In either case, both the funding of research and the distribution of its benefits are problems currently being negotiated in courts, parliaments and numerous intellectual forums around the world. We Americans, with our hyperactive legal system, are much in the lead in working out the issues of intellectual property. In the short run at least, the U.S. system of giving knowledge the same rights as property will no doubt prevail. In the longer term, the direction is not certain.

There are many who object to the way new knowledge is being consolidated and controlled through an interlocking web of patents, copyrights and licensing. This is especially vexing, they say, when such knowledge is produced at public expense. It slows progress for the many to give profit to the few. There are many "knowledge hackers" who take delight in undermining secrets and restraints, some of whom are tacitly supported by state power. The same digitalization of knowledge that accelerates progress makes theft and redistribution easier as well. We only need look at AIDS drugs, advanced electronics, or the fact that movies now appear on black market DVDs almost as soon as they're released to see the huge pressures to bypass established tollgates.

On the other side, defenders say that without a reasonable expectation of profit, research on the scale demanded today would be significantly reduced or not happen at all. Moreover, production must be supported by efficient distribution impossible without price protection. Those who steal secrets and the results of long years of research attempt to benefit from the work and investments of others at the risk of jeopardizing future progress.

There is no easy or consistent answer to this dilemma. Still, the ETH, through major efforts in technology transfer, is helping its researchers package and sell the results of their work. There is no single formula, but today an array of contracts has been worked out that smooth and simplify the process.

SWISS AND AMERICAN PERSPECTIVES

Americans will be concerned with how the ETH differs from U.S. institutions of comparable magnitude. How is the ETH meeting the challenges we all face? These questions are extremely important, since every advanced university today—whatever its location— faces a future that is anything but certain.

Our world is changing rapidly. The economic and cultural stakes are very high indeed. As Americans, we should not overlook solutions that are different from those of our own strategists and planners. The Swiss have created a model that clearly works, as have the Americans. While this work has focused primarily on the outstanding record of Switzerland's ETH, it should be noted that the leading 100 American universities, and within that number the top ten, have contributed an astonishing amount to human knowledge, and in the process have made the U.S. an economic superpower. A key question is to what extent both countries can learn and benefit from each other's institutions.

In 2005, the Rector of the ETH, Dr. Konrad Osterwalder, noted that in many respects Swiss universities at the graduate level are moving closer to where American universities are today. He was implicitly citing the top U.S. research centers both as benchmarks of development and as models for success. As the ETH restructures itself to achieve greater organizational flexibility and to embark on new directions in science, it is borrowing from the U.S., since Americans have already wrestled to earth many of the tough university management issues. Swiss academic and business leaders have long been particularly sharp and close observers of the American scene. Almost every ETH professor and, for that matter, most high-level executives in Swiss multinationals have spent a short or long period studying or teaching at a U.S. university or working in the U.S. Judging from their CVs, Caltech, Stanford, MIT, Harvard and UC Berkeley are like signposts on a Swiss highway.

Swiss multinational corporations have always been flexible and light-footed, evolving quickly to deal with complex foreign environments. But as a publicly owned and funded institution, the ETH's "board of directors," so to speak, are the people of Switzerland, and within Swiss society in general more conservative attitudes and priorities are slow to change.

Transforming a university involves what the Swiss call *Politik*—

not politics in the Tammany Hall sense, but the social and cultural side of the equation. You have to convince people—taxpayers, ultimately, because Switzerland is a direct democracy—to change the public consensus at a basic level. In the midst of today's information revolution, it's easy to forget that the broad base of citizens may not automatically buy into dramatic transformations. Some Swiss may not understand the ETH's vision of the future unless the school itself makes explaining its vision a priority. That is exactly what the ETH is doing now. You can call it "opening up" the university, but it's really making clear that the school's innovations, plans and investments will ultimately benefit everyone.

Swiss leaders have absorbed the lessons of American scientific success and are setting out to re-create the conditions which they think have made American science and industry so productive over the past 50 years. It's ironic, because a century or so ago, U.S. universities were themselves chasing European models, back when the ETH, Heidelberg, Berlin, Vienna and Göttingen were the names to emulate. Today, although the landscape of many U.S. schools may be what Dr. Osterwalder calls academic "flatlands," he also recognizes there are superb individual institutions forming "peaks"—and the "creative chaos" of the Palo Altos, Rt. 128s outside of Boston and Silicon Valleys is much admired in orderly Switzerland.

Thus Switzerland and the U.S. are linked in a realm and in ways that perhaps neither country fully realizes. The Swiss have transcended the strictures of a sometimes reticent culture to create a society and economy that are the envy of the world. The ETH has been an indispensable part of this achievement. The U.S., of course, also possesses an extraordinary record of accomplishment, with its own universities claiming much of the credit. As the world grows closer together during the 21st century, it would be particularly beneficial for the Swiss and Americans, through their leading educational institutions, to increasingly learn from each other.

CHAPTER TWELVE

Engaging the Future

In 1855, the Polytechnic first opened its doors with flags flying, cannons firing and bands playing. The guns could only salute the hopes the new school represented; as of yet, there was no record to celebrate.

In 2005 the ETH staged a festival to commemorate its first 150 years. By then the once humble school could celebrate one of the world's most splendid records of academic and scientific achievement. The festival consisted of an exhibition in Zürich's Platzspitzpark, displaying the technologies that the ETH was currently researching or developing. The two-week event, called *Welten des Wissens* (Worlds of Knowledge), was held in the incongruous shadow of Gustav Gull's towering medieval Landesmuseum.

To call it a mere science fair would be inaccurate—it was a science fair to end all science fairs. Hundreds of Zürichers stood in line, often in the rain, to enter the various pavilions, view videos and handle the actual hardware. A foreign visitor could not help but observe at least two things: perhaps nowhere else in the world but the hometown of the ETH could such an exhibition have been mounted so successfully and with such artistry and interest. And perhaps no other people but the Swiss, many of them returning day after day and some traveling from all over the country, would have thronged the event for two weeks with such a combination of intellectual curiosity and a sense of collective pride.

In formulating a final assessment, one is forced to ask: as the

ETH proceeds into the 21st century, will it be able to sustain the record it has achieved? All human institutions, even those with proud histories and enviable records, have a tendency to stagnate, ossify or become complacent. Can the ETH avoid this all too common human pitfall? While a positive answer to the question is by no means assured, the promise of continuing dynamism is bright. The school appears determined to sustain the high quality of its teaching and research and to foster an institutional culture that will continue to produce excellence.

Hönggerberg is the biggest and, at a cost of close to half a billion Swiss francs, certainly the most expensive bet the ETH is making—the creation of a new Science City of 10,000 people devoted to advanced research. There is little question that it will be the ETH of the future. If it succeeds, it will become the prototype of similar ventures across Europe and probably around the world. The ETH is banking on that success.

It is always pleasing to start from scratch and have brand-new state-of-the-art labs. And the ETH had no room to expand in the picturesque streets of Zürich itself. There is much to be said for having a compelling symbol and a real campus in an American sense. Hönggerberg's experiment in specialization and in assembling critical mass can be the best of both worlds for the ETH: a thoroughly 21st-century science campus near but not on top of the amenities of old-world Zürich.

How does one judge whether, after its opening, Hönggerberg is a success? That is an intriguing question bringing up the issue of *Indikatoren,* or "measures." Like the life sciences and nanotechnology, academic measurement of the success of new ventures can be very creative. But somewhere in the planning process there must be some hard equations of investment and return. The ETH has made a commitment in going to Hönggerberg, with all the excitement that new designs and the creation of new facilities entail. Whatever the result, there is no backing out. Will students and researchers like the place and relish living and working there? It is certainly a showplace. Will it also help recruit students and faculty to the ETH? Right now, it's too early to tell.

INTEGRATION WITH EUROPE

Among managers and professors at the ETH, there is a difference of opinion whether Switzerland should join the EU. Some say it is necessary and inevitable in the long term. Through treaties and arrangements of many kinds, Switzerland and the ETH already participate in many EU initiatives, the Bologna educational reform being the most prominent. The ETH has also been approved to take part in EU-funded research projects and is active in that area. In fact, EU research is a significant source of outside funding for some ETH departments.

Others say that if you asked any three German academics or businessmen chosen at random, they would tell you that Switzerland is better off staying out of the EU "mess." Certainly many Swiss believe that, with their lower taxes, lower unemployment and relative freedom of enterprise, they should avoid the European quagmire. And of course since medieval times the Swiss have never been "joiners." It was only in 2001 that they finally decided to join the United Nations, in a hotly contested referendum, though in that case too they had long participated in donating generously to UN humanitarian initiatives.

The dilemma is that Europe is Switzerland's primary export market, and the country is dependent on European prosperity and good will. Switzerland cannot afford to be independent in a way that other Europeans perceive as arrogant or hostile. So the Swiss, and the ETH, have both feet down in the European Community. For the ETH, this impulse has taken the form of the IDEA League, its association with other leading scientific institutions. More schools may join shortly. Yet, it seems certain that in the foreseeable future Switzerland will not formally join the EU, although informal or semi-formal partnering will continue or accelerate.

While European economies remain relatively depressed, there is no good reason to join, especially as the EU experiment itself seems to be unraveling with the rejection of its new constitution in France and the Netherlands. In any case, the Swiss reap an advantage from being able to manage their own fiscal policy. It is important to note that the EU as well as the nations that constitute it are making vigorous efforts to transform their economies into information economies. The Swiss are smaller, more flexible and share a stronger internal consensus. Moreover, their very independence allows them to move faster in putting educational reforms in place. The fact that the ETH is ranked higher today than any institution in Germany or France is indicative of the problems Germany and France are facing in overhauling their own educational systems.

THE SWISS NATION

Most Swiss believe the ETH should help Switzerland first. However, as the ETH proceeds to establish links with other schools and research hubs across the globe, it raises the question: is the ETH a Swiss or an international institution? Remember that over half of the ETH's current professors do not hold Swiss passports, and roughly the same percentage holds for doctoral degrees awarded each year. At the most advanced levels, Switzerland—like the U.S.—depends on foreigners to staff its research facilities. International recruiting of both students and high-level faculty is considered essential to the ETH's strategic plan, and more foreigners, not fewer, will be the rule for the ETH in coming years. More classes will be offered in English, and in some departments such as Finance it will be possible to earn an advanced degree without having to learn German.

In a prosperous and benign environment this kind of international support and cooperation is wonderful. Yet, the future ETH will have to be both Swiss and international, for as the ETH commits to a truly international model, it is also exposed to new pressures. Both Germany and France have large and growing immigrant communities that to a greater or lesser degree resist complete integration. Switzerland has a long tradition of helping and welcoming refugees, but its own immigrant population is now pushing 21 percent. Among such groups, Swiss nationality and heritage can lack meaningful resonance. Moreover, as with the intellectual class of elites in most Western democracies, there are individuals in Swiss universities, organs of culture and media who regard patriotism and national pride as anachronistic, or worse. A visitor can detect the sentiment in conversations with Swiss students at the ETH, who seem almost embarrassed by—or oblivious to—their founding myths and symbols, whether these be references to William Tell, the Rütli Meadow in 1291 and 1940, or the Lion Monument in Lucerne. This trend is not unique to Switzerland—indeed, an historical sense among U.S. young people may be even more lacking—nevertheless it is something the Swiss must contend with as they chart a path for the ETH, increasingly an international asset.

MAINTAINING THE FOUNDATIONS

As the Swiss grapple with the thorny issues and as yet unforeseen challenges of the 21st century, they are sensibly committed to maintaining the foundations of the ETH that they know account for its success. Among other bricks in the foundation are ample money, talented people, and an institutional ethos that encourages the pursuit of excellence.

When asked the reasons for the ETH's success, its leaders are clear that financial support has been a key. The initial commitment of funds from the federal government provided the Swiss a return on their investment that made them willing to sustain it, though at the school's founding in 1855 Switzerland was by no means a rich country. The subsequent success of the Swiss economy, the development of its domestic talent and the country's enhanced global presence have more than verified the wisdom of the national investment (although the Swiss economic powerhouse obviously owes its success to more than just the ETH).

Moreover, the federal money allocated to the school comes with relatively few strings attached, allowing the ETH to pursue its mission without looking over its shoulder for accountants, bureaucrats or investigative reporters. The academic departments and their research projects are audited by the federal government every six years. Then, but only then, they have to justify the direction they took and the money they spent. This six-year accountability period allows scientists to experiment and pursue the inevitable blind alleys without someone auditing their projects every step of the way. It balances accountability with the need for freedom to explore that is the perquisite for groundbreaking science. Ample funding and the freedom to use it wisely have made the school unusually successful in drawing the most innovative students and professors to the ETH over the decades.

THE BEST PEOPLE

Who are the "best people" in this context? Two categories, at a minimum: theoreticians and practical men.

The ETH is a two-sided place. There is the fundamental or pure research side, of whom Einstein is the universal example. In the early days, pure research most often came from such supremely gifted individuals working in simple or relatively simple labs. They made the theoretical breakthroughs that literally shook the world. But, for the most part, they had little concern for the business or economic implications of their work.

Then there is the applied side of ETH—the engineering side, especially. The thousands of superbly trained ETH engineers were practical interpreters who took the best available knowledge—by no means limited to knowledge produced at the ETH or even in Switzerland—and applied it to human problems. They designed and built the bridges, tunnels, hydroelectric generators and distribution networks, the new machines and processes. Like the original founders of the ETH, they were practical men, deeply involved in business, and often entrepreneurs. The nation may have supported the ethereal heights of pure research, but it was the ETH's practical men who used knowledge to create lasting wealth, ultimately for the entire nation.

THE INSTITUTIONAL ETHOS

In addition to ample and dependable funding, which attracted the best people, who in turn paid back the Swiss investment many times over, there is a final aspect to the ETH's foundations that the present administration recognizes—to its great credit—and appears determined to uphold. This aspect is less tangible than funds and personnel, though no less crucial in the school's success. It is the institutional ethos that inspires and sustains a commitment to excellence.

At the ETH, the pressure to excel is not so much external as it is self-imposed. The culture of the institution encourages people to be the best they can be. The faculty have the time and the resources to spend on research, study and cultivating the technical imagination. The extra ingredient is the culture that includes a high degree of trust—the best people are selected as faculty, and the school then trusts them and gives them the means and creates the environment for them to succeed

Finally, the leadership principle, from the President on down, is one of generating "emotional prosperity." Risk taking—imagining what is possible and pursuing it—is encouraged. Along with the taking of risks and the trust that supports it is a kind of "creative chaos" at the heart of the institute's culture. In the process of unveiling the future, which is the primary goal of scientific research, there will be few pat solutions, but a swirl of energy devoted to possibilities.

IN CONCLUSION

An institution like the ETH does not exist in a vacuum. It thrives within the culture that surrounds and supports it. As different as the U.S. and Switzerland are from each other, both maintain institutions largely dependent on the health, prosperity and culture of their respective nations. The ETH is a sterling example of an institution that has grown from and contributed back to its host culture.

The Swiss seem to have an innate ability to do science sensibly, and the ETH for the most part has avoided the common pitfall of imposing a set methodology on diverse disciplines. In the past, research has been hampered simply because it was deemed that proven methods were the only "respectable" way to do science. In his work *Human Nature and the Limits of Science*, British philosopher John Dupré calls this "scientific imperialism," by which he means "the tendency for a successful scientific idea to be applied far beyond its original home, and generally with decreasing success the more its application is expanded."

What the mind of man can conceive, man can build. Indeed, that is the story of the ETH. Yet this enormous power in the wrong hands, or driven by hubris or lust for power, can breed the most appalling results, which is why the mad scientist and his monstrous creation is one of the most enduring themes of modern literature. The tales of *Frankenstein* or *The Island of Dr. Moreau*, for example, warn mankind of a science that respects no limits of decency, piety or common sense because it echoes the oldest temptation of man, one that goes all the way back to Eden: the temptation to know, and then knowing all, "ye shall be as God."

The great boon of science and its handmaiden, technology, have enriched man immeasurably, but they also have their dark side. The secrets of the universe uncovered by that most peaceable and humane individual, Albert Einstein, followed two paths. One led to the benefits of peaceful nuclear energy, the other to Hiroshima and thence a dire threat to human existence.

The advances in biology, medicine and genetics that have saved lives and reduced pain and suffering have their dark side in Nazi Germany's campaign to eliminate the people it viewed as biological threats to the nation's health. Physicians, geneticists and anthropologists willingly participated in the Nazis' "racial health policies," beginning with the mass sterilization of "genetically diseased" persons, including the infirm and mentally disabled, and ending with the near annihilation of gypsies and European Jewry.

Switzerland is that rarest of nations which deliberately turned its back on the use of its legendary regiments abroad when it was at the height of its military renown. Through their collegial politics and their peaceful, stable society, the Swiss have shown they are anything but imperialists—of the scientific variety or any other. A humane, sensible, and decent approach to science flows from the character of the Swiss people themselves and is evident in the ethos of the ETH. Their modest nature, grounded in reality and balancing the pursuit of pure knowledge with practical uses, has helped save science at the ETH from its dark side. The ETH and the Swiss capture the essence of Aldous Huxley's words in his foreword to *Brave New World*. If he were to rewrite the terrifying classic of a future in which science and technology have run mad, he said, "I would offer . . . the possibility of sanity . . . in a community of exiles from the Brave New World. . . . In this community economics would be decentralist and politics cooperative. Science and technology would be used as though, like the Sabbath, they had been made for man, not (as at present and still more so in the Brave New World) as though man were to be adapted and enslaved to them."

The Eidgenössische Technische Hochschule is a place of high achievements. It has contributed for 150 years—and will surely continue to contribute—a harvest of theoretical and practical knowledge arguably unequaled by any comparable institution. It is also a gift the Swiss have given to the wider world. Hopefully more and more U.S. researchers will be represented on the Hönggerberg, and Switzerland and the United States—the Sister Republics who have always shared a vision of human freedom and human potential—will grow even closer, to the lasting benefit of both.

A Note on Sources

Much of this work has relied on personal interviews with members of the ETH "family," from the President, Rector, and faculty, to students and graduates, conducted during three extended visits to Switzerland from August 2004 through May 2005. For the early, historical chapters, however, the author is indebted to a number of secondary sources.

Two general texts on Switzerland's history, culture, geography and people were valuable for providing an initial context for the ETH story. These were Murray Luck's highly detailed *History of Switzerland* (Palo Alto: SPOSS, Inc., 1985) and André Siegfried's *Switzerland, a Democratic Way of Life* (London: Jonathan Cape, 1950), an interesting and discerning book. Both are valuable works, but may also suggest the contemporary need for an authoritative, up-to-date English-language history of Switzerland from its earliest period to the present.

An interesting sample of what Americans think about Switzerland and the Swiss can be found in the survey "Image der Schweiz in den USA," by the Institut für Marketing und Unternehmungsführung (IMB) der Universität Bern (November 20, 2000).

The material in Chapters 3 and 4 on the political struggle leading to the birth of the ETH, and its early days, is drawn heavily from chapters by Klaus Urner and Jean-Francois Bergier in *Eidgenössische Technische Hochschule Zürich, 1955–1980: Festschrift zum 125 Jährigen Bestehen* (Zürich: Verlag Neue Zürcher Zeitung, 1980). The *Festschrift* is the official history of the ETH by and for the Swiss, until it is updated or superseded by an expected volume in 2005. Dr. Bergier is the former head of the ETH History Department, and the author is indebted to him for a lengthy personal interview in Bern on May 4,

2005, in which he also provided valuable insights on the ETH's contribution to Swiss national defense, especially in World War II.

The discussion of Stefano Franscini's contribution to the founding of the ETH is drawn from Konrad Osterwalder, "Role and Influence of Stefano Franscini in the Educational System of Switzerland," *Proceedings of the Conference on Statistical Science* (Basel: Birkhäuser Verlag, 1997), honoring the bicentennial of Franscini's birth, in Monte Verità, Switzerland, and from personal interviews with Dr. Osterwalder, the ETH's Rector.

Chapter 5's tale of the electrification of Switzerland is based on an article by Dr. David Gugerli of the ETH History Department, "Sociological Aspects of Technological Change: The Rise of the Swiss Electricity Supply," *Science in Context* 8, no. 3 (1995), and an interview with Dr. Gugerli.

The section on the construction of the St. Gotthard and Simplon tunnels draws on *Sechs Schweizer Alpeningenieure* (Meilen: Verein für Wirtschaftshistorische Studien, 2000); Eva March Tappan, Ed., *The World's Story: Vol. VII. Germany, The Netherlands, and Switzerland* (Boston: Houghton Mifflin, 1914); K. Kovari and R. Fechtig (trans. E.G. Prater), *Historical Tunnels in the Swiss Alps: Gotthard, Simplon, Lötschberg* (Vol. 2) (Zürich: Gesellschaft für Ingenieurbaukunst, 2000); and a visit to the historical display at the Simplon.

The life and career of Wilhelm Röntgen is based on "Wilhelm Conrad Röntgen: Lebenslauf" (online at http://www.roentgen-museum) and the entries on Röntgen in J. L. Heilbron (Editor-in-Chief), *The Oxford Companion to the History of Modern Science* (New York: Oxford University Press, 2003). In fact, *The Oxford Companion* proved highly instructive to the author (not a scientist) throughout the story on all matters related to science and the scientists portrayed.

Material on the life and work of Albert Einstein and the revolution in modern physics relies on an excellent and readable work by physicist Jeremy Bernstein: *Quantum Profiles* (Princeton, NJ: Princeton University Press, 2001). Bernstein is also cited in the discussion of the Besso-Einstein relationship ("A Critic at Large: Besso," *The New Yorker*, February 27, 1989). Columnist George Will also had an interesting piece about Einstein in "The Mind That Changed the World," *The Washington Post* (January 6, 2005).

The discussion on the Jung-Pauli relationship is drawn from a video lecture on Pauli and Jung by Professor David Lindorff, 1979, in the ETH Archives, and from the fascinating *Atom and Archetype: The*

Pauli-Jung Letters, 1932–1958, edited by C.A. Meier (Princeton, NJ: Princeton University Press, 2001).

Chapter 7's discussion of the revolution in structural engineering and bridge building, and the career of Othmar Ammann, draws on two fine books, technically authoritative yet accessible to the nonspecialist: Darl Rastorfer, *Six Bridges: The Legacy of Othmar H. Ammann* (New Haven and London: Yale University Press, 2000); and David P. Billington, *The Art of Structural Design: A Swiss Legacy* (New Haven and London: Yale University Press, 2003).

David P. Billington's *Robert Maillart's Bridges* (Princeton, NJ: Princeton University Press, Princeton, 1979) and his parallel work, *Robert Maillart and the Art of Reinforced Concrete* (New York: The Architectural History Foundation; Cambridge, MA: The MIT Press, both 1990), were valuable sources on Maillart's life and career. An article by Marcel N. Barbier, "La formation des ingénieurs en Suisse," in *La Revue des Ingénieurs*, no. 54 (September 1954), also contributed to this section.

David P. Billington's works were also highly useful for the discussion of Christian Menn. The passage on Menn and the Zakim Bridge on the Charles River is from "Harvard's Help Spans Charles River," by Doug Gravel, *The Harvard University Gazette* (March 1, 2001) and http://www.bostonroads.com.

The discussion of Swiss national defense and deterrence in World War II is heavily indebted to the definitive work on the subject by Stephen P. Halbrook: *Target Switzerland: Swiss Armed Neutrality in World War II* (Rockville Centre, NY: Sarpedon Publishers, 1998). Other sources for Chapter 8 were Victor Davis Hanson's *The Wars of the Ancient Greeks* (London: Cassell & Co., 1999); Dr. Edwin Vieria, Jr., "Are You Doing Your Constitutional Duty for 'Homeland Security'?" (May 16, 2005), and his other essays on the role of an armed citizenry found at http://www.newswithviews.com; and Dr. Hans Halbheer, "To Our American Friends: Switzerland in the Second World War," *American Swiss Foundation Occasional Papers*, Spring 1999, and "What's Wrong with Swiss Neutrality?," a paper given at the Hoover Institution International Conference on Political Neutrality in Europe, at Stanford University, Stanford, CA, on May 2, 2005. The author is especially indebted to interviews and special research material on the ETH and Swiss national defense provided by Dr. Jürg Stüssi-Lauterburg, Swiss Army officer, prolific author and, since 1984, head of the Federal Military Library and Historical Service in Bern.

For the discussion of architecture in Chapter 10, a valuable resource was found in *Switzerland—A Guide to Recent Architecture* by Maya Huber and Thomas Hildebrand (London: Ellipsis Arts, 2001). Many prominent architects currently have websites, accessible by their names or the names of their firms, that feature illustrations of their designs.

The final chapters of this book, concerning the latest developments at the ETH and in global science, as well as current issues in the broader world of higher education, were partly the result of the author's several visits to the ETH, when he had the opportunity to interview the individuals named above and also in the Acknowledgments. An additional major source of insight was the internet with its ever-growing wealth of information on specialized subjects. For a list of the websites most helpful for this work the reader is encouraged to examine Appendix III: "Further Information About the ETH."

Of course, the internet starting point for anyone wishing to delve more deeply into this subject is the ETH's own website (www.ethz.ch), which underwent a vast expansion as part of the ETH's 150th anniversary activities. It provides a "virtual" tour of the school, past, present and future. Some of the material is posted in English, but (be forewarned) most if it as well as the navigational signposts are in German.

Another internet resource that deserves special mention is the series of sites sponsored by the Nobel Foundation (www.NobelPrize.org). Each Nobel laureate since the award's inception is featured with a biography and a description of his or her achievements. More recent Nobel laureates have also provided brief, often delightful, autobiographies. For this work in particular, ready access to the stories of Nobel laureates was highly valuable.

PHOTO CREDITS: The historical photos and those of Zürich in this work were provided by the Image Archive ETH-Bibliothek, Zürich. The photos of the Hönggerberg campus were provided by the ETH's Department of Corporate Communications. The photos of CERN are courtesy of CERN Geneva. The photo of the PSFS Building is courtesy of Bryn Mawr College and that of the Teatro del Mondo is courtesy of the Pritzker Prize Foundation.

Appendices

APPENDIX I

THE ETH DOMAIN

For more information about the six components of the ETH Domain (in German, *Bereich*), or the "Greater ETH," readers are encouraged to consult the following:

1. ETHZ—ETH Zürich: http://www.ethz.ch/about/index_EN

2. ETHL—ETH Lausanne (the French initials are EPFL, for Ecole Polytechnique Fédérale de Lausanne): http://www.epfl.ch/Ebornes.html

3. PSI—the Paul Sherrer Institute, which conducts basic research in new areas of science in Würenlingen/Villigen: http://www.psi.ch/ueber_das_psi/ueber_das_psi_e.shtml

4. WSL—Swiss Federal Institute for Forest, Snow and Landscape Research in Birmensdorf: http://www.wsl.ch/welcome-en.ehtml

5. EMPA—Swiss Federal Laboratories for Materials Testing and Research in Dübendorf and St. Gallen: http://www.empa.ch/plugin/template/empa/2/*/--/l=2

6. EAWAG—Institute of Aquatic Science and Technology in Dübendorf: http://www.eawag.ch/about_e/e_index.html

ETH DEPARTMENTS

With research and teaching becoming increasingly interdisciplinary, the ETH has become a complex organization. You can think of the ETH

departments as the pillars of the school. They retain significant autonomy and, research focus aside, are considerably different one from one
another in size, how they run themselves, spend their resources, and
fulfill their obligations to planners and university managers. Many of
the departments are relatively new and all fall into one of four "selective areas of excellence"—Science and Mathematics, System-Oriented
Sciences, Architecture and Building Sciences, and Engineering
Sciences—the new strategic focii of the university. Together with
Humanities, Social Sciences, and Political Sciences, these core areas
define the ETH identity. Here is a current list of departments (grouped
by area):

Civil Engineering and Geomatics
Architecture (ARCH)
Civil, Environmental and Geomatics Engineering (BAUG)
Engineering
Mechanical and Process Engineering (MAVT)
Information Technology and Electrical Engineering (ITET)
Computer Science (INFK)
Materials Science (MATL)
Management, Technology and Economics (MTEC)

Natural Sciences
Mathematics (MATH)
Physics (PHYS)
Chemistry and Applied Biosciences (CHAB)
Biology (BIOL)

System-Oriented Natural Sciences
Earth Sciences (ERDW)
Environmental Sciences (UWIS)
Agricultural and Food Sciences (AGRL)

Other Sciences
Humanities, Social and Political Sciences (GESS)

Departments are now considered components of a university portfolio and are ranked in terms of (1) their perceived importance and (2)
whether they are being aggressively grown, maintained at a constant
level, or being reduced. Existing federal funding and newly acquired

outside (nonfederal) funding are allocated across this portfolio, just as a corporation would fund its operational units.

ORGANIZING FOR THE FUTURE

Each of these independent departments, however, is networked into a complex web of centers, institutes, projects and initiatives—most inter-disciplinary—which are highly flexible, ever changing, almost virtual departments themselves. ETH strategic planners are laying emphasis on new research initiatives in bioengineering, biosciences and biotech-nology, energy, materials science, micro- and nanoscience and bio-imaging. These are the real bets on the future where the university is investing major resources of money and intelligence. They are to be the areas where ETH will build excellence in this century. All were chosen after considerable debate because of their potential to grow and pro-vide economic advantage for Switzerland. Some are essentially start-ups, others are fields where the ETH already has a strong lead.

These new problem-oriented, interdisciplinary centers—which more often than not consist of a small administrative center (a website) running a target-focused communications network of specialists—are the real heart of the new university model. They are essentially links between problems, people and resources. They spring up like mush-rooms and can draw in or discard resources quickly. This is the model a whole new generation of researchers is learning to set up and use effi-ciently. The ponderous process of paper information exchange, slow-motion peer review and publication has been sped up by light years.

Of course, many centers are larger and more formal infrastructure networks, with considerable staff and budget. But, as a rule, they are concerned with making information, including the latest research, available over communications networks. The importance of the net-work—its output—has less and less to do with where it is physically housed since a center can be utilized instantaneously in Tokyo, San Francisco, or Adelaide just as easily as in Zürich. It is the quality of the database portal—its completeness, relevance and ease of use—which is key. Indeed, making and branding a research portal in a given field is a large part of achieving excellence in that field. People come to you because they know you're good and offer the best and most efficient resource.

These portals, which are being set up to avoid the defects of elec-tronic exchange—which includes the mere listing of uncoordinated and overlapping information—are one of the huge new structural issues of university building. Is portal information to be free or virtually free—the traditional academic model—or are the portals to somehow be turned into profit centers? Needless to say, there are huge interests at stake on both sides of this divide. Already, in the enormous area of intellectual property rights and free information exchange, we can hear the shelling in the suburbs. Luckily the capital investment in networked centers is minimal. However, the consequences for the future of research may be enormous. There will be many creative solutions offered.

TEACHING AND RESEARCH FACILITIES OUTSIDE THE DEPARTMENTS

Collegium Helveticum. Founded in 1997 by the ETH to promote dialogue within the sciences, the Collegium Helveticum seeks to increase mutual understanding of the natural and technical sciences as well as of humanities and social sciences. A "Graduate College," it is composed of relatively few people, with young scientists of the University of Zürich and of the ETH Zürich representing the core of the Collegium. Associated members, chosen on the basis of their interdisciplinary interests and the scientific quality of their research project, spend two semesters at the Collegium while they are still working on their dissertations. Internationally renowned visitors of the domains of science, literature and art come to participate in the program and give lectures to members and the public.

Center for Languages. Foreign students can undertake language study here.

Centro Stefano Franscini (CFS; see Chapter 3). The ETH maintains this well-appointed international conference center in southern Switzerland, on the hill above Ascona called Monte Verità. Various conference rooms for up to 110 people, a restaurant with panoramic view and an experienced staff are at your disposal for 5-day international meetings organized by university professors or researchers working in Switzerland. Since 1989, the Center has hosted 20–25 scientific conferences every year.

Functional Genomics Center Zürich (http://www.fgcz.ethz.ch/). The Functional Genomics Center Zürich (FGCZ) is a state-of-the-art facility jointly sponsored by the University of Zürich and the ETH. It provides access to the latest technologies of transcriptomics, proteomics, and bioinformatics to research groups of both institutions. FGCZ is designed to help researchers cope with rapid changes in technology and information expansion.

Swiss National Supercomputing Center (CSCS; www.cscs.ch). The Swiss National Supercomputing Center provides, develops, and promotes technical and scientific services for the Swiss research community in the fields of high-performance and high-throughput computing.

Research Centers and Databases (there are hundreds). For more information see http://www.ethz.ch/research/services/index_EN.

Across networks, professors and institutes of different fields of the ETH coordinate their efforts under common strategic aims. some within the ETH, some with other universities.

ETH Research Database (RDB; https://www.rdb.ethz.ch/search/). In 2005 there were 5,001 published projects in this database. Obviously it can cover the ETH, the ETH domain, all the schools in Switzerland, all of the EU, all of the world. But, like a new-patent service, it allows virtually anyone to find what's been done in very specific areas.

The Center for Biosystems Science and Engineering (http://www. bsse.ethz.ch/(concept paper). http://www.bsse.ethz.ch/Concept Systems X_E_12_08_04.pdf).

This center, housed in Basel, is part of Project SystemsX, which is a national network for the future field of systems biology jointly supported by ETH and the Universities of Zürich and Basel.

EMEZ (www.cscs.ch). The Electron Microscopy Center of the ETH.

ETH Transfer (www.transfer.ethz.ch). Technology transfer office, relationships with the private sector.

Innovation Initiatives (INIT; http://www.vpf.ethz.ch/services/NIT/index_EN).

The ETH Innovation Initiatives Program is a means to promote new scientific endeavors that in the medium to long term may result in the establishment of new professorships or the creation of new centers of excellence. This program provides a limited amount of seed money for exploratory projects on a competitive basis. Successful applications will be funded for a maximum period of three years, and every project will be subject to a review two years after initiation. Depending on the outcome of these reviews and subsequent decisions of the ETH Executive Board, the projects may become scientific focal points at ETH.

Euresearch Zürich (www.euresearch.ethz.ch). Searchable bank of European research programs.

FIRST (www.first.ethz.ch). This is a technology and cleanroom facility for advanced micro- and nanotechnology located on the Hönggerberg campus. It is a sophisticated high-tech tool for science and education to be used and operated jointly by several departments and their institutes.

Computing Services (www.id.ethz.ch). Central provider of Information and Communications Technology (ICT) at the ETH.

ISN (www.isn.ethz.ch). International Relations and Security Network.

Swiss Institute for Business Cycle Research (www.kof.ethz.ch). Information concerning research on business cycles.

Aramis (http://www.aramis-research.ch/). All projects funded or undertaken by the Swiss government.

Avenirsuisse (http://www.avenirsuisse.ch/8.0.html). A think tank for Swiss economic and social issues.

ADDITIONAL CENTERS AND RESEARCH UNITS

Center for Comparative and International Studies
Center for Continuing Education (ZFW)
Center for Higher Education (LZ)
Center for Product Design (ZPE)
Center "History of Knowledge," jointly sponsored by the ETH and the
    University of Zürich (ZGW)
Center of Biosystems Science & Engineering, the new center of the
    ETH Zürich at Basel (C-BSSE)
Center of Competence Finance (CCFZ)
Center of Energy Conversion (CEC)
Center of Mechanics—IMES (ZfM)
Centre for Chemical Sensors, Technopark (CCS)
Centre for Energy Policy and Economics (CEPE)
Centre for Plantsciences
Centre of Excellence in Analytical Chemistry (CEAC)
Centro Svizzero di Calcolo Scientifico
Elektronenmikroskopie-Zentrum
Enterprise Sciences, ETH-Center for (BWI)
ETH-Zentrum für Unternehmenswissenschaften
ETHags
Functional Genomics Center Zürich
Geneva Centre for Security Policy

Geneva Centre for the Democratic Control of Armed Forces
Geneva International Centre for Humanitarian Demining
HEDC–HESSI Experimental Data Center
Language Centre
Mechanics, Center of (IfM)
Neurowissenschaftszentrum Zürich
Swiss Centre for International Agriculture (ZIL)
Swiss National Point of Contact for Satellite Images (NPOC)
Technology and Innovation Management
Technology and Management, Center for (CTM)
Zentrum für Internationale Landwirtschaft (ZIL)
Zentrum für Neurowissenschaften
Zentrum für Pharmazeutische Wissenschaften BS-ZH
Zentrum für Theoretische Studien
Zentrum für Fremdstoff- und Umweltrisikoforschung Zürich (XERR)
Zentrum für Mechanik
Zürich Information Security Center (ZISC)
Zürich-Basel Plant Science Center

APPENDIX II

THE SWISS EDUCATION SYSTEM

Switzerland's primary and secondary education system is a key factor in preparing young Swiss for the ETH, its sister the EPFL in Lausanne, or any of the fine cantonal universities. The high quality of Swiss schools is a factor in sustaining academic standards in higher education, and is thus a part of—or backdrop to—the ETH story.

In keeping with its bedrock political principles, Switzerland's education system is largely decentralized. The cantons make most decisions on the running of schools and provide most of the funds. Teachers are actually elected by and are accountable to the local community. It might come as a shock to Americans to learn that Switzerland does not have a federal minister of education, yet—*mirabile dictu* —no Swiss child is left behind. Each canton has its own chief education official. These individuals make up the Swiss Conference of Cantonal Ministers of Education and play an important role in coordinating education policy, although the cantons remain autonomous in education, as in many other matters.

The Swiss educational system is divided into four stages: preschool, primary, secondary (which encompasses two levels, I and II), and tertiary or higher education. The tertiary or final stage also includes adult education. Primary and secondary schooling are compulsory and typically last for nine years. Although a few private schools exist, the vast majority of children attend cantonal (public) schools.

Preschool or kindergarten (*école enfantine, scuola dell'infanzia*) normally lasts two years. Then, as in the U.S., six-year-olds start primary school and spend five to six years before proceeding to Secondary I, the second stage of compulsory schooling, where they receive a basic general education. Generally at the age of 16, students who wish to continue their education move into Secondary II, which generally lasts three to four years. Those who follow Secondary II either pursue vocational training for direct entry into the skilled labor market, or they prepare for tertiary (higher) education. Teachers and administrators at the local level, who are after all closest to the students and can best observe their aptitude and performance, make the decision whether the individual will proceed on a vocational track or take the academic track that leads to higher education. The end goal of the academic track is the coveted diploma known in Switzerland as the *Maturität* (equivalent to the German *Abitur*).

A *Maturität* diploma qualifies a student to attend a cantonal university or one of the two federal polytechnics, the ETH or EPFL. Roughly 20 percent of Swiss 19-year-olds earn their *Matura*. About two-thirds of 16–21-year-olds choose the vocational track and apprenticeships. This lasts three or four years, depending on the chosen field. Trainees spend most of their time working for an approved company but are released to attend a vocational school one or two days per week. Vocational students have a choice of about three hundred recognized apprenticeship categories.

All cantons operate *Matura* schools, built around a choice of a main subject—what we might call a "major" in the U.S. These schools are tough by U.S. standards, generally exceeding in content and rigor the education American students receive at a typical high school. In other words, the *Maturität* surpasses a U.S. high school diploma, but is not quite equivalent to a bachelor's degree.

The core curriculum includes languages, the humanities, social sciences, economics, mathematics, natural sciences, art and music, and physical education. In addition to the academic content, the *Matura* school also encourages intellectual openness and the ability to exercise independent judgment. Students are even required to write a research paper before the *Matura* examination.

At the end of the schooling process, normally twelve years, students take a written exam in at least five *Matura* subjects, covering the first national language and a second language, mathematics, the main subject, and an elective subject. The research paper is assessed as well. *Matura* examinations are also given at the federal level for students who do not attend a cantonal school (for example, private schools, evening *Matura* schools, and correspondence courses).

Proposals are on the table to make public education more uniform between the cantons, but that is still not the same as centralized control from Bern, the federal capital. Like the rest of the industrialized world, Switzerland is confronting major changes as its people become more mobile and families move to a new canton, where their children might enter school or change grades at different ages from the canton where they lived before.

Globalization presents further pressures to standardize education not only within Switzerland, but also within Europe at large. Globalization has also increased the need for linguistic competence. Once it was considered sufficient for a Swiss citizen to know one of the other national languages besides his own, but today English is becoming a prerequisite for success in the international marketplace.

In addition to the two main federal institutions—the ETH and EPFL—there are 10 cantonal universities in Switzerland. Three are in Francophone cantons: Geneva, Lausanne, and Neuchâtel. Five are German-speaking: Basel, Bern, Lucerne, St. Gallen and Zürich. One is Italian-language: Lugano in Canton Ticino. Fribourg is bi-lingual French and German. The Universities of Basel and Zürich rank among the world's top 100 schools.

APPENDIX III

FURTHER INFORMATION ABOUT THE ETH

Read more about or gain additional perspectives on the ETH through *Essays 2030—Visions of the Future of the ETH Zürich*, which contains about two dozen essays of what the ETH will be like in 2030. The essays, some solicited from individuals inside and outside the school, some chosen in an open contest, represent a wide range of opinion. From first-person "you are there" science fiction to the measured insights of today's leading scientists, the essays all stress different aspects of the school's growth—technical, organizational, teaching, cultural, societal, spiritual. Some point to a golden age of open research and accelerated human progress worldwide. Others echo the pessimism found in Europe today and warn of a litany of environmental or cultural catastrophes. They can be read at www.essays2030.ETHZ.ch.

SOME HELPFUL WEBSITES

University World Ranking by *The Times Literary Supplement*
    http://www.thes.co.uk/worldrankings/
ETH Zürich Homepage (English) comprehensive access to the complete ETH domain
    http://www.ethz.ch/index_EN
ETH Departments and Who's Who
    http://www.ethz.ch/people/whoiswho/index_EN
The ETH Board Site (English) ETH strategic planning
    http://www.eth-rat.ch/
ETH Science City (English) Hönggerberg campus
    http://www.sciencecity.ethz.ch/?lang=en
Welcome Tomorrow 150 Years ETH Zürich
    http://www.150jahre.ethz.ch/index_EN
Corporate Partners of Welcome Tomorrow
    http://www.150jahre.ethz.ch/partnership/index_EN
Resource Guide to ETH Student Life (English)
    http://www.ethz.ch/intranet/life/index_EN
ETHLife International (English) campus magazine with extensive archives
    http://www.ethlife.ethz.ch/e/
ETHistory Site 1855-2005 (English) compilation of tours, debates,

accounts, interviews, archives prepared for the 150th Jubilee
https://www.ethistory.ethz.ch/index_EN
Listing and Websites of All Universities in Switzerland
http://www.forumjam.co.uk/univ/europe/switzerland/
swissmain.html
Swiss Timeline
http://mypage.bluewin.ch/Ruegg/Tl_e_2.htm
Swiss Federal Statistical Office (English) comprehensive Swiss education statistics
http://www.bfs.admin.ch/bfs/portal/en/index.htm
Avenir Suisse (English)—Swiss think tank
http://www.avenirsuisse.ch/index.php?id=8&lang=2
Technopark Zürich (English) private tech-transfer
http://www.technopark.ch/estart.cfm
Swiss Economic Forum
http://www.swisseconomic.ch/en/
ETH RiskLab—Financial and Insurance Risk Management
http://www.risklab.ch/press/QuantitativeFinance2002e.html
Institute for the History and Theory of Architecture
http://www.gta.arch.ethz.ch/e/index.htm
Institute of Pharmacological Sciences
http://www.pharma.ethz.ch/
New Pharmacenter Basel–Zürich
http://www.pharmacenter.ch/index.html
Alliance for Global Sustainability
http://globalsustainability.org/
The Annual Crew Race between the University of Zürich and the ETH
http://www.asvz.ch/unipoly/
China–Switzerland Relations
http://www.fmprc.gov.cn/eng/wjb/zzjg/xos/gjlb/3366/t17000.htm

APPENDIX IV

ETH NOBEL PRIZE WINNERS

While the world of science and technology confers other plaudits upon its luminaries besides the Nobel Prize, the Nobel still stands out in the public imagination as the pinnacle of achievement in the recognized disciplines. ETH graduates and faculty have won an astounding 21 awards in science (in some cases sharing the award with others). Two ETH chemists won the prize in medicine.

The 21 ETH Nobel laureates are:

Wilhelm Conrad Röntgen, Physics, 1901
Alfred Werner, Chemistry, 1913
Richard Willstätter, Chemistry, 1915
Fritz Haber, Chemistry, 1918
Charles-Edouard Guillaume, Physics, 1920
Albert Einstein, Physics, 1921
Peter J.W. Debye, Chemistry, 1936
Richard Kuhn, Chemistry, 1938
Leopold Ruzicka, Chemistry, 1939
Otto Stern, Physics, 1942
Wolfgang Pauli, Physics, 1945
Tadeus Reichstein, Medicine, 1950
Felix Bloch, Physics, 1952
Hermann Staudinger, Chemistry, 1953
Vladimir Prelog, Chemistry, 1975
Werner Arber, Medicine, 1978
Heinrich Rohrer, Physics, 1986
Karl Alexander Müller, Physics, 1987
J. Georg Bednorz, Physics, 1987
Richard Ernst, Chemistry, 1991
Kurt Wüthrich, Chemistry, 2002

Index